Negotiating Difference in the Hispanic World: From Conquest to Globalisation

The *Bulletin of Latin American Research* Book Series

The *Bulletin of Latin American Research* publishes original research of current interest on Latin America, the Caribbean, inter-American relations and the Latin American Diaspora from all academic disciplines within the social sciences, history and cultural studies. The BLAR/SLAS book series was launched in 2008 with the aim of publishing research monographs and edited collections that compliment the wide scope of the Bulletin itself. It is published and distributed in association with Wiley-Blackwell. We aim to make the series the home of some of the most exciting, innovatory work currently being undertaken on Latin America and we welcome outlines or manuscripts of interdisciplinary, single-authored, jointly-authored or edited volumes. If you would like to discuss a possible submission to the series, please contact the editors at blar@liverpool.ac.uk

Negotiating Difference in the Hispanic World: From Conquest to Globalisation

EDITED BY
ELENI KEFALA

This edition first published 2011
Editorial organisation © 2011 Society for Latin American Studies, text © 2011 The Authors

Blackwell Publishing was acquired by John Wiley & Sons in February 2007. Blackwell's publishing program has been merged with Wiley's global Scientific, Technical and Medical business to form Wiley-Blackwell.

Registered Office
John Wiley & Sons Ltd, The Atrium, Southern Gate, Chichester, West Sussex, PO19 8SQ, United Kingdom

Editorial Offices
350 Main Street, Malden, MA 02148-5.50, USA
9600 Garsington Road, Oxford, OX4 2DQ, UK
The Atrium, Southern Gate, Chichester, West Sussex, PO19 8SQ, UK

For details of our global editorial offices, for customer services, and for information about how to apply for permission to reuse the copyright material in this book please see our website at www.wiley.com/wiley-blackwell.

The right Eleni Kefala to be identified as the author of this editorial material in this work has been asserted in accordance with the UK Copyright, Designs and Patents Act 1988.

Library of Congress Cataloging-in-Publication Data
Negotiating Difference in the Hispanic World: From Conquest to Globalisation/edited by Eleni Kefala.
         p. cm. – (Bulletin of Latin American Research book series)
     Includes bibliographical references and index.
     ISBN 978-1-4443-3907-9

A catalogue record for this book is available from the British Library.

This book is published in the following electronic formats: Wiley Online Library 978-1-4443-3907-9

Set in 10 on 13pt and Palatino
by Laserwords Private Limited, Chennai, India
Printed and bound in the United Kingdom by Page Brothers, Norwich

Contents

Acknowledgements

The editor and publishers wish to thank the following for their permission to reproduce copyright material: Fundación Casa de Alba, Madrid; Biblioteca Nacional de España, Madrid; Bibliothèque Nationale de France, Paris; Bodleian Library, University of Oxford; Glasgow University Library, Scotland; The Bridgeman Art Library; and IWGIA (International Work Group for Indigenous Affairs), Copenhagen. The editor would also like to thank David Howard and Ken Lestrange for exemplary editing. Finally, the contributors would like to express their gratitude to the editor for her professional commitment throughout the publication process.

Acknowledgements

Introduction

ELENI KEFALA

University of St Andrews

In the last three decades, studies on cultural translation and hybridity have thrived. Rather than comply with a particular strand of postcolonial or decolonial[1] criticism, this volume seeks to resituate Hispanic culture within the wider debate on identity, and to investigate the intricate mechanisms whereby the latter has been moulded and remoulded in the last 500 years. The ten chapters that comprise this interdisciplinary work by no means claim to offer a comprehensive or, even less so, a definitive image of cultural encounters in the Hispanic world – such aspirations would render any study on difference frivolous and contentious. Instead the principal aim of this book is to bring to the fore solid instances of aesthetic, ideological and cultural negotiations, some more conflictual and problematic than others, that have shaped Spanish American societies from the Conquest to the present day, and fashioned our own cultural apprehensions. In other words, it invites us to rethink that semiotic locus where the mutual complicity between identity and difference is both disruptive and recuperative due to the constant reconfigurations of the former through the latter. Difference, then, is not understood as a topological sign of alterity, nor simply as an

---

1 The term *decolonial* refers to what we could catachrestically call Latin American postcolonial theory. According to this line of thinking, the term *postcolonial* is misleading as it can only refer to the end of historical colonialism in its political-administrative form. Decolonial thinking distinguishes between historical *colonialism*, a form of political and administrative domination, and *coloniality*, which refers to a thorough and far-reaching global pattern of power that remains rampant in global capitalism – in this way, colonialism can be viewed as a particular historical manifestation of coloniality. Aníbal Quijano conceptualises the capitalist world-system, whose origins he traces back to the Conquest of America, as a 'heterogeneous historical-structural matrix', a system of domination, conflict and exploitation, whose global pattern of power creates a society of vertical relations, affecting all dimensions of social existence: labour, sexuality, subjectivity and authority (2000a and 2000b). He argues that coloniality 'se funda en la imposición de una clasificación racial/étnica de la población del mundo' (is based on the imposition of a racial/ethnic classification of the world population) (2000b: 342). The translations of Spanish quotations into English are mine unless a bibliographical reference is provided in parentheses.

essential component of the *Self*, but as the mechanism *whereby* the idea of the Self is negotiated, uttered and performed.

The volume is divided into three parts, which bring together contributions from the fields of literary and cultural studies, cultural history, art history, translation studies and cultural anthropology. Part I, *Found in Translation*, includes three chapters whose semantic axis hinges upon the issue of literary and cultural translation in the sixteenth, eighteenth and twentieth centuries. Part II, *Appropriations and the Rhetoric of Self-Definition*, consists of three chapters on the in-translation state of identity in Mexico, Argentina and Chile, focusing on the idea of the appropriation of the Other as a rhetorical trope of self-definition. Finally, the four chapters of Part III, *Liminality and the Politics of Identity*, expand on the processes of identity formation analysed in Part II, slightly shifting their attention from the act of appropriation to the notion of liminality. The purpose of this introduction is to map out the epistemic territory of the individual contributions while at the same time opening up the debate on difference within the context of Latin American studies. It is therefore meant to complement the ten chapters of the volume, not simply summarise its principal findings.

Difference is the beacon of identity, individual and collective. In the semiotic process, *selfness* stops where *otherness* begins, and conversely. My femaleness, for instance, comes to the fore most forcefully around men; likewise, I am *Greek* Cypriot when associated with *Turkish* Cypriots. Hence, beyond a rudimentary element of plurality (meaning, as Jacques Derrida has shown, is differential and plural), difference is the indispensable condition for the complex process of identity formation and self-definition to be set in motion. Such a view impels us toward what Sanford Budick calls 'a reconceptualisation of the experience of alterity' (1996: 1), and the formulaic tropes whereby identity is gestated. In a way, life is a constant journey of the Self *in difference*, and identity, as James Clifford suggests, 'an itinerary rather than a bounded site – a series of encounters and translations' (1997: 11). We negotiate difference at all times, when talking, reading, surfing the web, pondering, dreaming, travelling, falling in and out of love, interpreting and translating. Paradoxically, when seen in this way, difference is no longer what keeps us apart but in fact what brings us together in a dialectical relation, by means of notional and emotional transference and transcendence; for this reason, it is of utmost importance in the micro- and macro-development of individual and cultural identities.

Difference presupposes two or more entities, yet it is *through* difference that these entities are conceptualised as id-entities. If we agree for a moment to shift our attention from *identity* (the case of *being a female*, which still requires the presence of the male) to *self-definition* (the enunciation of *femaleness*), then we realise that self-defining and self-differentiating are the two simultaneous reciprocal acts of discursive enunciation. Difference is the relational fluid zone that *emerges from* and *because of* the encounter between X and Y, who, nonetheless, emerge *as such* through and because of their mutual contact. We could think of identity as the outcome of osmotic processes that are historically and culturally specific, and that are set in motion through difference during the encounter of two or more entities. Consequently, identity is socially constructed and historically produced according to structures of power and domination, and for this reason needs both to be de-naturalised and de-essentialised.

The interstitial topography in which difference is inscribed is formative, transitional and translational. Formative because it is the operative playground that paves the way for self-realisation and self-definition to surface through processual confrontations with, and mirrorings in, the Other (we could think of Jacques Lacan's mirror stage (1999), as well as of the palindrome with its two complementary strands that are mirrored in each other). Therefore, beyond and before a space of 'newness', as Homi K. Bhabha argues, this is primarily the recuperative place of selfness. Transitional because the osmotic processes of identity (re)formulation, enacted and mediated by difference through necessity, persuasion or conflict, lead to the establishment of a new order of things – which in turn will be subject to new reorderings, and so on and so forth. Bhabha's hybrid 'third term' (1994: 113), the undecidable *neither–nor* that he borrows from Derrida (1992: 163) – the 'newness [that] comes into the world' (Bhabha, 1994: 227) –, is the natural but not singular outcome of this transition. If we take the case of sixteenth-century Mexico, for instance, in racial terms Bhabha's new, hybrid *third* term would be Martín Cortés el Mestizo (Z) (neither Spanish nor Nahua), the offspring of the union between Hernán Cortés (X) and La Malinche (Y). Does this imply that X and Y remained unaltered by the encounter? The answer is negative, otherwise we would be yielding to essentialist notions of identity. The new reorderings issued by such negotiations concern not just the third, *neither–nor* term (Z), but all the terms of the encounter (X, Y and Z). Neither the Europeans nor the indigenous were left unchanged or 'uncontaminated' when confronted with the Other,[2] notwithstanding that this change was largely apportioned unevenly due to what decolonial thinkers, in particular Aníbal Quijano

---

2 Bhabha's *newness* could, of course, indicate any changes related to the three terms of the encounter, but the use of the word 'third', which is identified with hybridity, sounds somewhat problematic. As a matter of fact, only in racial terms could Bhabha's hybrid thirdness stand entirely conspicuous on this particular occasion, and this is a reminder of the limitations of theoretical concepts borrowed from biological sciences to analyse cultural phenomena. For more information on hybridity and its origins in biological studies, see Young (1995).

(2000a), call the 'coloniality of power' – a hegemonic model of power that resulted from the alleged supremacy of the European religion, knowledge and culture over their non-European counterparts.[3]

Finally, since no entity comes into this new order unswayed, it means that this liminal space, which Bhabha associates with hybridity, is ultimately translational (translation in the etymological sense of the term, as transference, transformation), allowing for the hybrid to emerge. Bhabha identifies the translational zone of hybridity as the 'Third Space' or 'space of thirdness' (1994: 217). Specifically, he argues that

> the intervention of the Third Space of enunciation, which makes the structure of meaning and reference an ambivalent process, destroys [the] mirror of representation in which cultural knowledge is customarily revealed as an integrated, open, expanding code. Such an intervention quite properly challenges our sense of the historical identity of culture as a homogenising, unifying force, authenticated by the originary Past, kept alive in the national tradition of the People. [. . .] It is that Third Space, though unpresentable in itself, which constitutes the discursive conditions of enunciation that ensure that the meaning and symbols of culture have no primordial unity or fixity; that even the same signs can be appropriated, translated, rehistoricized and read anew. (1994: 37)

There is no doubt that the translational space to which Bhabha refers problematises any notions of homogeneity and fixity with respect to identity and culture. We have seen, however, that this liminal area of contact is first and foremost formative; hence, strictly speaking, it constitutes not the *third* space but the *primary* space of negotiation and contestation *through* which the 'identities of culture' (in the case of Cortés and La Malinche, European and Nahua) have been historically formed and reformed. To put it differently, 'the discursive conditions of enunciation' concern not only cultures but also individuals, families, communities, tribes, city-states, and so forth. In fact, *before* they ever concerned cultures, they principally concerned individuals, families, communities, tribes and city-states, which gradually developed a sense of 'common' cultural identity, always through the contact with the Others, and always by excluding or silencing what was perceived as difference within a given social entity (the Tlaxcaltecs, for instance, that once defined themselves *against* the Nahuas, now fall under the same undifferentiated category of the

---

3   See also fn. 1.

'indio' when confronted with Europeans and *criollos*;[4] the same applies to the Zapotecs, Tojolabales, Olmecs, Mixtecs, Chichimecs, Toltecs, Mayas, and so on). The *Self* and the *Other* are concepts in perpetual revision, and otherness changes according to the vicissitudes of selfness. Furthermore, if we agree that this translational space allows for the third (hybrid/*neither–nor*) term to be formed, then Bhabha's second concept, 'space of thirdness', may be more appropriate, although still not wholly unproblematic in so far as the *neither–nor* represents only one (surely the most visible) of the many (often more subtle) changes generated by such negotiations. Yet how do we distinguish between primary spaces of contact and 'spaces of thirdness', especially in the contemporary era of the media, diaspora and globalisation? We may provisionally say that, for all the obvious limitations of Bhabha's notion, it may still be useful when indicating what we could call 'border' or 'hyperbolic encounters', that is, negotiations between different cultural systems of signification. In other words, contacts that create outcomes that are *hyperbolically* visible, as in the case of European and indigenous negotiations in Latin America – the religious festivals of Corpus Christi, Inti Raymi and Qoyllur Rit'i in Cusco are salient examples of the religious syncretism stemming from such negotiations.

However, there seems to be a graver problem with Bhabha's concept, which is to be found in the equation of the third (*neither–nor*) term with hybridity.[5] The latter is not free of controversy due to its links to racialisation, which is equally contentious. Quijano argues that the categorisation of people as 'indigenous', 'black', 'white' and 'mestizo' did not exist before 1492: 'el racismo y el etnicismo fueron inicialmente producidos en América y reproducidos en el resto del mundo colonizado, como fundamentos de la especificidad de las relaciones de poder entre Europa y las poblaciones del resto del mundo' (racism and ethnicity were initially produced in America and reproduced in the rest of the colonised world, as a way of establishing the specificity of the relations of power between Europe and the rest of the world) (1993: 167). He adds that the idea of 'race' is based on the assumption that there is a 'desigual nivel de desarrollo biológico entre los humanos, en una escala que va desde la bestia al europeo' (variable level of biological development among humans, on a scale that goes from the beast to the

---

4 In Spanish America, the term *criollo* refers to people of European ancestry who were born and bred in the 'new' world, and who distinguished themselves for that reason from Europeans; however, in the Caribbean the term *Creole* could indicate people of Afro-European origins, while in Brazil the word *crioulo* refers to people of African ancestry. Here, I am using the term in its former sense. The term *mestizo* refers to people of mixed European and Amerindian origins.
5 See also fn. 2.

European) (1993: 169). The racialisation and consequential subalternisation
of the colonised came to justify their enslavement and exploitation in general.
In this sense, and despite their merits, from a decolonial point of view,
postcolonial theories of hybridity still adopt an intra-modern perspective
as they fail to question race as one of modernity's[6] most powerful social
inventions;[7] instead, they perpetuate a way of social classification that is
impregnated with the logic of coloniality. In addition, although Bhabha gives
a strong political reading to hybridity when he says that 'it creates a crisis
for any system of authority' (1994: 114), this 'space of thirdness' could be
seen as just *another* locus of enunciation, *another* way of thinking, which is
epistemically and politically privileged over the others, thus reproducing
modernity's logic, only this time in reverse. Besides, there is no warranty
that this 'third space', the space of the mestizo *par excellence*, will result in the
subversion of the colonial order – in Latin America, for instance, the project
of modernisation very often was carried out by the *criollo* and mestizo élites.

Walter Mignolo, among other decolonial thinkers, has stressed the need
for *un pensamiento otro* (thinking otherwise),[8] *un pensamiento fronterizo* (a
border thinking), which refers to non-Eurocentric ways of thinking from the
perspective of coloniality (2003: *passim*) – what Frantz Fanon calls the colonial
wound. This should not be understood as a fundamentalist, anti-modern
or anti-European call (there is hardly any space that has been untouched
by modernity and any notion of an absolute outside is fallacious, to say
the least) but, in the terms of Santiago Castro-Gómez, as an *amplification*
of the scope of visibility (2007: 90), which will allow us to go beyond the
dualisms of modernity and profit from the perspectives of those who have
been inferiorised, subalternised, dehumanised and silenced by it. This is what
Enrique Dussel (2002: 221) and Mignolo (2005: *passim*) define as *exteriority*
and *colonial difference* respectively. In the case of Latin America, for instance,
we could think of the various indigenous and African communities, but also
of other subaltern groups, such as women, gay communities, the poor, and

---

6   Decolonial thinking distinguishes between two phases of modernity. Specifically,
    Enrique Dussel uses the term *first* or *early modernity* to refer to the 'discovery'
    and subsequent colonisation of America by the Spaniards and the Portuguese
    (fifteenth to eighteenth centuries), reserving the term *second modernity* for what
    is widely known as modernity (2002: 227–228) – the latter is roughly defined
    as the Enlightenment, the French Revolution and the Industrial Revolution that
    opened the way to the second wave of European colonialism in the nineteenth
    and twentieth centuries (Escobar, 2003: 60).
7   For more information on race and colonialism, see Quijano (1993 and 2000b).
8   The concept of 'pensée-autre', as a reaction to the epistemic hegemony of the
    West, belongs to the Moroccan intellectual Abdelkebir Khatibi (1983).

so on. However, the exteriority or difference of these groups, including the 'indio' and the 'afro', can only be relative because all of them have been involved in many ways and to varying degrees in the project of modernity. Hence, Mignolo's and Dussel's notions should be understood in terms of marginalisation rather than absolute difference, but also as integral parts of modernity. For example, the natural resources of the American continent, formerly owned by indigenous people, played a major role in the establishment of the capitalist world-system; similarly, the indigenous and African people were needed as cheap or free labour (slavery) for the advancement of European modernity. As Nelson Maldonado-Torres argues, 'la modernidad como discurso y práctica no sería posible sin la colonialidad, y la colonialidad constituye una dimensión inescapable de discursos modernos' (modernity as discourse and practice would not be possible without coloniality, and coloniality constitutes an inescapable dimension of modern discourses) (2007: 132). Coloniality then is the negative, constitutive exteriority of modernity, its darker side (Mignolo, 1995) or its underside (Dussel, 1996). Modernity's scope therefore cannot be fully revealed unless we *also* look at it through the perspective of this relative exteriority, which is precisely the colonial subaltern.[9] Besides, we should not forget Aimé Césaire's remark that colonisation dehumanises both elements of the colonial subject, the oppressor and the oppressed – what he calls 'the boomerang effect of colonization'.[10]

---

9 As Mignolo points out, one can either speak from the locus of the colonial subaltern or adopt its perspective. If the locus of enunciation and perspective coincide, then we have a 'strong border thinking' – this is the case of Fanon. If the locus of enunciation is not that of colonial difference yet the perspective is, then we have a 'weak border thinking' – this is the case of Bartolomé de Las Casas. Both are necessary 'para conseguir transformaciones sociales efectivas. El uno sin el otro es, en última instancia, *políticamente débil*' (in order to achieve effective social transformations. One without the other is ultimately *politically weak*) (Mignolo, 2003: 28). However, the locus of enunciation does not guarantee the perspective; for instance, an indigenous woman who works in a multinational company in Mexico may sympathise less with the status of indigenous women in her country than an Englishman who is sympathetic to feminism. Therefore, the colonial difference does not presuppose an epistemic or political difference, and herein lies one of the risks of decolonial thinking, which, despite its claims, tends to privilege (politically and epistemically) the perspective of the indigenous and African communities in the Andes.

10 '[Colonization] dehumanizes even the most civilized man; that colonial activity, colonial enterprise, colonial conquest, which is based on contempt for the native and justified by that contempt, inevitably tends to change him who undertakes it; that the colonizer, who in order to ease his conscience gets into the habit of seeing the other man as an animal, accustoms himself to treating him like an animal, and tends objectively to transform himself into an animal' (Césaire, 1998: 225).

With regard to Bhabha's 'space of thirdness', I would finally argue that there are not one, nor two, nor three but many spaces, all of which have an equally limited perspective. They are temporally, culturally, socially and epistemically situated, and therefore none of them can raise any claim to universality. In this context, Mignolo's notion of *pluriversality* is particularly relevant. Drawing on Édouard Glissant's concept of diversality (1993: 54), Mignolo envisages a world (I would also add, an identity) that is pluriversal, a world where many *and* incongruous worlds (and identities) are possible (in Escobar, 2003: 62–63). The incongruous dimension of pluriversality differentiates it from the politically correct multiculturalism of globalisation that aspires to function as a melting pot of difference.[11] This brings to mind the comments of the Uruguayan poet Cristina Peri Rossi on the 'multiplicity of being':

> Tengo las múltiples personalidades del yo del poeta y del yo narrador . . . la atribución de un sexo es casi siempre neurótica. Querer ser hombre, o querer ser mujer, o querer ser homosexual, siempre es neurótico y lo es porque crea una tensión entre *la multiplicidad del ser* y las exigencias sociales. [. . .] No creo para nada en la unidad del Yo . . . la identidad es un proceso y como proceso es contradictorio, admite los opuestos . . . Entonces *una* identidad es *una reducción del ser*. (Quoted in Dejbord, 1998: 72–73; my emphasis)

> I have the multiple personalities of the I of the poet and the I of the narrator . . . gender attribution is almost always neurotic. Wanting to be a man, or wanting to be a woman, or wanting to be a homosexual, is always neurotic and it is so because it creates a tension between the *multiplicity of being* and social exigencies. [. . .] I do not believe at all in the unity of the I . . . identity is a process and, as such, is contradictory, it accepts the opposites . . . Therefore *an* identity is *a reduction of being*.

I have referred earlier to the dialectical relation between the Self and the Other, which, to some extent, resonates Hegelian ontology. In light of Mignolo's and Peri Rossi's conceptualisations, I can now clarify that this complex process of self-definition is not so much dialogical but plurilogical, as it establishes a nexus of relations between the multiple selves/others of the Self and the multiple selves/others of the Other, a nexus that is realised on a differential ground that is always shifting and that allows for mutual influence and penetration, thus ruling out any fixed and essentialist notions of identity. For Hegel, this differential ground would be the constant flux of *becoming*, which sets in motion the dialectical relation between *being* and *nothing* (1969: 82–83).

---

11   Mignolo rightly argues that globalisation 'masks the fact that the geo-politics of knowledge and economy remains anchored firmly in the West' (2005: 153).

Yet as Derrida has shown, in Hegel's scheme difference as contradiction is interiorised and resolved:

> I have attempted to distinguish *différance* (whose *a* marks, among other things, its productive and conflictual characteristics) from Hegelian difference, and have done so precisely at the point at which Hegel, in the greater Logic, determines difference as contradiction only in order to resolve it, to interiorize it, to lift it up (according to the syllogistic process of speculative dialectic) into the self-presence of an onto-theological or onto-teleological synthesis. (Derrida, 1981: 44)

Obviously pluriversality as incongruity is much closer to Derridean *différance* than it is to Hegelian difference because *différance* opens up identity to infinite re-articulations and upholds difference as contradiction. Both pluriversality and *différance* transcend the dualism that characterises the Hegelian economy of identity/difference (Chueh, 2004: 20), which undercuts the logic of modernity and identifies the Other with the non-modern and non-European. As Dussel remarks, '[for Hegel], the "Orient" was humanity's "infancy" (*Kindheit*), the place of despotism and unfreedom, from which the spirit (*Volksgeist*) would later soar toward the West, as if on a path toward the full realization of liberty and civilization' (2002: 222).

So far we have talked about Bhabha's formulation of cultural translation and its shortcomings, as seen through a decolonial lens, but we have not said much about literary translation and the sort of changes the target language undergoes when it comes into contact with the source language and its cultural system. In her chapter 'The "Acculturation" of the Translating Language' (Part I), Anna Fochi, whose work belongs to the field of culturally oriented research on translation, namely the key issue of foreignising translation *versus* domesticating and neutralising strategies, probes Gregory Rabassa's transposition of Gabriel García Márquez's *Chronicle of a Death Foretold*. On the one hand, there is a translator whose relevance has been stressed to the point of being identified as one of the main factors determining the so-called 'Boom' of Latin American literature in the 1960s, and who believes that 'language is culture' (Rabassa, 2002: 91); on the other hand, there is a writer whose prose is uniquely rich in cultural connotations. Fochi carries out a systematic reading of Rabassa's target text (TT) by following Peèter Torop's six translatability parameters for cultural translation criticism (i.e. language, space, time, text, work and socio-political commitment). For all that Rabassa's text clearly strives not to hide the source text (ST) (most evident in the creative manipulation of language), his foreignising tactics become less conspicuous when dealing with the macroscopic cultural elements of the novel, for instance, *realia* or other geographically specific terms. Fochi suggests that the stimulating aspect of his translation is rather to be found in the English of the TT, affected by a deliberate tension with the language of the ST. Signs of this, she says, can be traced already in the peculiar syntax, and the Biblical and apocalyptic ring of the title of the TT, which indicate that, at least in this regard and mostly in line with those contemporary theories advocating literalism to register the 'foreignness' of the foreign text, Rabassa has been faithful to his precept: that is, in order to preserve 'whatever slim shards of the culture', it is necessary 'to acculturate our English' (2002: 91).

The acculturated English that Rabassa proffers is obviously the outcome of the confrontation of his language with linguistic and cultural differ-ence. Referring to Jorge Luis Borges's famous story 'Pierre Menard, Author of Don Quixote', Julio Cortázar signalled 'the subtle transmigrations and transgressions that take place in the translation of any text [...], and the more subtle distortion that historical and cultural distance imposes' (2002: 21). The Menardian encounter with difference (temporal, linguistic, cul-tural and ideological) corroborates the transmigrations, transgressions and distortions that underwrite all ontological reformulations, whether con-cerning people, texts or cultures, no matter how elusive they are. In his essay 'The Translators of *The Thousand and One Nights*', Borges exalts the 'happy and creative infidelity' (1999c: 106) of J. C. Mardrus's translation of the Arabic text, an idea related to the concept of translating (and writ-ing) *against* (Kefala, 2007: 102). Similarly, in 'The Homeric Versions' he claims that 'every modification is sacrilegious', and that the 'concept of the "definitive text" corresponds only to religion or exhaustion' (1999b: 69). Very close to Borges's ideas, which we could easily trace back to the nineteenth-century German commentary on translation (namely Schleirma-cher [2007] and Goethe [2007]), are those of the Brazilian theorist Haroldo de Campos and Peri Rossi. The former understands poetic translation as 'transcreation' and 'hypertranslation' (1982: 184); the latter as 'vampiric' and 'phagocytic' appropriation (2002: 58–60). Beneath the observations of Borges, de Campos and Peri Rossi, there is the latent assumption that identity is sacrilegiously modified, transcreated and (hyper)translated *against* and *through* alterity – the latter presupposes Peri Rossi's phagocytic appropria-tion. The fact that identity is happily and creatively unfaithful to essentialist pedigrees inescapably renders unilateral notions of *definitive* ontological cat-egories untenable and unattainable. Borges's semi-autobiographical story 'The South' [1956] (1998) is a fine example of the tensions and contradictions underscoring identity. The text recaptures the Sarmentine[12] debate on

---

12 For Domingo Faustino Sarmiento (1811–1888), the dictatorial regime of the Pampean caudillo, Juan Manuel de Rosas (1793–1877), was a manifestation of

civilisation (European/urban modernity) and barbarism (local/rural *criollismo*). Juan Dahlmann, an exemplary case of Argentina's antagonistic lineages (he is of German and *criollo* ancestry), is a librarian from Buenos Aires who, after having been hospitalised for septicemia, purportedly travels to the South of the country to recover from his illness, and to recover his *criollo* origins. This gauchesque story, grafted on José Hernández's epic poem *Martín Fierro* [1870s] (2004),[13] is subtly permeated by Borges's favourite philosophical themes (paradoxes of time and space, circularity and the double, among others), and bears out his aesthetic blueprint (a blend of universal and local traditions). Textual duality stands for national duality, in particular, the liminality of Argentine identity situated on the edge of European and local cultures. 'The cult of books' and 'the cult of courage' that Ricardo Piglia attributes to Borges's family genealogy (his paternal grandmother was English; his maternal great-grandfather a *criollo* who fought in the War of Independence)[14] are synecdochically bestowed upon the nation (1981: 90). 'The South' arguably is divested of monologic and monolithic notions of Argentine identity conspicuously present in Domingo Faustino Sarmiento's championing of 'the man of letters', and *Centenario*'s siding with the gaucho Martín Fierro as 'a man of courage' and therefore a 'proper' national symbol.[15] This is because the unresolvable tension between the two residual identities is

---

'barbarism', which imprisoned Argentina in its 'uncivilised' past (associated with gauchos [cowboys] and *indios* [Indians]). Sarmiento along with Esteban Echeverría, Juan Bautista Alberdi and Bartolomé Mitre were the major representatives of the so-called Generation of 1837, whose main task was 'to devise a programme that would make Argentina a modern nation', and in so doing 'they borrow[ed] heavily from their European contemporaries' (Shumway, 1991: 112). In particular, this pro-British/German (and strongly anti-Spain) intellectuals were greatly influenced by European writers like Goethe, Schiller, Hugo and Byron. Sarmiento's major work is his polemical essay *Facundo: civilización y barbarie* (*Facundo: Civilisation and Barbarism*) [1845] (2001).

13 *Martín Fierro*, which celebrates the free-spirited *criollo* gaucho of the Pampa, was originally published in two parts: *El gaucho Martín Fierro* (1872) and *La vuelta de Martín Fierro* (1879).

14 His great-grandfather, Colonel Isidoro Suárez (1799–1846), fought under Bolívar in the battle of Junín in Peru (1824) during the War of Independence, and was later called 'el héroe de Junín' (the hero of Junín) (Balderston, 1993: 116). His grandfather, Colonel Francisco Borges Lafinur (b. 1883), died in the battle of La Verde (1874) fighting for his mentor Bartolomé Mitre, in the civil war between Unitarians and Federalists (Balderston, 1993: 90).

15 The poet Leopoldo Lugones was one of the major representatives of the so-called Generation of the *Centenario*, which came to prominence around 1910 when Argentina celebrated its Centenary of Independence from the Spanish Crown. Lugones (1916) saw in *Martín Fierro* the text that would give racial, cultural and linguistic unity to the Argentineans, much in line with European epic poems like

sustained throughout the story, with Dahlmann repeatedly shifting between books and duels, reading and fighting, dreaming and living, almost incapable of fully settling on any of them. This intrinsic irreconcilability is reinforced by the ambiguous ending: is Dahlmann dying in a physical fight in the South, being true to his *criollo* origins and rejecting his Europeanised outfit? Or is he hallucinating back in the hospital that he never left, merely dreaming of his courageous Other before waking up in a sterile 'civilisation'? In either case, death seems to be the only way in which the tension could be resolved permanently and irreversibly. If he dies in the fight, he will have opted for his *criollo* side; if he dies in the hospital, he will have never truly embraced it. Through the aesthetic and semantic duality of the story, Borges vindicates the impossibility of definitive and unilateral classifications, underpinning the staggering plasticity of identity both in national and notional terms. Yet as I argue later on, Borges remains entangled in Sarmiento's Eurocentric approach as he does not escape the binary logic of civilisation/barbarism, although, as we have seen, he does refuse to resolve the apparent contradiction between the two – a mid-way between Hegelian difference and Derridean *différance*.

Once again I reflect on my personal case as an example of the malleable politics of self-definition: I am a Cypriot, born in Athens into a Cypriot family, who grew up in Cyprus, studied in an English university, lived in the United States for a short period and now works in a Scottish institution. I recall that when I first came to the United Kingdom, I was feeling Greek to the bone, and as most Greeks I was not entirely free of certain anti-Western sentiments. Back in Greece, however, I was always very conscious of my Cypriotness. Conversely, in the United States I was feeling European with a pinch of Britishness, not least because of a slight accent; but after a decade abroad, I can sense my Britishness rather pungently every time I go back to Cyprus. In London I feel almost obligated to my Scottishness, while in Spain my accent makes me sound like an Argentinean. My strong Greek 's' convinced the Peruvian Andeans, a few years ago, that I was Spanish, and compelled me to identify, albeit unwillingly, with European colonialism – and whatever this entails; nevertheless, I come from an island that has gone through innumerable occupations and colonisations, and thus I would instinctively side with history's disenfranchised. Do I feel like a confused, identity-less chameleon in a post-national, globalised world? I would firmly rebuff such indictment. Yet do I feel more Cypriot than Greek? More Greek than Scottish? More Scottish than British? I reckon that by now I am all of these and none of them solely since identity is contingent upon difference, and its

---

the French 'Chanson de Roland' and the Spanish 'Mío Cid'. For more information, see Kefala (2007: 49–51).

semantic grid is susceptible to continuous redrafting. In the last ten years, my notion of identity has become more porous, pliable and adaptable to the environment, and is being shaped according to the differential negotiations and transcodifications that occur sometimes hesitantly, occasionally readily and most of the times inadvertently. As Emily Apter notes referring to Walter Benjamin's 1916 article 'On Language as Such and on the Language of Man', 'everything is translatable and in a perpetual state of in-translation' (2006: 7). It is precisely this *in-translation* state of identity enacted and re-enacted *through* difference that this volume seeks to explore.

Yet how will I define myself (or how will others define me) in 20 years from now, if I am still in St Andrews? Will I be considered a Cypriot in Scotland or a hyphenated persona – a Scottish-Cypriot? In his book *Life on the Hyphen: The Cuban-American Way*, Gustavo Pérez Firmat speaks of the hyphenated Cuban-American culture as a precarious 'balancing act' between 'two contributing cultures', for which he reserves the term 'biculturation' (1994: 6). In the chapter 'Transatlantic Deficits; or, Alberto Vilar at the Royal Opera House' (Part III), Roberto Ignacio Díaz presents the case of a Cuban-American businessman, a liminal, hyphenated persona who was allegedly born in Havana and fled Castro's revolution to become known 'in the last years of the twentieth century [...] as the most generous philanthropist in the history of opera, with colossal and highly publicised donations to various companies on both sides of the Atlantic'. Díaz analyses Vilar's rise and fall in the context of opera in Cuba, especially the Havana-based companies that took Italian operas to the United States, as well as against the eventual effacement of Cuba from updated accounts of his biography, following the discovery that he was not born in Havana but in East Orange, New Jersey. Balancing, in this case, is negotiating different cultural systems, whether in reality or in the individual's fancy, while hyphenation seems to be as precarious as the bicultural condition that Pérez Firmat and Díaz describe.

Negotiations of difference, although abiding and ubiquitous, are reliant on the intensity, level and length of the encounter with the Others. These negotiations have been heightened by complex socio-political and cultural conjunctures such as colonialism and globalisation, which vehemently pre-cipitate reorderings of all sorts and at all levels. Naturally those topographies that have experienced such conjunctures first-hand lend themselves to the kind of analysis that this volume proposes, not because they are unique cases (the reverse is true), but because they disclose *hyperbolically* the mechanisms whereby identity is cast and recast anywhere, at anytime. In this regard, the case of what we nowadays call Latin America is cogent. From Mexico to Argentina, the American subcontinent once known as Tawantinsuyu (Andes), Anáhuac (valley of Mexico) and Abya Yala (Panama) (Mignolo, 2005: 2) has been a paradigm of what we have called 'border' or 'hyperbolic encounters'.

An example of these encounters can be found in the hybrid codes of Mexican heraldry, one of the few spaces in which the indigenous élites of post-Conquest Mexico could express their own worldview and authority claims. In 'Claiming Ancestry and Lordship: Heraldic Language and Indigenous Identity in Post-Conquest Mexico' (Part II), Mónica Domínguez Torres observes that local leaders, following the example of Spanish soldiers, 'requested to the King of Spain his approval for their coats of arms, as part of the rewards they were entitled for their steadfast acceptance of Christianity and for their assiduous help to Hernán Cortés in the Conquest of Mexico'. The area surrounding Lake Texcoco, she says, offers striking examples of Mesoamerican codes of ancestry and lordship introduced within the 'European vocabulary of heraldry'. She argues that these hybrid codes expose 'intricate negotiations meant to secure a political niche for the indigenous allies to the Spanish Crown'. Concentrating on the case of Antonio Cortés Totoquihuaztli's armorial, Domínguez Torres explores some of the ways in which the 'natural Lords' of New Spain used to justify their position within the colonial system. She concludes that Don Antonio's coat of arms, which combined local and foreign symbols, was key to the reconstruction of Tlacopan's past, and as such proved to be an operative political tool for negotiating its future.

Border encounters presuppose border crossing, which is the topic of Christina Karageorgou-Bastea's chapter, 'Transatlantic Crossings: Don Álvaro as a Threshold' (Part III). The author examines the aesthetic, psychological and ethical effect of border crossing in the Duke of Rivas's *Don Álvaro and the Force of Fate* ([1835] 1990, 2005). She argues that over and above the geographical *topoi* through which don Álvaro, the main character of the Duke of Rivas's play, passes, his own body and desire become fluid thresholds, unstable and precarious, where the Self and the uncanny, Europe and America come together. Along the different stages of his adventures, the protagonist is gradually transformed through processes of social and self-rejection. Karageorgou-Bastea holds that survival becomes a matter of border crossing: don Álvaro – the mestizo, the assassin, the soldier, the monk – takes up and abandons life projects and occupies interstitial spaces whose internal inadequacy turns into the moving force of the plot. He passes through crossroads where urban formations challenge rural customs; battlefields in which different countries dispute territorial expansion; entrances where secular life defies sacred mandates. In the play, she says, even gender and *ethos* become topological signs of the Other: a lad and a holy man, both on the edge of their male identity, prove themselves to be a fugitive woman; the declaration of friendship and loyalty turns into treachery and revenge; heroism is a disguise for escaping one's own fate and a subterfuge; holiness is a concealment for passion. Finally, don Álvaro himself is a living threshold: the offspring of the union between a female member of the Inca's imperial family and an unlawful Spanish viceroy. In this sense, the play is shaped aesthetically on that liminal space between the past and the present, the individual and his/her origin, the discourse and its obliteration, the inscription and the blur; in other words, the limit where memory and forgetting struggle for mastery.

The first colonial confrontation with difference, a literal and figurative crossing of the threshold between distinct civilisations, was a moment of great discovery for the Spaniards who translated the *new* world (or what they initially thought as part of the West Indies) in terms of wealth, territorial expansion, free labour and the conversion of the 'uncivilised' natives (presumably some more 'savage' than others) to Christianity. The contact from the colonial point of view has been well documented in Christopher Columbus's diaries and the several letters and chronicles of the conquistadors. 'They should be good servants', Columbus hastens to note on Friday, 12 October 1492: 'I believe that they would easily be made Christians, for they appeared to me to have no religion' (1969: 56). For Columbus, and indeed for the European coloniser, the Indians, in the best case, could have 'culture' but hardly civilisation. In 'Genealogies and Analogies of "Culture" in the History of Cultural Translation' (Part I), John Ødemark concentrates on the dislocations of the colonial religious discourse. He points out that the so-called 'spiritual conquest' of the Americas was accompanied by vast efforts of the religious orders to describe the language and customs of the local populations. Notwithstanding that friars like Bernardino de Sahagún and José de Acosta have been designated 'fathers of anthropology', 'the purpose of the knowledge produced was manifestly the conversion of the natives'. The author mentions that the semantic differential between missionary and modern ethnography lies in the anthropocentric criteria of the latter, which intend to grasp the viewpoint of the natives. He focuses on the translation of ethnographic knowledge and conceptual schemes from early missionary ethnography to the emergent field of cultural history and anthropology in the eighteenth century, and uses as a platform the work of Lorenzo Boturini Benaduci, a Milanese who after a long stay in New Spain published his 'new idea' of Mesoamerican history in Madrid in 1746 (*Idea of a New General History of Northern America*). The book was based upon his *museo indiano*, the largest collection of ethnohistorical sources from Mesoamerica ever collected, and is mainly remembered today as the first attempt to apply Giambattista Vico's *New Science* [1744] (1968) to a local culture. In a way, Vico is seen as the 'father' of the concept of culture as a historical category and therefore, in Boturini's work, two genealogies of early modern 'cultural' investigation come together. Ødemark explains that in order to proffer the new, Boturini had to relate it to prior Spanish knowledge of the Americas and naturally to his Spanish target culture. Through Boturini, the author approaches the broader issue of the translation of 'culture', and shows 'how "others" looked upon "others"' before the term became a conceptual category and a common place in the interpretation of human difference. In doing so, he historicises our own understanding of cultural pedigrees.

As regards the Europeans' perception of the indigenous as people without religion, Maldonado-Torres argues that this formed the basis for the later assumption that they lacked, or had less, humanity (the colonised as an inferior human being), which was exemplified in the sixteenth century in the debate between Juan Ginés de Sepúlveda and Bartolomé de Las Casas (2007: 145).[16] Drawing on Dussel's distinction between Descartes's *ego cogito* and modernity's *ego conquiro* (I conquer), which preceded the former by more than a century (Dussel, 1996: 133),[17] he says:

> Si el *ego cogito* fue formulado y adquirió relevancia práctica sobre las bases del *ego conquiro*, esto quiere decir que 'pienso, luego soy' tiene al menos dos dimensiones insospechadas. Debajo del 'yo pienso' podríamos leer 'otros no piensan', y en el interior de 'soy' podemos ubicar la justificación filosófica para la idea de que 'otros no son' [...]. (Maldonado-Torres, 2007: 144)

> If the *ego cogito* was formulated and acquired practical relevance on the basis of *ego conquiro*, this means that 'I think, therefore I am' has at least two unforeseen dimensions. Beneath 'I think' we could read 'they do not think', and inside 'I am', we could trace the philosophical justification for the idea that 'others are not' [...].

The *ego conquiro* is the invisible side of the *ego cogito*, in the same way that coloniality is the darker side of modernity – much like photograph negatives. For Maldonado-Torres, the syllogism 'Others do not think, therefore they are not', implicit in the Cartesian *ego cogito*, explains philosophically Columbus's 'doubt' as regards the humanity of the others, and justifies, in the eyes of the European, their subsequent colonisation and racialisation (2007: 145). This misanthropic scepticism, as he calls it, creates a 'sub-ontological difference' or a 'colonial ontological difference', which is the difference between Being and what lies below it – that is, the 'damnés de la terre' (wretched of the earth) in Fanon's terms (1963), Dussel's exteriority and Mignolo's colonial difference. This sub-ontology discloses the presence of what he calls 'coloniality of being'

---

16   For more information, see Hanke (1974).
17   See also 'Toward a Phenomenology of the Ego Conquiro', Chapter 1 of *The Invention of the Americas* (Dussel, 1995).

(2007: 146–147),[18] which refers to the ontological dimension of Quijano's 'coloniality of power'.[19]

Needless to say, Columbus's translation of the natives was utterly partial and misleading. Their conversion would prove much more troublesome than the admiral had ever anticipated, forcing the European faith to compromise its purported purity and authority by allowing, reluctantly more often than not, for the syncretic to emerge. For the natives, on the other hand, the encounter with European difference, both an 'emblematic and problematic moment' as J. Jorge Klor de Alva notes (2006: xxii), brought about an even more sweeping change. King Moctezuma's messenger describes this moment eloquently and movingly: 'Their trappings and arms are all made of iron. They dress in iron and wear iron casques on their heads. Their swords are iron; their bows are iron; their shields are iron; their spears are iron. Their deer carry them on their backs wherever they wish to go. These deer, our lord, are as tall as the roof of a house' (León Portilla, 2006: 30). The strangers in iron that disembarked on Good Friday, 22 April 1519, 'from a small mountain floating in the midst of the water, and moving here and there without touching the shore' (2006: 16) were not gods, as Moctezuma repeatedly misjudged, but a bunch of soldiers in search of gold that were about to change for ever, albeit unknowingly, the historical course of at least two continents and initiate a long period of Eurocentrism. The Aymara in what is now Bolivia and Peru interpreted this confrontation as a dragonish shattering of the previous order, a radical epistemic break, which they called *Pachakuti* – literally, 'the world upside down' (Mignolo, 2005: xiv and 161). The *icnocuicatl* (or songs of sorrow) composed by Aztec poets soon after the Conquest of Mexico-Tenochtitlan are telling of the profound wound inflicted upon the Indians: 'Weep, my people:/ know that with these disasters/ we have lost the Mexican nation./ The water has turned bitter,/ our food is bitter!/ These are the acts of the Giver of Life. . .' (León Portilla, 2006: 146).[20]

Regretfully, very few native accounts of the Conquest have survived. Among them is Sahagún's *Universal History of the Things of New Spain* ([ca. 1577] 1950–1982, 2000), also known as the *Florentine Codex*, which comprises reports on the Conquest of Mexico from the Nahuas' point of view. In 1558 Fray Bernardino de Sahagún, a Franciscan missionary in sixteenth-century Mexico, was commissioned to compose a work on the world of the Aztecs or Nahuas. Sahagún spent 20 years gathering data from Nahua

---

18   The term 'coloniality of being' is first mentioned by Mignolo (2001: 30).
19   See also fn. 1.
20   Extract from the song 'The Fall of Tenochtitlan' (most likely composed in the year 1523).

respondents, giving cohesion to an amalgam of heterogeneous material in Nahuatl, and translating his first written version into Spanish. The resulting text, *Universal History of the Things of New Spain*, consists of twelve books that comprise information on Nahua gods and mythology, ceremonies, omens, soothsayers, astronomy, rhetoric, kings and lords, professions, flora and fauna, and the Conquest of Mexico-Tenochtitlan. Victoria Ríos Castaño's chapter, 'Translating the Nahuas' (Part I), reveals how Sahagún interpreted the world of the Nahuas in accord with his own mindset, target audiences and purposes. He departed from the basis of an Occidental classification of knowledge and included within a range of categories the indigenous material that he deemed most adequate and representative. The author analyses two of the several intellectual models that most likely Sahagún had used as his sources: Bartholomaeus Anglicus's medieval encyclopaedia *De proprietatibus rerum* and the medieval religious compilation of vices and virtues.

Right from the outset, the meeting of two worlds with no common language was vested in mistranslations and dislocations, and set up an endless series of border encounters that continuously assessed and reassessed epistemic premises on both sides. In his first letter to the Emperor Charles V and Queen Doña Juana dated 10 July 1519, Cortés relates the first recorded incident of mistranslation when he refers to the peninsula of Yucatán in the southeast coast of Mexico: 'We have reason to believe that Your Royal Highness have been informed, by letters of Diego Velásquez, the admiral's lieutenant in the island of Fernandina (Cuba), of a new land that was discovered in these parts some two years ago more or less, and which was first called Cozumel and later Yucatan, without it being either the one or the other as Your Royal Highness shall see from our report' (Cortés, 2001: 3). The land was 'discovered' by Cortés's political rival, Diego Velásquez, governor of Cuba, who allegedly misunderstood the Mayas, assuming that the place was called *Yucatán* when in fact the locals were saying that they could not understand their language. Anthony Pagden clarifies that the word *Yucatán* is a Spanish corruption of *Ci uthan*, meaning 'they say so', and that the correct name was *uluumil cutz yetel ceh* ('The Land of Turkeys and Deer') (Cortés, 2001: note 2, 449). The name Yucatán subsequently appeared in maps, with the first one dating from as early as 1527 (see Diego de Landa's *Account of the Things of Yucatan* [1941]).[21] According to Stephen M. Hart, 'the scene epitomises the drama of the conquest: on the one hand, we have a native population which finds the words and actions of the Europeans incomprehensible, while, on the other, we have the European coloniser mapping out a new world based on a misreading' (2007: 15).

---

21   Reference given by Pagden (Cortés, 2001: 450).

The colonial mapping of the 'new' world, an ultimate deed of epistemic reordering, was in this case not only partial but based on a false premise. Sadly this epistemic revisionism continued to be asymmetrical, in so far as the power, even in the post-Independence era, lay in large part with the Europeans and European descendants, namely with *criollos* and less with mestizos (with the exception of Evo Morales in Bolivia), typically attuned to the Western system of knowledge; at the same time, the indigenous and African populations, ontologically and epistemologically subalternised (Walsh, 2005: 17), were consigned to the fringes of the officialdoms, inhabiting the breaches and silences of their double marginalisation (citizens on the periphery of the world-system and of their own countries), and producing historical hiccups within the official national narratives. Even writers like Borges failed to acknowledge non-European cultures in Argentina (the Collas, Chiriguanos, Tobas, Mapudungun, Guaranies, Wichi, Mapuches and Tehuelches, among others),[22] as he espoused only one of the three constituents of the supposed primitivism of the country (the *criollo* gaucho of European descent), conspicuously overlooking the *negros* (Afro-Argentines) and the *indios*; in 'The South' the latter are depicted negatively, in the figure of the ill-mannered 'young thug with the Indian-looking face' who challenges Dalhmann to a duel (Borges, 1998: 179). In most of the cases, the Indians and those of African descent have been forced into a spatialised marginality (shanty towns, hapless suburbs and remote rural areas), which stands as a signifier of their social and cultural invisibility (in Argentina, for instance, those who had survived the nineteenth-century systematic extermination of indigenous tribes were expelled to the northern and southern extremes of the country).

Sarmiento's conceptual grid civilisation/barbarism, which has marked ideological discussions in Latin America since Independence, is a paradigmatic case of the *criollo* élite's identification with the West as the unequalled locus

---

22 'There are 16 to 20 indigenous groups in Argentina that dwell primarily in the northern part of the country, bordering Bolivia and Paraguay. The larger groups are the Collas (35,000), the Chiriguanos (15,000), the Tobas (15,000), the Mapudungun (40,000) of the Chaco, the Guaranies (10,500) of Misiones and the Wichi (25,000). Further south, about 36,000 Mapuches live in the province of Nequen and Tehuelches, bordering on Chile [...]. There are also varying estimates of Quechua and Quichua speakers in Argentina depending upon seasonal employment. In the Tierra del Fuego, there are also some Selk'namgon people. [...] Chiringuan, Choroti, Mataco, Mocovi, and Toba are spoken in the Gran Chaco. In Mesopotamia, Guarani is the main language for indigenous people. Aruacano-Mapuche and Tehuelche is spoken in Patagonia, while Yamana, Ona, and Selk'namgon are spoken in Tierra del Fuego' (Minorities at Risk Project, 2003: np).

of epistemic enunciation, to secure a political, social and cultural niche within the incipient networks of power. As his fellow Europhile Juan Bautista Alberdi had put it: 'Nosotros, europeos de raza y de civilización somos los dueños de América' (We, Europeans of race and of civilisation, are the owners of America) (Terán, 1996: 58). There are three chapters in this volume that reconsider the ideological legacy of the Generation of 1837. In 'A European Enclave in an Alien Continent?' (Part III), Leslie Ray revisits in a polemical fashion the enduring dichotomy between European civilisation and indigenous barbarism in Argentina today. The author contends that in contrast with its Latin American neighbours, who at least pay lip service to their indigenous roots in their official histories, Argentina has evolved the guiding fiction that it was founded by Europeans and wholly upon European values, and that, following the so-called 'Conquest of the Desert' in the late nineteenth century, its original cultures 'were as good as wiped out'. In this way, from very early on Argentina endorsed a sanitised version of history full of absences and epistemic breaches, where the non-European Other was officially obliterated from collective memory. As a consequence, notes Ray, its indigenous peoples often find themselves in the unenviable position of being seen as aliens in their own land, with no prospect of the emergence of an Evo Morales to represent their interests and express their pride. Ray imparts an analysis of the theories of the major figures of the Generation of 1837 (Alberdi, Sarmiento, Esteban Echeverría), who contributed to the formation of the guiding fiction of European cultural superiority, disclosing 'the idealising and denigrating assumptions that underpin them'. He stresses that such theories 'did not emerge in a vacuum, but were in accord with the requirements of a new state founded on immigration', yet surprisingly they continued to be pervasive in periods when immigrants were 'scapegoated for the country's problems' – an issue discussed in Michela Coletta's chapter. He concludes that despite some modest signs of improvement, the picture that appears to emerge of Argentina today is of a hierarchical society, still divided along racial lines, in which urban indigenous youngsters in particular find themselves in a liminal position, neither able to embrace and be fully embraced by mainstream society, nor to return to the noble 'authentic' life in rural communities that is idealised by their parents and grandparents.

In 'The Role of Degeneration Theory in Spanish American Public Discourse at the *Fin de Siècle*' (Part II), Michela Coletta considers the representation of race and immigration in relation to the idea of the degeneration of the national character in Chile and Argentina at the turn of the twentieth century. In Chile, the debate around the opposition between the so-called Latin race and the Anglo-Saxon race exploited the category of degeneration as a discursive tool: while ideas of disease and decay were attributed to the former, the latter was perceived as being younger and less intellectualised, and therefore more able to survive. The economic, social and cultural implications of this paradigmatic opposition came fully to the surface during the first decade of the twentieth century, when many Chilean commentators strongly criticised the heavy influx of 'Latin' immigrants. Coletta thinks over the reasons and the extent to which the category of degeneration was employed to create and justify a supposed '*Latin* American' modern identity. She corroborates that a historical conception of race echoing the French tradition, which became consolidated from Augustin Thierry onwards, was adapted to the Spanish American context. However, she observes that while the acquisition of European blood was seen to be a way out of the racial impasse since the mid-1800s, in the last few years of the nineteenth century there seemed to be a progressively ambivalent attitude towards European immigrants, especially those coming from Southern Europe. In Argentina, modern European culture was increasingly represented as old and stagnant through the depiction of the 'Latin' immigrant. One of Coletta's main contentions is that the idea of Latinity, which was strongly marked by notions of moral and racial degeneration, was instrumental to shaping discourses of 'modernity' in the region. She looks into the role that this ambivalence played in the process of self-definition at the turn of the century, which led to the reconfiguration of the traditional dichotomy of *civilisation versus barbarism*.

Finally, Emilse Hidalgo's '(Mis)appropriating Europe' (Part II) surveys the ways in which the cultural crossings between Argentina and Europe inform the symbolic representation of history, politics and cultural memory in Ricardo Piglia's novel *Artificial Respiration* ([1980] 1994, 2001), through the use of voice, translation, quotation and the proper name. Hidalgo studies how these textual strategies subvert the antagonism between the ideologemes of civilisation and barbarism as they are set in a relational strain, following Benjamin's concept of the dialectics between civilisation and barbarism. She further discusses 'the tensions that arise when European culture is "transposed", "grafted" or "translated" into the social and political coordinates of a peripheral country', thus problematising the socio-political and cultural opposition between Self/Other. The strategies of displacement, paradox and irony are studied as literary forms that vindicate the tradition of those who were vanquished, silenced and subjugated by the hegemonic Other. She argues that Piglia's novel suggests new forms of reading the literary, cultural and political tradition of Argentina that work as a 'correction' or a (mis)reading – that is, a reading *against* the grain – of a previous social text, resituating those readings in the present context of post-default Argentina.

In a conversation we had a couple of years ago, Piglia referred to the juxtaposition between civilisation and barbarism as a self-legitimating ideologeme utilised by those in power to relay (official) history: 'Esa oposición la plantean siempre las clases dominantes, digamos que esa oposición es el modo que tienen los vencedores de pensar la historia' (This opposition is always presented by the dominant classes, let's say that this opposition is the way in which the victors think of history).[23] In a different interview, Noé Jitrik disclosed the underlying fallacies of such epistemic enunciations, concentrating on two major moments of world history:

> La Revolución Mexicana, por ejemplo, fue vista por la clase dominante como barbarie enfrentada con la civilización porfiriana. [. . .] Los principales actores del nazismo [. . .] pretendían representar la civilización (porque sostenían que los judíos, gitanos, homosexuales, etcétera, eran infrahumanos). (Kefala, 2008: 267)

> The Mexican Revolution, for example, was seen by the dominant class as barbarism against the Porfirian civilisation. [. . .] The principal actors of Nazism [. . .] claimed to represent civilisation (because they held that the Jews, gipsies, homosexuals, etc., were sub-humans).

No sooner had the nascent nations got rid of colonial rule and grappled with a sense of 'postcolonial' identity than they were cast anew, as if in a time loop, into another type of socio-economic coloniality veiled under the label of modernisation and, more recently, of neoliberalism and globalisation. In the final chapter of the volume, 'McOndo, Magical Neoliberalism and Latin American Identity', Rory O'Bryen proposes that we review the tropes that have traditionally underpinned thinking about identity and identification in Spanish America, in response to a burgeoning of engagements with globalisation and post-nationalism in post-Boom fiction. He remarks that since the mid-nineteenth century, when Spanish and American writers looked to Europe and North America in their efforts to define national and continental identities, there has been considerable debate as to whether the dialectic of self-identification through the foreign entails the homogenisation or loss of an original cultural ground (acculturation), or whether, indeed, it involves the symbolic densification of such ground, and the mutual-transformation of all parties in the equation (transculturation). Such a debate reached its apotheosis at the moment of the Boom, which dwelt at length on the struggle between subaltern cultures and a nascent capitalism that threatened to erase them, or on the struggle between commoditisation and the singular role of the aesthetic. Now the debate between acculturation and transculturation,

---

23   For a Greek version of the interview, see Kefala (2009).

observes O'Bryen, seems to have been firmly resolved in favour of the latter, and is accompanied by a broader desubstantification of identity *per se* that stresses its relational, processual nature. Nowhere is this clearer than in recent Spanish American engagements with popular culture. He postulates that since Manuel Puig at least, such engagements have disembedded identity from primordialist narratives that align the practice of culture with the reproduction of affective attachments to place through language. He also adds that they have exposed the Boom writer's contradictory claim to artistic autonomy precisely at the moment of his/her integration into a globalised consumer market. O'Bryen develops these issues further by exploring the implications for identity in which the practice of culture is explicitly placed within neoliberal economies of production and consumption. Through a close reading of Alberto Fuguet and Sergio Gómez's manifesto-collection *McOndo* (1996), he argues that consumption within de-nationalised scenarios of cultural exchange entails neither homogenisation nor loss, and adds that the symbolic shift from *Macondo* to *McOndo* calls for a thorough interrogation of discourses that place cultural *identity* at the intersection of traditional oppositions between First and Third World, Centre and Periphery. We have seen that Fuguet's and Gómez's call for a reconsideration of the locatedness of cultural identity is shared by decolonial thinkers. They, however, stress the need for an extra-modern perspective, which requires that we step out of the neoliberal epistemic paradigm in as much as *coloniality* is rampant in global capitalism. For this reason, they argue that we can speak of postcolonialism as the end of historical colonialism, that is, of colonialism in its political-administrative form, as opposed to postcoloniality which is still an incomplete project.

After 500 years of border negotiations and self-differentiations, the lingering question about national identity remains robust in all parts of Latin America, and discussions on culture loom over the continent poignantly now more than ever. The twentieth century has been prolific in critical essays, with Alejo Carpentier (1949) being the first to kick off a series of incisive theorisations of culture. Difference naturally rests at the heart of any project to conceptualise it, and thus mapping out the liminal space of identity development has been the principle objective of anthropologists, cultural critics and literati in the last 60 years or so, giving shape, as Julio Ortega points out, to a new 'geotextuality' (2006: 9). Below is a brief list, by no means exhaustive, of post-Independence theorisations in Latin America, whose major aim has been to register the aesthetic, cultural and epistemic conjunctions and disjunctions taking place in the interstitial precinct of contact and negotiation, and to explicate the palimpsestuous, pluriversal and plurilogical configurations that ensue from these negotiations: Alejo Carpentier's 'the marvellous real' (Latin American reality is marvellous because it is saturated by heteroclite traditions that withstand reason) (1949, 1990); Jorge Luis Borges's irreverent *orillas* (the indeterminate in-between territory of the suburbs of Buenos Aires where the rural *criollo* tradition and urban modernity meet and merge; metonymically within this liminal zone Latin Americans in general are free to appropriate irreverently elements from different cultures) (1999a); Xul Solar's *neocriollo* (an Esperanto-like concoction based on American Spanish, Brazilian Portuguese, English and German); Oswald de Andrade's anthropophagy (Latin American identity is formed through the digestion of heterogeneous traditions) (1991); the magical realist trend inaugurated by Gabriel García Márquez (a variation of Carpentier's notion, according to which ordinary and extraordinary events occur side by side in a continent imbued with mutually exclusive systems of knowledge); Aimé Césaire's *négritude* (an attempt to defy the invisibility of the disenfranchised otherness in the Caribbean) (1998); Frantz Fanon's violent zones of contact between cultures (1967); José María Arguedas's bilingual and bicultural consciousness (the indianisation of Spanish through bicultural processes in the Andes) (1985); Roberto Schwarz's misplaced ideas (Latin America is a pool of contrapuntal ideas, originating in different times and cultures) (1992); Rodolfo Kusch's *fagocitosis* (the engulfing of the European by the indigenous) (1970); Édouard Glissant's transversality (cross-cultural convergences) (1992); Silviano Santiago's 'in-between discourse' (an inter-mediate discourse on Latin American cultural encounters) (1978); Roberto Fernández Retamar's Calibanism (the devouring of the master/coloniser by the slave/colonised) (1971); Haroldo de Campos's cannibalism (akin to Oswald de Andrade's anthropophagy) (1986); Fernando Ortiz's (1987) and Ángel Rama's (1982) transculturation (mutually influential exchange of cultural capital); Antonio Cornejo Polar's heterogeneity (2004); Ricardo Piglia's appropriation (it fastens on Borges's irreverence) (1995); Gloria Anzaldúa's reconceptualisation of *mestizaje* (the border Chicano experience in the United States) (1987); Gustavo Pérez Firmat's biculturation (a balanced, mutual exchange between two cultures) (1994); Néstor García Canclini's hybridity (the hybridisation of the traditional and the modern in Latin America) (1997); Ariruma Kowii's (2005) and Catherine Walsh's (2006) interculturalism (the fair collaboration between dominant and subaltern cultures, as well as between subaltern cultures); Enrique Dussel's transmodernity (2002) and Santiago Castro-Gómez's transculturalism (2007) (a creative dialogue between different cultures, logics and perspectives); Walter Mignolo's border thinking (it conforms to Kowii's interculturalism) (2005); and Luís Madureira's cannibal modernities (2005) (see anthropophagy and cannibalism).

All of these theorisations are cognitive maps of the same liquid playground of difference, yet their perspectives can differ markedly; while some focus on its embedded creativity (Borges speaks of 'fortunate consequences' [1999a: 426]), others see it as a violent haven fostering mismatched distributions of epistemic power – what has recently become known as 'coloniality of knowledge', which highlights the epistemic dimension of Quijano's 'coloniality of power'.[24] If 'Occidentalism', for Mignolo, 'is an imperial malady' whose major symptom is 'the ongoing reproduction of a colonial Self-Other polarity' (1996: 76), the realisation of the formative, transitional and translational function of this frontier area should empower the deterritorialisation and defetishisation of monologic and monolithic notions of identity and history. In this way, the postcolonial shift from Occidentalism and Eurocentrism to 'globalcentrism', as outlined by Fernando Coronil, can indeed 'emphasiz[e] subalternity rather than alterity in the construction of cultural difference' (2004: 240). Only in these terms, however, could a postcolonial world be viable for all, and for Latin America in particular; not as a homogenisation of the subaltern (variously labelled as colonised, marginal, belated, peripheral, disenfranchised, vanquished, Third World and underdeveloped) accomplished through appellative monopolisations and an inordinate display of epistemic power, which strive to subjugate everything to an undifferentiated flux; but, as Timothy Brennan puts it, as 'a new openness' (2004: 123) to that in-translation space, unveiling the organic niche of difference in the politics of self-definition, and to what Benjamin called the *foreignness* of culture and identity. Difference ultimately is not something we have to live with side by side, as manifestos of a politically correct multiculturalism often proclaim, but the key agent in the continuous reassessment of selfness, a type of currency that identity inexorably depends upon.

Dussel proposes 'transmodernity' as an ethical project, 'a fertile multicultural moment', which could *trans*cend (but not negate) Western modernity. For him, transmodernity is a true, creative dialogue among the multiple cultures of the planet:

> I have called 'transmodernity', a worldwide ethical liberation project in which alterity, which was part and parcel of modernity, would be able to fulfill itself. The fulfillment of modernity has nothing to do with a shift from the potentialities of modernity to the actuality of European modernity. Indeed, the fulfillment of modernity would be a transcendental shift where modernity and its denied alterity, its victims, would mutually fulfill each other in a creative process. The transmodern project is the mutual fulfillment of the 'analectic' solidarity of center/periphery, woman/man, mankind/earth, western culture/peripheral postcolonial cultures, different races, different ethnicities, different classes. It should be noted here that this mutual fulfillment of solidarity does not take

---

24   See Castro-Gómez (2007), Lander (2000) and Walsh (2007).

place by pure denial but rather by subsumption from alterity. (2000: 473–474)

Similarly, Walsh suggests that in order to decolonise knowledge we need to develop a critical thinking in the area of cultural studies that takes seriously the intellectual contribution of indigenous and African social movements in the Andes (2005: 14), thus agreeing with William F. Fisher and Thomas Ponniah in that alternative visions to neoliberal globalisation – what Frei Betto calls 'globocolonisation' (2001 and 2004) – are to be found in contemporary social movements (2003: xi). The objective, according to Walsh, is to think 'fuera de los límites definidos por el neoliberalismo y la modernidad, y [...] construir mundos y modos de pensar y ser distintos' (outside the limits defined by neoliberalism and modernity, and [...] construct different worlds and ways of thinking and being) (2005: 15). Interculturalism, for her, is a powerful instrument in the struggle towards a truly postcolonial society:

> No nos referimos aquí a un pensamiento, voz, saber, práctica y poder más, sino unos pensamientos, voces, saberes, prácticas y poderes *de* y *desde* la diferencia que desvían de las normas dominantes radicalmente desafiando a ellas, abriendo la posibilidad para la descolonización y la edificación de sociedades más equitativas y justas. (2006: 35)

> We are not referring here to another way of thinking, another voice, knowledge, practice or power, but to ways of thinking, to voices, knowledges, practices and powers *of* and *from* difference that deviate from the dominant norms, radically challenging them, thus opening the possibility of decolonisation and the construction of more equitable and just societies.

Despite the obvious shortcomings of Walsh's conceptualisation of interculturalism, which at times appears to simply invert modernity's self/other polarity by seemingly privileging the indigenous and African populations as bearers of an ethically superior epistemology, the truth is that postcoloniality will remain a utopian project unless a true dialogue between different logics and cultures is initiated on an equal basis. To this end, we need to change both the content and the terms of the conversation (Mignolo, 2005: 149) by transcending modernity's bipolar legacy. In other words, privileging the formerly unprivileged alters the content but not the terms or the logic of the dialogue as it empowers a reverse coloniality, instead of eliminating it in all its forms (coloniality of power, coloniality of being and coloniality of knowledge).

Dussel's transmodern world envisions an ethically friendly society where the world's cultures could exist not hierarchically but, in Kyriakos Kontopoulos's terms, *heterarchically:*[25]

> Samuel Huntington, an ideologue of U.S. hegemony, sees as a 'clash', as a 'war' between civilizations, what is simply and positively the irreversible uprising of universal cultures excluded by modernity (and postmodernity). These cultures, in their full creative potential and together with a redefined Western culture [. . .] constitute a more human and complex world, more passionate and diverse, a manifestation of the fecundity that the human species has shown for millennia, a 'transmodern' world. A humanity that only spoke in English and that could only refer to 'its' past as an Occidental past would testify to the extinction of the majority of historical human cultural creativity. It would be the greatest castration imaginable and irreversible in humanity's world history! (Dussel, 2002: 236–237)

This vision of a heterarchical, transmodern world, however, lies, to a great extent, within the perimeter of utopian thought. The greatest challenge of postcolonial and decolonial theories today is, indeed, to break the barriers of academia and become praxis in the outside world where the future of humanity is being negotiated.

---

25 As opposed to hierarchy, heterarchy is 'a partially ordered level structure implicating a rampant interactional complexity' (Kontopoulos, 1993: 381).

1

Translating the Nahuas: Fray Bernardino de Sahagún's Parallel Texts in the Construction of *Universal History of the Things of New Spain*

VICTORIA RÍOS CASTAÑO

The Franciscan missionary, Fray Bernardino de Sahagún (1499–1590), arrived in Mexico-Tenochtitlan in 1529 to engage in the zealous indoctrination of the Nahuas or Aztecs. Yet, unlike the majority of his fellow missionaries, he spent over 50 of his 60 years of evangelical mission in three further proselytising-related objectives: firstly, the education of an élite of Nahua neophytes, aimed at governing and controlling a new Christianised indigenous society; secondly, the composition of doctrinal works in their language, Nahuatl, crucial for efficient indoctrination and orthodox celebration of Catholic rituals; and thirdly, an investigation of the Nahuas' culture designed to document religious practices the Spaniards considered idolatrous, with the specific aim of providing means for their eradication.

Regarding the latter aim, in 1558 the Franciscan Order commissioned Sahagún to compile a text on the world of the Nahuas, which he completed in Nahuatl around 1569 and translated into Spanish, this time under royal request, until 1577. The resulting work, *Historia universal de las cosas de Nueva España (Universal History of the Things of New Spain)*, was divided into twelve books: I Gods, II Ceremonies, III the Origin of the Gods, IV Soothsayers, V Omens, VI Rhetoric, VII Astronomy, VIII Kings and Lords, IX Merchants and Craftsmen, X The People, XI Earthly Things (Fauna and Flora), and XII The Conquest of Mexico.[1]

---

1 Sahagún's title 'Historia universal de las cosas de Nueva España' has been incorrectly superseded by 'historia general'. For further discussion, see Browne (2000). In this chapter, I will refer to Sahagún's work as *Historia universal*. The titles of the twelve books are those suggested by Arthur J. O. Anderson and Charles E. Dibble, translators of the Nahuatl text and Sahagún's prologues (originally written in Spanish) into English, in *Florentine Codex: General History of the Things of*

Of particular interest for this study is Sahagún's own statement that he set off to conduct research by designing

> en lengua castellana, vna minuta, o memoria, de todas las materias, de las que auja de tratar: que fue lo que esta escripto en los doze libros. (*Florentine Codex*, 'Prologues': 53)

> an outline or summary in Spanish of all the topics to be considered. This is that which is written in the twelve Books.

Several Sahagún scholars like Alfredo López Austin (1974) and Miguel León Portilla (1999a) have viewed his outline or summary, which is unfortunately lost, as a series of questionnaires created by a pioneer anthropologist with the purpose of data collection. Focusing on this perception, López Austin reconstructed the questions that Sahagún may have posed by analysing parallel contents in all the chapters of the twelve books.[2] Here, however, I regard López Austin's rewriting of the hypothetical questions as insufficient to understand the nature of Sahagún's summary. An examination of the material gathered in *Historia universal*, by establishing links with reference texts that Sahagún could have known, proves an omnipresent Western categorisation of the world, and helps uncover his summary as a manifestation of how he began a cultural translation process: the relocation of the world of the Nahuas into a European target-text. He applied a Spanish classification of knowledge, for he wrote that he made his outline in Spanish, and aimed at gathering the indigenous material that he considered most adequate and representative in Nahuatl.

In this chapter, I am concerned with the identification of two of the Western reference texts that Sahagún could have used to categorise the world of the Nahuas. I name these models, which reflect the cultural conventions and textual norms inherent in Sahagún's Old World, *parallel texts*. In translation studies this term has two definitions. It refers both to the source-language text and its translated version, as well as the target-language text imitated in translation training and in the translation process, which provides information on the patterns of target texts into which the source text is to be most effectively accommodated (Baker, 1995: 230). Adopting the second meaning of the term, I seek to demonstrate that in the construction of *Historia universal*, and particularly in the creation of his outline, Sahagún deployed two types of parallel texts: encyclopaedias like the

---

New Spain vols. 1–13 (Sahagún, 1950–1982). This edition is hereafter referred to as *Florentine Codex*.

2   See López Austin 'The Research Method of Fray Bernardino de Sahagún: The Questionnaires' (1974).

English Franciscan Bartholomaeus Anglicus's *De proprietatibus rerum*, composed between 1240 and 1260, and religious texts such as treatises on vices and virtues.

Starting with *De proprietatibus rerum*, this magnum opus was strongly influenced by the arrangements and contents of Pliny's *Historia naturalis* and Isidore of Seville's *Etymologiae*, from which Anglicus quoted on many occasions. *De proprietatibus rerum* circulated widely during the early Renaissance in both Latin and vernacular languages; the Spanish translation, for example, was written by Fray Vicente de Burgos around 1470 in the Basque town of Tolosa. Donald Robertson (1966) and León Portilla (1999b) hold the view that this is probably the work on which Sahagún relied most when planning his *Historia universal*. For Robertson, the fact that Anglicus and Sahagún were Franciscans implies that the latter knew about his fellow brother's work. He could have consulted Anglicus's encyclopaedia either in the library of the friary of San Francisco in Salamanca, where he took his vows and studied Arts and Theology, or in the library of the Imperial College of Santa Cruz of Tlatelolco in New Spain. Here Sahagún spent long periods of his life teaching Latin and medicine, for the purposes of which he could have resorted to this text.

To sustain his argument, Robertson also pinpointed striking correlations in both the arrangement and the contents of the two works, as this chart he created shows (1966: 627):

Historia universal	*De proprietatibus rerum*
Book I, The Gods	Book I, The Trinity; Book II, The Angels
Book II, The Calendar	Book IX, The Divisions of Time
Book III, The Gods	Book I, The Trinity; Book II, The Angels
Book IV, Astrology	Book VIII, Zodiac
Book V, Divination	
Book VII, Astronomy	Book VIII, Astronomy
Book VIII, Ch. 8–21, Rulers	Book VI, Virtues and Vices of Man
Book IX, Merchants and the Arts and Crafts	
Book X, Ch. 1–26, Virtues and Vices of the Indigenous People	
Book X, Ch. 28, Illnesses and Medicines	Book V, Parts of Human Body; Book VIII, Illnesses and Medicine
Book XI, Ch. 1, Animals	Book XVIII, Animals
Book XI, Ch. 2, Birds	Book XII, Birds
Book XI, Ch. 3, Animals of the Water	Book XIII, Fish
Book XI, Ch. 6, Trees	Book XVII, Trees and Herbs
Book XI, Ch. 7, Other Herbs	
Book XI, Ch. 8, Precious Stones	Book XVI, Stones, Minerals and Metals
Book XI, Ch. 11, Colours	Book XIX, Colours, Odours, Tastes
Book XI, Ch. 12, Waters and Land	Book XVIII, Waters; Book XIV, Earth and Hills

De proprietatibus rerum and *Historia universal* begin with the Divine (Sahagún's Books I, III, Anglicus's Books I, II), proceed to the Human (Sahagún's Books VIII, IX, X, Anglicus's Books III–VII) and subsequently to the Mundane. This final section contains information on nature, namely herbs, animals and geological/geographical material (Sahagún's Book XI, Anglicus's Books VIII–XIX). Moreover, within each of these divisions, readers proceed from the superior to the inferior: trinity to angels, man to his illnesses, the heavenly bodies to the earth, and the animal and vegetable kingdoms to the mineral world (Robertson, 1966: 622–623).

Robertson indicated that the most enlightening coincidence in Anglicus's and Sahagún's texts is found in Anglicus's Book VI 'the ages of man and his properties', and in Sahagún's Book X 'in which are told the different virtues and vices which were of the body and of the soul, whomsoever practised them' (1966: 625). In Anglicus's Chapters VI, VII, X, XI, and XV to XIX, people are described as sinful and virtuous according to age, status and profession. The following is a passage from Chapters XVI and XVII on the properties of bad and good servants. I quote here the translation into Spanish by Fray Vicente de Burgos:[3]

> Del sieruo malo, capitulo xvj. Cosa co[n]teniente es co[n] las cosas q[ue] dicho hauemos d[e]l sieruo digamos algo de sus miserables propiedades por las quales assi & a los otros haze mucho mal. El mal sieruo comunme[n]te es borracho & negligente enlos seruiçios de q[ue] deue seruir a su señor/ y es ladron q[ue] le hurta los bienes. E destos dize salamon enlos .xxx. capitulos delos proverbios q[ue] seruidor neglige[n]te y borracho no sera jamas rico. El es comunme[n]te oçioso qua[n]do deue ser diligente [...]. Del buen seruidor, capitulo xvij. Ha el buen seruidor muchas buenas co[n]diçiones dignas de nos sser oluidades. Ca es de buen ygenio y entendimie[n]to. E de tal dezia salamon a los .xvij. capitulos d[e] sus proverbios. El sabio sieruo avra señoria sobre los hijos locos. (Anglicus, [1494] 1992)

> On the bad servant, Chapter xvi. Concerning what we have already said about the servant, let's say something about his bad properties, which lead him to act sinfully. A bad servant is commonly a drunkard, negligent in his chores for his lord, and a thief who steals his goods. In

---

3 For further references see John of Trevisa's translation into English (ca. 1398), *On the Properties of Things: John Trevisa's Translation of Bartholomaeus Anglicus 'De Proprietatibus Rerum', a Critical Text* (Anglicus, 1975–1988); and the Spanish translation of Vicente de Burgos *De las propriedades de las cosas* (Anglicus, [1494] 1992).

Chapter xxx of his proverbs Solomon says that a drunken and negligent servant will never become rich. He is commonly lazy when he should be diligent. On the good servant, Chapter xvii. The good servant has many qualities which are worth remembering, for he is wise and intelligent. Thus said Solomon in Chapter xvii of his proverbs. The wise servant will govern over fool sons. (My translation)

The passage lists the qualities of the servant, which vary from 'drunkard', 'negligent', 'thief', 'lazy' to 'witty', 'intelligent', 'respectable', 'bold' and 'faithful to his lord'. The maxims borrowed from the *Book of Proverbs* of the Old Testament authorised the description; that is, they validated the reliability of the human properties chosen.

Similarly, in Chapters I–XXVI of Sahagún's Book X in *Historia universal* there is a series of virtues and vices portraying a wide spectrum of people: from family members (good and bad fathers) to rulers (good and bad lords), and professions such as craftsmen (good and bad carpenters). For instance, in Chapter I an account of the virtuous and the sinful daughter is provided in Nahuatl:

> yn tecuneuh yn ichpuchtli, quiztica, macitica vel nelli ichpuchtli in iectli in qualli, in qualli ichpuchtli, tecacqui, mimati, tlacaqui, mozcalia, iollo timalli, yxtilli imacaxtli, tlanonotzalli, tlazcaltilli, tlauapaualli, tlamachtilli tlanemachtilli, chipauacanemilice, mimattinzli. Tecuneuh in amo qualli in amo iectli, in tlaueliloc, teuhio tlaçollo, cuecuech, cuecuel, ciuatlaueliloc, mihimati, moquequecimmati, moieiecquetza, muchichiua, apan vpan nemi, auilnemi, auilquiztinemi, mahauiltia, ahauiltzoncaloa, cuecuenocini, iuinti. (*Florentine Codex*, X: 2–3)

> One's daughter: the daughter [is] untouched, pure, a virgin. The good daughter [is] obedient, honest, intelligent, discreet, of good memory, modest, respectful, well reared, well taught, well trained, well instructed, prudent, chaste, circumspect. One's daughter [who is] bad, evil, perverse [is] full of vice, dissolute, proud; a whore, she is showy, pompous, gaudy of dress, garish; she is a loiterer, given to pleasure; a courtesan, given to amusement, always vicious, crazed, besotted.

Like the aforementioned description of the bad and the good servant, this passage supplies a copious list of adjectives so as to describe a daughter or a woman in general: discreet and modest *versus* proud and showy; prudent *versus* crazed. Although this coincidence of contents and classification of human characteristics according to sins and virtues prompted Robertson to underscore the influence of *De proprietatibus rerum* on *Historia universal*, he did not explain the reason why and the way in which Sahagún included these depictions. In the Spanish version of Book X (The People), Sahagún himself offered some clues when addressing his reader:

> No se debe ofender el lector prudente en que se ponen solamente vocablos y no sentencias en lo arriba puesto, y en otras partes adelante, porque principalmente se pretende en este tratado aplicar el lenguaje castellano al lenguaje indígena para que se sepan hablar los vocablos propios desta materia, de *viciis et virtutibus*. (*Historia general*, 2: 860)

> The wise reader must not get tired or offended while reading only words and sentences, as written above and in subsequent pages. The main aspiration of this book is to apply the Spanish language to the indigenous language so that vocabulary on this matter, of *viciis et virtutibus*, can be spoken. (My translation)

Sahagún expressed his wish to gather words and sentences in an attempt to conform to a religious textual tradition: the treatises on vices and virtues. These treatises, which he mentions as inspirational reference texts, probably when outlining the topics of what eventually became Book X in *Historia universal*, could be branded as another parallel text or intellectual model.

The compilation of vices or sins and virtues dates back to Aristotle's treatise *De virtutibus et vitiis*. In his eighth chapter he examined virtues such as prudence, humility, soberness, magnanimity, and their opposites; stupidity, wrath, cowardice and vileness. Medieval scholasticism, following the philosopher's example, gave rise to the appearance of further texts akin. In the thirteenth century the Italian rhetorician Guido Faba (ca. 1190–1245) wrote *Summa de vitiis et virtutibus*; and the Dominican preacher Guillaume Perrault (d. 1271) wrote *Summa de viciis et virtutibus*. In the same vein, in his *Summa theologiae* (1265–1272), volume *Secunda secundae*, Thomas Aquinas, fervent admirer of Aristotle, devoted 170 chapters to virtues and sins in light of what classical and religious authorities had discussed. Aquinas divided virtues into theological (faith, hope and charity) and cardinal (prudence, justice, fortitude and temperance). In his analysis of the virtue of temperance, he wrote: 'Macrobius holds that temperance produces modesty, sensitiveness of shame, chastity, honourableness, moderation, sparseness, soreness and purity. Andronicus also lists gravity, continence, humility, simplicity, refinement, discipline, and contentment with one's lot' (Aquinas, 1963–1981: 49). As this passage shows, treatises on vices and virtues were rich in vocabulary. In fact, they provided rhetorical training in the sense that their readers could learn a wide range of synonyms and antonyms. More importantly for this chapter, these treatises constituted a valuable proselytising aid. Priests, who aspired to inculcate Christian values and moral perfection *versus* sin in the minds of their audiences, used these texts in their speeches, homilies and in the administering of the sacrament of penance. In England, for instance, several ordinances decreed in Councils and Synods from the thirteenth to the fifteenth centuries compelled every priest to secure for themselves a *summula* or compilation on vices and virtues. At the beginning of the sixteenth century, these treatises still flourished throughout Europe, and were translated from Latin into the vernacular languages. For example, the *Somme le roi* of Lorens d'Orléans was translated into Spanish around 1450, and the international best-seller *Fiori di virtù* into *Flor de virtudes y vicios* around 1470 (Francis, 1942: ix–xxx).

In the friary of San Francisco in Salamanca, Sahagún would have deployed some of these treatises in order to improve his fluency in Latin to become more eloquent in Spanish, and to write inspiring and effective sermons. Once in New Spain he could have consulted the editions of Aquinas's *Summa theologiae* and the *Summa uirtutum* under the name of Guillaume Perrault, which were available in the library of Tlatelolco (Mathes, 1982: 63). After reconsidering the study and use he probably made of these works either in Spain or New Spain, it is very likely that in his outline or summary he incorporated a section on vices and virtues, which involved gathering terminology in Nahuatl and information about the Nahuas. Linguistic and cultural data could be utilised for the creation of sermons or in the auricular confession of his Nahua neophytes. In an attempt to develop this argument, the following pages illustrate how data within *Historia universal* was drawn on to the administering of this sacrament.

The Franciscans introduced aural confession in New Spain in 1526. Sahagún voiced concerns regarding this arduous task in the first prologue of *Historia universal* when urging his fellow missionaries to learn how to

> preguntar lo que conuiene y entender lo que dixeren tocante a su officio [porque] los peccados de la idolatria [. . .] no son aun perdid[os] del todo. Y los confesores ni se [los] preguntan ni piensan que ay tal cossa: ni sauen lenguaje para se lo preguntar ni aun lo entenderan aunque se lo digan. (*Florentine Codex*, 'Prologues': 45–46)

> ask what is proper and understand what they may say pertaining to his work [because] the sins of idolatry [. . .] are not yet completely lost. [. . .] And the confessors neither ask about them, nor think such thing exists, nor understand the language to inquire about it, nor would even understand them, even though they told them of it.

In this revealing paragraph, Sahagún's experiences as a confessor resonate strongly. When attempting to administer the sacrament he would have wrestled to understand what his penitents articulated, whether they had performed idolatry, and if so, of which type, in order to absolve or urge them to do penance. Confessors, as he argued, did not know how to ask and interpret what they heard. Unaware of the existence of idolatry they consequently contributed to its perpetuation.

Historia universal in Nahuatl was written with the intention of supplying the linguistic and cultural information that according to Sahagún missionaries needed to convert the Nahuas. Book X (The People) is one of the texts that best exemplify Sahagún's evangelical mission, in this case, the achievement of appropriate confessions. Bearing in mind the different types of Nahua penitents, Sahagún included a depiction of people depending on their virtues or vices; in other words, their good or bad properties. The people contained in this list ranged from family members to professionals, which coincided with Spanish ones, as in the case of the physician, or attested to a new reality. An interesting example is the cacao seller:

> In tlaueliloc cacaoanamacac: cacaoananauhqui, teixcuepani, cacaoachichiuh [.] In quinamaca cacaoatl tlanexquetzalli, tlâcectli, tlatletomaoalli, quiticeoacatlapiquia, in xoxouhqui, quinexuia, quinexpopoxoa, quiti-çauia, quitlaltiçauia, quitlaluia, quitlalpopoxoa, tzooalli, xicocuitlatl, aoacaiollotli, quicacaoatlapiquia, cacaoaxipeoallotl ic quiquimiloa, caca-oacacalotl conaaquia, in ticeoac in xoxouhqui, in patzaoac, in chi-lacachtic, in xamanqui, in cacaltic, in quimichnacaztic, quicenneloa, quicepanneloa, quimotlaltia, itlan caquia, quicepanmictia, nel quap-patlachtli itlã quitlaça quimotlaltia, inic teca mocaiaoa. (*Florentine Codex*, X: 65)

> The bad cacao seller, [the bad] cacao dealer, the deluder counterfeits cacao. He sells cacao beans which are placed in [hot] ashes, toasted, made full in the fire; he counterfeits by making the fresh cacao beans whitish; he places them in [hot] ashes – stirs them into the [hot] ashes; [then] he treats them with chalk, with chalky earth, with [wet] earth; he stirs them into [wet] earth. [With] amaranth seed dough, wax, avocado pits he counterfeits cacao; he covers this over with cacao bean hulls; he places this in the cacao bean shells. The whitish, the fresh cacao beans he intermixes, mingles, throws in, introduces, ruins with the shrunken, the chilli-seed-like, the broken, the hollow, the tiny. Indeed he casts, he throws in with them wild cacao beans to deceive the people.

In this passage a confessor who had to administer the sacrament to a cacao seller could grasp the variety of techniques a bad or sinful one adopted when mixing his merchandise with spurious substances. The confessor could also reproduce specific Nahuatl terminology and collocations related to the cacao seller's activity, such as to make 'toasted, whitish, shrunken, chilli-seed-like beans' and 'to treat and mix cacaobeans' either 'with chalk' or 'chalky earth'. All in all, confessors were able to figure out what kind of questions they could pose, and were more likely to understand their penitents' answers.

Fray Alonso de Molina was one of Sahagún's fellow missionaries who turned to the material collected in Book X of *Historia universal* to compose his bilingual confession manual *Confessionario mayor en lengua mexicana y castellana* ([1569] 1984).[4] Both Franciscans maintained a peer-reviewed relationship in their creation of lexical and doctrinal texts in Nahuatl. Sahagún ([1579] 1993) approved Molina's first dictionary of Nahuatl *Vocabulario en lengua castellana y mexicana* ([1555] 1571) and Molina probably proof-read Sahagún's biblical translations of Latin into Nahuatl included in Sahagún's doctrinal work *Postilla* (Bustamante García, 1989: 488).

An example to demonstrate that Molina copied material from Book X is found in Molina's questions tailored to the cacao-seller penitent:

> Y tú que vendes cacao ¿revolviste el buen cacao con el malo, para que todo se emplease y vendiese, engañando a las gentes? ¿Encenizaste el cacao verde o revolvístelo con tierra blanda para que pareciese bueno o pones masa de tzovalli dentro del hollejo del mismo cacao o masa de cuescos de aguacate, falseando el dicho cacao? ¿Y los cacaos pequeños y delgados tuéstaslos para los hacer parecer grandes y gruesos? (de Molina, [1569] 1984: Folio 37, 19–20)

> And you cacao seller, did you mix good cacao beans with bad ones so that everything was sold? Did you deceive your customers? Did you mix green cacao beans with ashes or with soft earth so that the cacao looked good? Did you add amaranth seed dough or that of avocado pits to counterfeit the cacao bean? Do you roast small and thin cacao beans to make them look big and thick? (My translation)

Molina seems to have transformed the description included in *Historia universal* into questions for his confession manual. In Sahagún's text a bad cacao seller 'counterfeits cacao' in general, whereas Molina urged confessors to ask the cacao seller whether he mixed good and bad cacao beans to cheat his customers. The information on the bad cacao seller as someone who 'places them [the cacao beans] in [hot] ashes – stirs them into the [hot] ashes; [. . .] stirs them into [wet] earth' (*Florentine Codex*, X: 65) is changed by Molina

---

4   The confession manual is divided into two columns; the Nahuatl version on the left and Molina's translation into Spanish on the right.

into the question: 'Did you mix green cacao beans with ashes or with soft earth so that the cacao looked good?'. As we have seen, Sahagún also wrote that the bad cacao seller '[with] amaranth seed dough, wax, avocado pits he counterfeits cacao' (*Florentine Codex*, X: 65). In relation to this idea Molina suggested the following question: 'Did you add amaranth seed dough [masa de tzovalli] or that of avocado pits?'.

Molina's queries evidence that Sahagún's intention of passing on to a missionary audience a work that best aided them in their proselytising endeavours was somehow fulfilled. Molina adapted relevant passages that Sahagún had codified by applying a classical and Christian dichotomy to his gathering of information on the Nahuas.

Sahagún's usage of this binary characterisation of people in treatises on vices and virtues stresses the predicament that in the composition of *Historia universal* he behaved as a cultural translator at the service of the Spanish Empire, for he transferred Nahua source data into his European categories with the aim of evangelisation. The first translation decision that he took was to outline a list of topics on which he would extract information to eventually complete *Historia universal*. He chose western models or parallel texts that contained the material he wished to cover. Medieval encyclopaedias and religious and liturgical texts offered him a template to classify the world of the Nahuas, and the Nahuas themselves. Book X (The People) clearly illustrates how Sahagún proceeded. Instead of portraying their personal physical appearance or behaviour, he classified them into a rigid Christian categorisation of sinful versus virtuous in order to guarantee a more effective administration of the sacrament of penance to Nahua neophytes. It is this relocation of the Nahuas into Sahagún's religious worldview that leads us to question to what extent labelling him a pioneer anthropologist has limited discussion on his proselytising motivation, which ultimately triggered and shaped both his linguistic and cultural interests when composing *Historia universal*. To label Sahagún a cultural translator invites us instead to explore how he understood and interpreted the Nahuas at the service of the empire.

2

Genealogies and Analogies of 'Culture' in the History of Cultural Translation – on Boturini's Translation of Tlaloc and Vico in *Idea of a New General History of Northern America*

JOHN ØDEMARK

> If the ideas and the basic terminology of Aristotle or the Stoics or Pascal or Newton or Hume or Kant did not possess a capacity for independent life, for surviving translation, and indeed, transplantation, not without at times, some change of meaning, into the language of very disparate cultures, long after their own worlds had passed away, they would by now, at best have found an honourable resting-place beside the writings of the Aristotelians of Padua or Christian Wolff, major influences in their day, in some museum of historical antiquities. (Isaiah Berlin, *Vico and Herder*, 2002: 8)

This chapter explores the cultural history of the translation of Giambattista Vico's 'first civil metaphor' to New Spain and Spain. Vico, a Neapolitan teacher of rhetoric, published three versions of his *Scienza Nuova* during his lifetime (in 1725, 1730 and 1744). The later history of its reception, not least the so-called discovery of Vico beginning with Jules Michelet in the nineteenth century, has seen his new science as a harbinger of historicism and modern cultural anthropology. Along with the text in which it appears, the first civil metaphor thus forms part of the canon of the human sciences. What role did the metaphor have in his *Scienza Nuova*? And how was it translated to the New World?

According to the Bible, after the Deluge men had been dispersed all over the earth. Vico asserted that they had forgotten how to live in society during their lawless wanderings. This lawless state of affairs, however, ended with the appearance of Jove, who, communicating angrily with lightning and thunder, drew men back into civil life. Vico referred to this event as 'that first civil metaphor in which Jove, identified with the Sky, would write his laws in lightning and promulgate them in thunder' ([1725] 2002: §411).[1] I am interested in how this metaphor was used to frame and interpret the Mexican deity Tlaloc in a historical work published in Madrid in 1746. The author's name was Lorenzo Boturini Benaduci, a Milanese traveller who, after his stay in New Spain, published the work entitled *Idea de una nueva historia general de America septentrional*[2] (*Idea of a New General History of Northern America*; hereafter *Idea*). Boturini based this 'new history' upon a collection of manuscripts he had assembled in New Spain, which he called *museo historico indiano* (Indian historical museum). According to John B. Glass, Boturini's *museo* was 'the most important [. . .] collection for Mexican Ethnohistory ever assembled' (1975: 473). Unfortunately for Boturini, the authorities in New Spain confiscated his collection. The official reason was that the Milanese traveller not only had collected funds for the coronation of the image of the Virgin of Guadalupe, but he entered the territory without the required permission from the Council of the Indies. For this reason Boturini was incarcerated, and eventually expelled and sent to Spain. There he presented his *Idea* to the Council of the Indies, and in December 1745 the Council licensed the publication of the work.[3]

In addition to the part Boturini played in the history of Mesoamerican antiquarianism and the historiography of the apparition of the Virgin of Guadalupe, he also fulfilled a remarkable role in the history of the early reception of Vico's *New Science* (hereafter *NS*). In fact, the *Idea* can be considered the first attempt to adapt the 'universal' and 'ideal' history of the *NS* to the history of a particular 'culture'. However, Boturini's use of Vico was not wholly felicitous in eighteen-century Spain. He quoted extensively from Vico, but never identified the Neapolitan author as his source; consequently he was accused both of 'translating' the *NS* and of 'accommodating' Vico's explanation of Greek fables to Mesoamerican mythology.

Even if Boturini signals that his is a *'new* history', and thus promises – through a performative speech act inscribed in the title – a break with prior

---

1   References to the *Scienza Nuova* are to paragraphs, not pages.
2   Boturini's spelling is awkward. He uses tildes in unexpected places and omits them in those places where we would expect them. Here, and in the following citations from Boturini, I transcribe his text with the original spelling intact. The translations of Boturini are mine.
3   José Torres Revello published documents pertaining to the Boturini case in Argentina in 1933. These were republished in Mexico in 1936 (Torres Revello, 1936).

Spanish historiography of the Indies, he must also relate the announced novelty to his target culture, that is, to previous Spanish knowledge of the subject. The so-called 'spiritual conquest' of the Americas was already accompanied by extensive efforts by the religious orders to describe the language and customs of the natives. But although such friars as Bernardino de Sahagún, José de Acosta and Bartolomé de Las Casas have been called the 'fathers of anthropology', the purpose of the knowledge produced was manifestly the conversion of the natives. This distinguishes missionary ethnography from modern ethnography written according to anthropocentric criteria with the intention of grasping the 'native's point of view'.[4]

Boturini had to adapt to his Spanish target culture not least because the *Idea* was written with a clear objective in mind; that is, to obtain the position of 'Royal Chronicler in New Spain' and regain control over the confiscated museum. This early 'translation' of Vico – performed by a Milanese foreigner in Spain – makes Boturini's case a privileged example in what one could call the cultural history of cultural translation. *Idea* articulates two genealogies of 'cultural' thought from what Peter Burke has called the period 'before the concept of culture came into general use' (1997: 2). How does Boturini, a marginal figure from the historical archive, incorporate a metaphor from the text of one of the canonised voices of the human sciences in his proposition for a new history of *America septentrional*? By answering this question, I also intend to approach some aspects of the broader issue of how 'cultures' were translated before the term came into general use, in order to address questions of human difference and sameness.

One particular Vico reception has seen the Neapolitan teacher of rhetoric as the founding father of the modern human sciences. Donald P. Verene (2002) dates the current interest in Vico on the Anglo-American scene back to Isaiah Berlin's *Vico and Herder*.[5] Berlin claimed that 'Vico is the true father of the modern concept of culture and of what one might call cultural pluralism, according to which each authentic culture has its own unique vision, its own scale of values' (1990: 59–60). Many have heavily contested this casting of Vico in the role of precursor (see, for instance, Lilla, 1993). Nevertheless, the identification of where the break with 'tradition' occurs in Vico still amounts to what one could call the historico-narrative premise of a particular 'Vico discourse', almost obsessed with the question of the newness of the *NS* (see Said, 1975; White, 1976).[6] This historical narrative has had a strong

---

4   For more information, see Ødemark (2004).
5   Now republished as *Three Critics of the Enlightenment* (Berlin, 2002).
6   See, for instance, Anthony Grafton, who recently applied this topology in his introduction to the Penguin translation of the *NS*: 'Vico bestrides the modern

impact on the (rather negligible) reception of Boturini's *Idea* – even from a decolonial scholar such as Walter Mignolo. He sees Boturini's *Idea* as the first interpretation of Amerindian scripts that breaks with the conceptual grid that governed previous understandings of non-alphabetic Amerindian writing. As such, it represents an escape from the 'trap of the Renaissance celebration of alphabetic writing'. According to Mignolo, this was the 'trap' that friars had fallen into (1995: 148). Mignolo emphasises Vico's influence in his account of this event in the historiography of Mesoamerican script:

> Vico introduced, nevertheless, a new way of looking at the history of writing and the writing of history. The happy coincidence that Boturini read Vico and went to Mexico to see in Mexican writing what missionaries of the first century failed to see: the Amerindian's magnificent and exemplary (to paraphrase his own [Boturini's] expressions) ways of writing history, which could be positively compared – according to Boturini – with the most celebrated histories written anywhere in the world. (1995: 149)

Here Vico's theory in the *NS* becomes the 'cause' of the elimination of an interpretative 'failure', while Boturini's work on Mesoamerican culture is the practical effect.

Berlin based his claims of Vico's paternity to 'culture' upon the Neapolitan's use of the so-called *verum/factum* principle, an epistemological precept according to which only makers can have true knowledge of objects: to make is to know (the truth of) the object constructed. In his early book *On the Most Ancient Wisdom of the Italians*, Vico ([1710] 1988) restricts the knowledge of

---

social sciences and humanities like a colossus. Historians, anthropologists and philosophers around the world agree in seeing his *New Science* as a work of dazzling prescience. Vico argued systematically that the understanding of a past society – even of an earlier period in the history of one's own society – was a demanding, if rewarding, intellectual task. The modern reader opening a work by Homer or Livy had to realize that it did not describe individuals like himself, men and women whose experience, feelings and ideas would be immediately recognizable. Only by mastering the general laws of social and cultural evolution that Vico himself had formulated could one avoid committing basic errors. Vico's contemporaries envisioned the ancient Greeks and Romans as robed sages moving decorously down perfect colonnades. In fact, they had been brutal primitive warriors' (Grafton, 1999: xi and 2001: 259). Here a certain 'heterology of the past', in its turn based upon an awareness of historical anachronism, is singled out as Vico's contribution. A scrutiny of the Vico literature makes one rather uncertain of what the 'agreement' between 'historians, anthropologists and philosophers' is about.

nature to God (since he made it), while the knowledge of human creations is still open for human cognition. Thus, a modern distinction between the fields of the natural and the human sciences appears to be prefigured here – at least when it comes to the point of *where* the boundaries between nature and culture are to be drawn, and the constructivist criteria for drawing them. This epistemological principle from *Ancient Wisdom* is rephrased in what appears to be an anthropological key in the later *NS*:

> But in the night of thick darkness enveloping the earliest antiquity, so remote from ourselves, there shines the eternal and never failing light of a truth beyond all question: that the world of civil society has certainly been made by men, and that its principles are therefore to be found within the modifications of our own human mind. Whoever reflects on this cannot but marvel that the philosophers should have bent all their energies to the study of the world of nature, which, since God made it, He alone knows; and that they should have neglected the study of the world of nations, or civil world, which, since men made it, men could come to know. (Vico, [1744] 1968: §331)

According to Berlin, it was precisely in the 'leap' between the two texts that Vico founded a conceptual field for the study of 'culture'. In the *NS*, 'the *verum/factum* formula could be applied to human history conceived in its widest sense, to all that men have done and made and suffered' (2002: 141). Here *il mondo civile* appears to be a pure product of a human art of making. Moreover, it would seem to follow that other human subjects who share this anthropological potential for making could also understand the social arrangements of other humans. The ultimate result of this transposition, claims Berlin, was the discovery of 'the very conception of culture as a category of historical thought, and indeed of thought in general' (2002: 141). However, 'civil society' is also founded upon a rhetorical art. This is so because 'civil society' as a product of human *poiesis* has its origin in what Vico calls the 'first civil metaphor', the metaphor Boturini applies in interpreting Tlaloc.

Below, I shall use Boturini's translation of Vico's first civil metaphor to approach some aspects of the relation between early modern, theocentric and emergent anthropocentric forms of cultural investigation. But before doing so, I shall situate my subject matter within the broader theoretical field of translation; first, by taking into account Homi K. Bhabha's theory on translation and secondly, by presenting a primal scene of cultural translation taken from the work of the anthropologist Roy Wagner.

How should we analyse Boturini's translation of Vico's first civil metaphor? In *The Location of Culture*, Bhabha states that

it is not adequate simply to become aware of the semiotic systems
that produce the signs of culture and their dissemination. Much more
significantly, we are faced with the challenge of reading into the present
of a specific cultural performance, the traces of all those diverse disciplinary discourses and institutions of knowledge that constitute the
condition and context of culture. [. . .] Such a critical process requires a
cultural temporality that is both disjunctive and capable of articulating,
in Lévi-Strauss words, 'forms of activity which are both at once ours
and other'. (1994: 163)

Thus, any cultural performance (like our translated metaphor) should not
be reduced to the effect of a unified and underlying semiotic system that
functions as a code and/or 'cause'. Rather, one has to investigate all the
'traces' that impinge upon it. Bhabha defines these as follows: 'I use the
word "traces" to suggest a particular kind of interdisciplinary discursive
transformation that the analytic of cultural difference demands. To enter into
the interdisciplinarity of cultural texts means that we cannot contextualise the
emergent cultural form by locating it in terms of some pre-given discursive
causality or origin' (1994: 163). This approach liberates us from the model
of influence (still having an impact on Mignolo's account of a break with
the tradition of the friars) and from seeing Boturini's translation of Vico as
an American appendix to the text of the 'strong poet' from Naples. On the
contrary, any given cultural performance should be understood as overde-
termined, as responding to and incorporating signs from various centres of
culture. This also makes it possible to give agency to Boturini the 'translator',
and (eventually) to the Mesoamerican material he articulates through Vico's
theories. But in the case of Boturini's translation and the citation of Vico's
first civil metaphor, the metaphor, and the concept of culture itself – in its
historical temporality – is one of the disciplinary and institutional 'traces' in
play. Thus, the very concept that demarcates the field of investigation is
inevitably implicated in the analysis. How are we to meet the 'challenge'
in this case? To accomplish this task, albeit partially, we have to tackle the
question of the historical constitution and temporality of culture – precisely
the conceptual space that Bhabha uses to qualify 'temporality' and 'performance'. In addition, one should also tackle the issue of what it implies to
inscribe the relation between 'us' and 'them' as sameness and difference
in terms of a *cultural* relation ultimately grounded in the unconscious (the
meeting place of 'forms of activity which are both at once ours and other'). To
situate the relation of self and other in the unconscious is after all a strategy
with a long theological prehistory.[7] What is 'culture's' historical location at a

---

7   See, for example, Asad (1986, 1993) and Argyrou (2002).

level between the surface of the text and the registers of the archaic and the unconscious? Is 'culture' translatable across time and space?

As I have already mentioned, in order to approach this more extended problem, I shall discuss what might be called a primal scene of cultural translation found in Wagner's book, *The Invention of Culture* (1981). Wagner writes that a possible translation of 'culture' in Melanesian languages is the term *kago* (the pidgin word that has become a part of the terminology of religious and cultural studies in a term spelled slightly differently, 'cargo cult').[8] The author performs his translation of 'culture' in the following way:

> If we call such phenomena 'cargo cults', then anthropology should perhaps be called a 'culture cult', for the Melanesian 'kago' is very much the interpretive counterpart of our word 'culture'. The words are [...] 'mirror images' of each other, in the sense that we look at the natives' cargo, their techniques and artefacts and call it culture, whereas they look at our culture and call it 'cargo'. These are analogic usages. (1981: 31)

This translation underlines Wagner's argument that 'culture' belongs (and this comes as no surprise) to our culture. It is a sobriquet that 'we' use to classify and explain the otherness of 'others'.[9] Here then 'culture' is made relative to a certain cultural and conceptual history. On the one hand, this scene of cultural translation obviously conjures up a whole range of familiar paradoxes of relativism. On the other hand, in Wagner's translation, the concept – almost immediately after the apparent suspension of 'cultural authority' – is assigned a secure place in the tribunal of experience, as Wagner's analogy of culture clearly presupposes that the experience of collective human difference is registered at some kind of *border*. Borders must exist, must have a real presence in the experience of the human world. It is actually only at such borders that the Melanesian *kago* can function as a dynamic or pragmatic equivalent to 'culture', as a way of naming a relation to 'others' who are felt to be different (but still somehow the 'same'). It is here, then, at

---

8   The *Penguin Dictionary of Religion* defines the term 'cargo cult' as follows: 'The name given to [...] movements occurring primarily [...] in Melanesia, expecting a new order of equality with whites and human fulfilment to be achieved supernaturally, and symbolized by the arrival of a cargo of Western-type goods' (Hinnels, 1984: 76).

9   'The study of culture is culture, and an anthropology that wishes to be aware, and to develop its sense of relative objectivity, must come to terms with this fact. The study of culture is in fact our culture; it operates through our forms, creates in our terms, and borrows our words' (Wagner, 1981: 16).

this border that culture begins to present 'itself' as difference in the same. We are witness here to an encounter between two different terms (*kago*, culture) pointing towards what we must take to be the *same* border from different linguistic vantage points.

If 'culture' is translated into *kago*, and in a certain sense 'vanishes' cross-culturally, this last term is also dissolved into 'cult'. Thus, we also have a 'vanishing point' in historical time. It is the term 'cult' that functions as the *tertium comparationis*, and which establishes a linguistic location where 'we' can be compared to 'them' ('culture cult' [i.e. anthropology] vs. 'cargo cult'). The term 'cult', historically derived from *cultus* – a Latin term bearing the age-old traces of serving as a mark for religious difference, and a precursor of 'culture' itself – , thus turns out to be a prerequisite for Wagner's staging of this particular scene of cultural translation. But if 'cult' in this way functions as the middle term, it also means that the boundary, in the last instance, is wholly contained within the history of the language of the 'culture cult' – anthropology.

Some salient semantic aspects of this vanishing point could be captured by invoking the linguistic concept of collocation (see Catford, 1967: 101).[10] Even if *kago* and 'culture' in certain respects 'mirror each other', the terms involved are undoubtedly embedded in different languages with different semantic histories where they collocate with a range of different words and meanings. In addition, they are also related to different pragmatics, to different ritual practices and intentions (in the cargo cult, preparing for the dead ancestors' return – the latter will come with valued Western goods as a gift to the living;[11] in the culture cult, writing anthropological literature to further academic knowledge – and careers). I shall approach the translation of the first civil metaphor from these two angles. I shall be concerned with traces

---

10 In the final chapter of *A Linguistic Theory of Translation*, in a section devoted to 'The limits of translatability', John C. Catford explains cultural untranslatability in purely linguistic terms: 'To talk of "cultural untranslatability" may be just another way of talking about collocational untranslatability: the impossibility of finding an equivalent collocation in the T[arget] L[anguage]. And this would be a type of linguistic untranslatability. We might define collocational untranslatability thus: untranslatability arising from the fact that any possible TL near-equivalence of a given S[ource] L[anguage] lexical item has a low probability of collocation with TL equivalents of items in the SL text which collocate normally with the given SL item' (1967: 101).

11 See, for instance, the practices described in the *Penguin Dictionary of Religion*: 'Wharves, airstrips, and warehouses may be built, and to hasten the event new rituals and behaviour replace the traditional customs and economy' (Hinnels, 1984: 76). Thus, the living create the infrastructure that will allow the dead ancestors to come back to life with a surplus of valued Western goods.

of a theological discourse that 'still' influences Vico's 'cultural' investigation, and a pragmatics of collecting that makes Boturini depart from Vico's *NS*.

The full title of Boturini's *Idea* is: *Idea de una nueva historia general de America septentrional fundada sobre material copioso de Figuras, Symbolos, Caractères y Geroglificos, Cantares y Manuscritos de Autores Indios ultimamente descubiertos* (*Idea of a New General History of Northern America founded upon copious material of figures, symbols, characters and hieroglyphs, songs and manuscripts by Indian Authors recently discovered*). Boturini's *museo historico indiano* was to serve as the 'foundation' for the history proposed in *Idea*, and the 'copious material' consisted of the sources 'recently discovered' by Boturini himself during his stay in New Spain. The second part of the publication consisted of a catalogue of the *museo*, and on the title page of this section, Boturini writes that 'el siguiente Tesoro Literario [. . .] puede servir para ordenar, y escribir la historia general de aquel Nuevo Mundo, fundado en Monumentos indisputables de los mismos Indios' (the following Literary Treasure [. . .] can serve to organise and write the general history of the New World, based upon the Indians' own indisputable Monuments) (Boturini, 1746: np). In addition to being referred to as a particular 'cultural' and 'racial' authorship (*manuscritos de autores indios* [manuscripts of Indian authors]), these authentic 'monuments' are presented as a personal possession. This can be understood from the title page of the catalogue:

> Catalogo del museo historico indiano del Cavallero Lorenzo Boturini Benaduci, Señor de la Torre y de Hono, Quien llegó a la Nueva España por Febrero del año 1736. y à porfiadas diligencias, è inmensos gastos de su bolsa juntò, en diferentes Provincias, el siguiente Tesoro Literario. (Boturini, 1746: np)

> Catalogue of the Indian historical museum of the gentleman Lorenzo Boturini Benaduci, Lord of Torre and of Hono, who arrived in New Spain in February of the year 1736, and with persistent efforts, and immense expenses from his own purse, gathered, in different provinces, the following literary treasure.

In this paratextual space, at the border between *Idea* and the *Catalogo*, Boturini frames 'his' collection in an economic idiom; it has been made a possession as a result of hard work accompanied by huge monetary expenses. In the introduction to the catalogue section (immediately after the title page), Boturini, in the same idiom, claims that the collection is his only 'estate' (*hacienda*) in New Spain. Moreover, this literary *hacienda* is so valuable that he is unwilling to exchange it for other, more mundane treasures. If the museum is a personal possession, and as such part of a 'personal economy', it has also entered an altogether different economic sphere: 'Esta es la unica Hacienda, que tengo en Indias, y tan preciosa, que no la trocàra por oro, y plata, por diamantes, y perlas' (This is the only estate I have in the Indies, and [is] so precious that I will not exchange it for gold and silver, for diamonds and pearls) (1746: np). Thus, the collection is 'so precious' that it cannot be traded back into the economy within which it was in play when it was established.

Taking the disciplinary traces of practical antiquarianism and a certain economy of collecting seriously would have consequences for the reading of *Idea* – not least with respect to its assessment of the script of native culture. As Mignolo has observed, Boturini praised Mesoamerican script for its 'figures, symbols, characters and hieroglyphs, which envelop a sea of erudition', and eulogised Mesoamerican history as 'the most eloquent of all that to this day has been discovered' (Mignolo, 1995: 149–150, see Boturini, 1746: 2). However, Boturini's assessments of the history and script of the 'other' could also be read in relation to the 'literary treasure' which the collector claims as his 'only *hacienda*'. Every statement regarding Mesoamerican script and history in Boturini's text can be seen as part of a system of split references. By this I mean that statements on the worth of Mesoamerican culture also implicate the value of Boturini's 'own' museum, a copious collection of sources on the history of *America septentrional*. Consequently, statements on the 'culture of the other' would also refer back to the author/collector. In between the 'self' and the 'other' there emerges the mediatory space of the *museo historico indiano*. On the one hand, this is a product of 'other' producers (*autores indios*), but on the other, it also forms part of the 'hacienda economy' of the collector. In this way, the text of the *Idea*, the museum and the historical referent represented in the historical narration – in its turn 'founded' upon the sources gathered in the museum –, can be seen as forming a 'unit' of cultural production. Inside this unit, we find a feedback loop where the enunciator, as collector/historian, ultimately is implicated in the statements referring to his historical referent, namely Mesoamerican culture. How do the traces of the institutional and disciplinary practice of collecting and antiquarianism relate to Boturini's translation of Vico's first civil metaphor – the metaphor that creates 'culture', or perhaps something analogous in the period 'before the concept of culture came into general use'?

Boturini's misfortunes were not to end in New Spain. In April 1745, he presented *Idea* to the Council of the Indies, which first responded positively to his historical project (Cañizares-Esguerra, 2001: 137). It appointed its *fiscal* for New Spain, José Borull, to review the work and he delivered a report that judged *Idea* very favourably. Borull recommended that Boturini should be appointed *escritor general de la Nueva España* (general writer of New Spain), that the collection should be returned to him and that he should be given the necessary money to go to New Spain and assume his newly awarded office (Cañizares-Esguerra, 2001: 140). In December 1745, in accordance with Borull's recommendations, the Council approved the publication of *Idea*, and appointed Boturini royal chronicler of New Spain. A few months later, however, the council changed its mind and Antonio López (a *nahua* interpreter working for the *audiencia* in New Spain who had made the first inventory of the Boturini collection) was assigned the task of establishing an academy of history in New Spain (Cañizares-Esguerra, 2001: 140). During this time, people in the circles around the Royal Library in Madrid had levelled certain accusations at Boturini. In July 1746, the Jesuit and courtier Andrés Marcos Buriell wrote that

> ahora se publica que en la obra es mero traductor de Juan Bautista Vico, napolitano, que el año de 25 de este siglo imprimió una idea de una ciencia y Derecho natural y de Gentes contra Grocio, Puffendorf [*sic*] y Seldeno, al qual tengo aquí pero no he podido leer. (Andrés Marcos Buriell to Gregorio Mayans 1746-IV-30. Carta nr. 75, in Mayans y Siscar, 2002)

> now it is divulged that in the work he is merely translating Juan Bautista Vico, a Neapolitan who in the 25th year of this century printed an idea of a science and natural Law and of Nations against Grotius, Pufendorf and Selden, which I have here, but have not been able to read. (My translation)

As mentioned above, it is true that Boturini never explicitly named Vico in his *Idea*. In fact, the closest he comes to identifying the Neapolitan author in *Idea* is in a section where he discusses the Mesoamerican god Tlaloc. It is precisely here that Boturini cites Vico's first civil metaphor:

> Y aunque los Indios de la segunda y tercera Edad tuvieron à este Idolo [Tlaloc] por Dios de la lluvia, no obstante, los de la primera le reverenciaron como Pregonero de la Providencia, pensando que ella escribia las leyes con los rayos, y las publicaba con los truenos, que es lo mismo, que de Júpiter dixo con elegante metafora un Poeta Italiano.
> *Ne la primera etade*
> *Gli Eroi leggevan le leggi in petto a Giove.*
> (Boturini, 1746: 13; italics in the original)

And even if the Indians of the second and third age held this idol [Tlaloc] as the God of Rain, those of the first nevertheless revered him as the promulgator of Providence, thinking that she wrote the laws with lightning and published them with thunder – the same was said of Jove in an elegant metaphor by an Italian poet.

> *Ne la primera etade*
>
> *Gli Eroi leggevan le leggi in petto a Giove.*

The 'elegant metaphor' appears in a part of the text where Boturini describes the thirteen gods of the *Mexica* pantheon. The paragraph ends with a quote from an 'Italian poet' – Vico. Vico himself never treated the Mesoamerican deities explicitly, but in terms of the general system of his 'ideal, eternal history', every gentile nation has a Jove. After the deluge, men had been dispersed all over the earth and during their wanderings had forgotten how to live in society. The appearance of Jove, however, communicating angrily with lightning and thunder, drew men back into civil life. Identifying a 'Jove function' in Mexican mythology would therefore only be an empirical consequence of the general theory of the *NS*. The source text for the 'elegant metaphor' cited in *Idea* is the *NS* of 1725:

> Of all the children of the Sky, Jove was imagined to be the father and king of all the gods. Hence he was the origin of idolatry and divination, i.e. the science of auspices, because of the mode in which, as demonstrated above, he was the first god to be born in the Greek imagination. And, as our principles of poetry tell us, idolatry and divination were twin daughters born of that first civil metaphor in which Jove, identified with the Sky, would write his laws in lightning and promulgate them in thunder. From this metaphor came the first poetic civil sentiment in which the sublime and popular were united, more wonderful than anything to which poetry later gave birth: 'in the first age/the heroes read the laws on Jove's breast'. (Vico, [1725] 2002: §411)

The verse cited by Boturini (in Italian) refers back to the metaphor that Vico calls 'that first civil metaphor in which Jove [was] identified with the Sky'. The metaphor further creates what Vico calls 'the first poetic civil sentiment', the first social bond. In the imagination of 'the heroes', the language of the god is thought to be a sequence of *writing* and *speech*. However, the trope will also have further offspring, namely the 'twins' idolatry and divination. In other words, it seems to follow that the society that here comes into being will be doomed to idolatry and divination. A further consequence of this would be that the 'cultural' aetiology offered is strictly limited to 'gentile cultures'. Thus, a religious concern seems to interfere with the discovery of 'culture' as a 'category of thought'. How is this 'primal scene' adapted in Boturini's text? How is it used to interpret his *museo historico indiano*? And, to what extent does this general theory of a pagan 'cultural field' become an instrument of translation in *Idea*?

Boturini's aim when he quotes the 'elegant metaphor' is to explicate what he calls 'the hieroglyph Tlaloc'. He also announces that he has the 'effigy' of this deity 'in his museum'. Thus, the target of the metaphor is not only a product of the 'cultural other', it is also an object belonging to the collection that the collector claims as his own. Perhaps to supplement the reader's lack of access to this as a source, Boturini adds that the Neapolitan travel-writer Giovanni Francesco Gemelli Careri, in the volume on New Spain in his *Giro del mondo*, printed a copy of this effigy:

> TLALOC, cuya efigie tengo en mi Archivo; y de quien trae la copia en su Historia del *Giro del Mundo* el Doctor Francisco Gemmelli Carreri [*sic*] *tom.6. pag. 83* es Geroglifico de la Segunda Deidad, y casi Ministro de la Divina Providencia. (Boturini, 1746: 12; italics in the original)

> TLALOC, whose effigy I have in my Archive, a copy of which is provided in Doctor Francisco Gemmelli Carreri's [*sic*] history of the *Giro del Mundo vol. 6. pag. 83.* is Hieroglyph of the Second Deity, and almost minister of Divine Providence.

This reference to an illustration in the work of another Italian traveller also underlines that the following description and explication of the 'hieroglyph' will be an *ekphrasis* of an object forming part of Boturini's museum. It functions both as a reference and as a way of expressing that the effigy in the *museo* is a better source:

> En dicha estampa se vè à Tlaloc coronado con diademas de plumas, que deben ser blancas, y verdes, teniendo en la mano derecha una Centella, y en la siniestra una Rodela, hermoseada de otras muchas plumas de color celes[te]; en cuyos tres colores symbolizaban, en el blanco, aquellos primeros hijos, que candidos havian de nacer en la hermosura de los matrimonios; en el verde, la propagacion de sus linages; y en el celeste, el cuidado, que se les encargaba de mantener pura la Religion, y constantes los sacrificios para con los Dioses. (Boturini, 1746: 12)

> On the mentioned picture, one sees a Tlaloc crowned with feather diadems, which must be white and green. In the right hand he holds a bolt of lightning, and in the left, a shield adorned with many other feathers of a sky-blue colour. These three colours symbolised the following: white, those first children that were born innocent within the harmony of matrimony; green, the propagation of their lineages; and sky blue, the care they took in keeping religion pure and providing regular sacrifices to the gods.

Figure 1.   Tlaloc, illustration from Gemelli Careri, G. F. (1728) *Giro del mondo del Dottore D.Gio. Francesco Gemelli Careri. Nuova edizione accresciuta, ricorretta, e divisa in nove volumi. Con un Indice de' Viaggiatori, e loro opera. Tomo sesto. Contenute le cose più ragguardevoli vedute nella Nuova Spagna.* Presso Sebastiano Coleti: Venice

Boturini not only supplements Gemelli Careri's black-and-white illustration with the colours of the feather-diadem on Tlaloc's crown, he also deciphers their symbolic meaning (cf. Gemelli Careri, 1728: Figure 1). Contrary to Gemelli Careri, who wrote that the hieroglyph of the 'idol' signified 'rain and abundance' (1976: 59–60), the Milanese seeks the social meaning of the colours; they are to be seen as symbols representing social institutions: matrimony, the propagation of the lineage, i.e. family, property and inheritance, and, lastly, religion. This exposition of the iconological significance of Tlaloc's crown is perfectly consistent with the *NS*. Vico argues that the common sense of humankind is based upon three customs: belief in a divinity, marriage and burial, which by demarcating the land around the graves gives rise to property held in common in families (see Vico, [1725] 2002: §10). These customs are all a consequence of the first civil metaphor and the sequences of events that are set in motion with the appearance of Jove.

The hieroglyph of Tlaloc, then, is the 'material base', the 'fundament' of the historical narration from the museum upon which Vico's first civil metaphor is inscribed. While the appropriation of Tlaloc as a figure in the collector's *museo* introduces the paragraph, the quote of the 'elegant metaphor' of the 'Italian poet' comes towards the end. Tlaloc is the promulgator of Providence, but Boturini identifies Tezcatlipoca with Providence itself. We have seen that in 'the first age', the Mexicans believed that Providence 'wrote the laws with lightning and promulgated them with thunder'. This, claims Boturini, is 'the same' as what an 'Italian poet' said about Jupiter. Hence, what at first appears as a principle of 'cross-cultural identity' is postulated around this 'sameness'. What is the principle behind the equivalence? We have also seen that this principle applies both to the manner of fabricating gods (rhetorically, by metaphor) and to the 'natural' and/or literal referent of the trope (thunder and lightning). Metaphor thus serves as the bridgehead between the worlds of Jove and Tlaloc. However, the space between the pagan deities and their different worlds is taken by Providence; the pagan gods do the work of Providence. These deities, with their different iconographies and proper names, are, in the last instance, surface manifestations of a latent theological principle.

The verse taken from the Italian poet clearly functions as a window that enables Boturini to 'see', in a theoretical vision, Tlaloc and Jove as objects belonging to the same theoretical field, susceptible to the same explanation. But is this a cultural field produced by a purely human *poiesis*?

The first civil metaphor – in the source text *and* the translation – is based upon a schema:

1. There is a *belief* in a personified divinity who
2. *communicates* with the natural signs of lightning and thunder, which are seen
3. *metaphorically* as if they were
4. *writing and speech*, semiotic forms through which
5. the law was *promulgated* in both the New and the Old Worlds.

The law manifests itself through a sensory process that goes from vision to voice, from lightning to thunder, rather instantly, like the passage from eye to ear when reading aloud. This semiotic sequence of writing and speech serves as a 'trans-cultural' constant. At a level between the sameness of nature (lightning and thunder) and the surface difference of the gods, the projection of the semiotic and cultural forms of writing and speech upon the events taking place on the sky is the same. But, this is not purely a scene of human *semiosis*, of a projection of human, cultural meaning onto a non-signifying nature. On the contrary, it is willed by Providence who functions as the main actor. Although they take a local cultural form, the signs read by the heroes are *given* to be read by a super-natural and hence 'super-cultural' being – a being belonging to another ontological realm than that of culture producing humans.

The semantic field of the first civil metaphor – and its underlying ontological commitment – is, in this way, radically different from that found in any 'secular' oppositions between nature and culture, and the natural and the supernatural. Consequently, this is not the initial movement in the game of a purely human construction of culture through metaphor and poetic making, but rather a response where the activity of reading is inextricably linked to the passivity of receiving signs given in nature by a divine author. We are, then, rather far from the anthropocentrism of cultural modernity, as this, for instance, is expressed in Max Weber's definition of culture as 'a finite segment of the *meaningless infinity* of the world process, a segment on which human beings confer meaning and significance' (Weber, 1969: 81; my emphasis).

Vico regarded hieroglyphs and the first civil metaphor as primitive men's cognitive response to events that they were unable to comprehend. Due to the absence of abstract thought in what he called the 'childhood of the world', the gods and hieroglyphs of the early men who lived outside the space where God intervened directly (only the Hebrews received divine assistance directly – and literally – from God) were personified and animated as deities representing the necessities of life. This collocation of 'primitivism' and 'idolatry' thus defines Vico's unit of investigation. Moreover, it also enables him to compare 'cultures' from different historical times and places, and to inscribe them all in what he calls the 'first age'. One example (from the *NS* of 1744) captures his way of processing information from different historical and ethnographical zones and transforming it into a unit of investigation. It is taken from a section of the text where Vico treats the 'language of the gods' – i.e. the hieroglyphs of 'the first age', where Boturini's Tlaloc-hieroglyph would also belong. Here Greeks, Romans, Amerindians and Egyptians are all turned into instances of 'the same':

> There can be no doubt that among the Latins Varro occupied himself
> with the language of the gods, for he had the diligence to collect thirty
> thousand of their names, which would have sufficed for a copious
> divine vocabulary, with which the peoples of Latium might express

all their human needs, which in those simple and frugal times must
have been few indeed, being only the things that were necessary to
life. The Greeks had gods to the number of thirty thousand, for they
made a deity of every stone, spring, brook, plant, and offshore rock.
[...]. *Just so* [*appunto come*] the American Indians *make* [*fanno*] a god
of everything that exceeds [*supera*] their limited understanding. *Thus*
[*talchè*] the divine fables of the Greeks and Latins must have been *the
first true hieroglyphs, or sacred or divine characters, corresponding to those of
the Egyptians.* (1968 [English] and 1990 [Italian]: §437; my emphasis)

In this dense passage, Vico undertakes a comparison of world-historical
scope. The cited text begins in the past, with Greek and Roman polytheism.
Rather abruptly – in the clause beginning with 'just so' – he then turns to his
present-day America and assimilates this into the same 'cultural' unit with
the manner of creating the gods as the criteria of identity. From 'our' point of
view, this obviously erases the historical and cultural difference between the
Greco-Roman past and the ethnographic present of the *americani* (although
the verbs in this clause are in the present tense and thus retain traces of a
certain difference). The concluding clause, beginning with 'thus' (signalling
continuity of subject and a coming conclusion), returns to the Mediterranean
past, adds the Egyptians, and reaches a form of 'trans-cultural' conclusion
that applies to all the times and places that have furnished ethnographic
and historical evidence for the proposition put forward here. In this passage,
the fables of the gods from classical antiquity and the hieroglyphs of the
Egyptians are equated. In the last instance, these semiotic forms are not only
about 'the same' (gods who represent basic human needs) but they signify
their basic socio-economic referent in the same way (hieroglyphically) as well.
Thus, information from the Americas can serve as evidence for an argument
that begins and ends in the Old World, and concludes by postulating the
sameness of Greco-Roman fables and Egyptian hieroglyphs.

The common trait that makes these huge leaps in cultural-historical time
possible is the identification of fables with hieroglyphs, but added to this
is a collocation of 'primitiveness' with 'idolatry'. This, then, is not a 'primitiveness' defined entirely in evolutionary terms as it is (still) influenced by
theological concerns. This is evident if we turn to an earlier assimilation of
Amerindian 'culture' in Vico. Already in *The Constancy of the Jurist* (a part of
the *Universal Right* [1719–1721] 2000), Vico had quoted Acosta on the topic of
how 'the sublimity of the fables proceeds agreeably from prejudices carried
on from infancy'. Here Vico writes that 'the Peruvians, a most illiterate people
[*stupidissima gens*], admitted that whatever exceeded the average size, like an

immense river, a mountain, a tree, as Acosta narrates in the *Historia*, were believed to be gods' ([1719–1721] 1936: 374 and [1719–1721] 2000: 372).[12]

Boturini is far from seeing Mesoamerican writing as the semiotic and cognitive means of a *stupidissima gens*. On the contrary, he praises it because hieroglyphs, like Tlaloc, 'envelop a sea of erudition' (Boturini, 1746: 2; see Mignolo, 1995: 149–150). Even if Boturini follows Vico and places 'his' Tlaloc in 'the first age', stating that the 'same' was said about Jove in the first civil metaphor, he refuses to translate the constellation of primitivism, idolatry, hieroglyphs and fables as a total 'unit' with all its 'cultural' and theological collocations. This refusal should be related to what I called the split references of his museum and text: every statement of the value of Mesoamerican 'culture' and its 'sources' also refers to the symbolic value of Boturini's own 'museum' as a 'possession'. Placing Mesoamerican 'culture' in a primitive and idolatrous zone would imply a devaluation of the *museo*. This also means that a certain hybridity that dislocates clear-cut binaries between the cultural 'self' and the 'other' enters already at this practical level of antiquarianism, long before we turn to the unconscious.

We have seen that the description of acts of transfer or translations in the early modern period as 'cultural translations' itself amounts to a cultural translation into our 'culture cult'; an inscription into a conceptual framework that the actors did not share. Erasing this difference – paradoxically – is the same as erasing the culture of actors and authors like Boturini and Vico. The pragmatics of collecting applies mainly to the singularity of the 'Boturini case'. The broader semantic and conceptual issues of how 'cultures' were translated before the term came into general use, however, offers us the possibility of studying how 'others' looked upon 'others' before 'culture' became a common place in the interpretation of 'otherness' – and through this it also offers a way of historicising the common sense of the present.

---

12   The source seems to be a passage from the fifth chapter of Acosta's *Historia natural y moral de las Indias* where he treats Mexican and Andean idolatry: 'Porq[ue] en la mayor parte de su adoració[n] y ydolatria se ocupaba en ydolos, y no en las mismas cosas naturales, aunque a los ydolos se atribuyan estos efectos naturales, como de llover, y del Ganado, de la Guerra, de la generación, como los griegos y latinos pusieron también ydolos de Febo, y de Mercurio, y de Júpiter, y de Minerva, y de Marte' (Because in the main part of their adoration and idolatry they were concerned with idols, and not the natural things in themselves, although they attributed natural effects – like those of rain, the livestock, war, and generation – to the idols, in the same way as the Greeks and Romans raised idols of Phoebus, Mercury, Minerva, and Mars) (1590: 310; my translation).

3

The 'Acculturation' of the Translating Language: Gregory Rabassa and Gabriel García Márquez's *Chronicle of a Death Foretold*

ANNA FOCHI

Translation is a crucial moment of communication and contact between cultures, which inevitably leads to an 'experience of the other'; yet cultural encounters can range from mutual interpretation and influence to cultural assimilation and suppression.[1] Therefore, translation is never a neutral act of communication, but has important consequences for the delicate dialogue between cultures. Gregory Rabassa is particularly aware of these nuances. He is often referred to as the English translator of Gabriel García Márquez, almost his translator *par excellence*, notwithstanding that he has not translated all of García Márquez's works. For this reason, he has also been seen as an important factor in the so-called 'Boom' of Latin American literature in the 1960s. García Márquez himself openly praised Rabassa to the point of saying that there are some passages from his own works that he liked better in the English translation than in Spanish, despite the strong cultural specificity of his writings (2002: 25).

This explains why Rabassa, of all translators, is invited to take part in the international debate about translation and Latin America in Daniel Balderston and Marcy E. Schwartz's (2002) volume *Voice-Overs: Translation and Latin American Literature*, with a paper entitled 'Words Cannot Express... The Translation of Cultures'. Albeit not a theorist, Rabassa proves to be a translator who does not limit himself to mere practice, but, on the basis of his immense experience, mulls over problems in order to develop a more systematic approach to translation, and to take a stand in the crowded arena of translation studies. For example, with regard to the antithesis between a

---

1 In particular, see Bhabha (1994), Budick and Iser (1996), García Canclini (1997), Iser (2000), and Venuti (1998 and 2008).

source-oriented or a target-oriented approach to translation, Rabassa opts for a solution that prefers to avoid too drastic dichotomies, although he reveals a clear break with functional theories of language. Ultimately, language for Rabassa cannot be identified with mere communication. He argues: 'The fact that language is culture and culture is language is brought out most sharply when one tries to replace his language with another. A person can change his country, his citizenship, his religion [...] more easily and smoothly than his language (2002: 91). Such awareness that 'language is culture' (in other words, language as hermeneutics) also implies recognition of the difficulties of creating a translation that tries to foster 'a mutual mirroring of cultures', to use Wolfgang Iser's phrase (2000: 19), rather than a neutralising translation leading to cultural assimilation. In this regard, Rabassa specifically mentions the difficulties linked to differences in syntax between languages: it is often because of differences in the way words are 'strung together' that even apparently simple texts, which had not created any problems of interpretation when read, were then proved to be a sort of nightmare for the translator. Rabassa comments that unfortunately this is a rather forgotten field and that there are no systematic studies of grammar and syntax from a cultural point of view, except for a few notions concerning personal pronouns and forms of address. Not that he believes it is possible to preserve the grammatical structure of the original, so as to show that behind the translation there is actually another text, because 'to do so would be to produce some kind of gibberish that would be unintelligible to both sides'. However, 'there ought to be some kind of undercurrent, some background hum that lets the English-speaking reader feel that cultures do not translate easily' (2002: 89).

Here lies the problem: to preserve the individual identities of cultures and the richness they convey, without turning translation into an 'unintelligible gibberish'. Is this a possible or an impossible task? As is well known, behind this question there lies a long debate in Translation Studies between those who favour a complete negation of the foreign work and those, on the other hand, who advocate approaches that register this 'foreignness'. Although Rabassa does not use the key notions of foreignising, domesticating and neutralising translation, we can infer that he is certainly against hiding and assimilating a foreign text into a target language and culture, while, at the same time, he does not seem to forget the difficulties and risks involved in a foreignising approach to translation. Similarly, when he focuses on the thorny issue of rendering regional voices, he ponders and rejects the 'handy' solution of replacing a territorial language with another dialect or jargon from the target culture, which, just to give one notable example, was more or less what D. H. Lawrence had done in order to translate the unique language of Giovanni Verga's *Mastro Don Gesualdo* (Laurence had turned to the jargon of the miners of Northern England).[2] Referring to Latin American literature, Rabassa confidently affirms that to make Martín Fierro sound like a North American cowboy would simply be a disaster:

> To make Martín Fierro a cowboy is to ruin the poem. The gaucho and the cowboy lived on the plains, rode horseback, herded cattle, and fought Indians, yet it is ludicrous to think of John Wayne as a gaucho. It is the culture that matters, and culture is often made up of the lesser details [. . .]. These small things add up to make the similarities disappear. The talk of the gaucho is peculiar to his caste, as is that of the cowboy, but they are not interchangeable, and to translate gaucho speech into cowboy dialect would be to ruin the effect. Here is where the translator cannot follow the writer from the other side of the fence, but must be most creative himself. Keeping custom in mind, he must conceive of an English that the gaucho would speak if he spoke English. This will, of course, be pure invention, but if successful it will not only bring a language across the divide, it will bring a culture. (2002: 90)

These statements reveal a personal approach to translation, which, siding with the foreignising line, apparently hints at very innovative translating and experimental solutions. With such premises, we are clearly encouraged to have high expectations when approaching Rabassa's translation of *Crónica de una muerte anunciada* (García Márquez, 1981). Even more if we consider the evolution of the notion of foreignising translation and the relative debate within Translatology, which raises the question as to where exactly Rabassa's translation of García Márquez's novel has to be located. Answering this question constitutes the main aim of this chapter.

One of the scholars devoting great attention to these issues is Lawrence Venuti, who has repeatedly dwelt on the topic, pointing out how it has been approached from different perspectives throughout recent decades. On the one hand, fluent strategies of translation 'that make for easy readability and produce the illusion of transparency' (2000: 341) lead to domestication and assimilation, and have long dominated British and American cultures; on the other hand, according to Venuti, an oppositional history can be traced:

> [Fluency] can be countered by 'foreignizing' translation that registers the irreducible differences of the foreign text – yet only in domestic terms [. . .]. This line of thinking revives Schleiermacher and Berman, German Romantic translation and one of its late twentieth-century avatars. But

---

2   See Fochi (1982).

following poststructuralist Philip E. Lewis (and modernist poet-theorists like Pound), it goes beyond literalism to advocate an experimentalism: innovative translating that samples the dialects, registers, and styles already available in the translating language to create a discursive heterogeneity which is defamiliarizing, but intelligible [. . .]. (2000: 341)

García Márquez's short novel was almost immediately translated into English, in 1982, that is, the year after its publication, with the title, *Chronicle of a Death Foretold*, which is only partially a literal translation of the source text (ST). The original title is in itself open to evocative echoes and varying interpretations, namely the two words, *crónica* and *anunciada*. With regard to the first one, *crónica*, at first sight the choice of the corresponding noun *chronicle* would seem almost a binding choice, and yet, it is not a completely neutral rendering, but already a subtle form of interpretation. If in Spanish the word *crónica* can mean both a historical chronicle, or account, as well as a news report, or feature and article (and it is this second meaning that here seems to have greater relevance, especially thanks to García Márquez's interest and personal experience in journalism), in the English version, however, the word comes to be divested of its reference to journalism and to the complex inter-action between it and literature. It does not mean a 'feature story', a 'report', but rather introduces a new literary and historical connotation. In this way, the first word of the title comes to raise other evocative echoes for the English reader. Unlike its Spanish equivalent, '*chronicle* may evoke memories of King Alfred and the Venerable Bede' to Anglo-Saxon readers, as Ambrose Gordon comments (1985: 84). Moreover, 'chronicle' is not merely connected to history, but also to a past and glorious stage of writing of history, as the *Penguin Dictionary of Literary Terms and Literary Theory* (Cuddon, 1988) explains.

Even more strategic seems to be the choice of 'foretold' for *anunciada*, which, still according to Gordon, becomes in the title of Rabassa's target text (TT) a 'clear hint at dark prophesy' (Gordon, 1985: 89). If we check 'foretell' in *Collins English Dictionary and Thesaurus*, these are some of the synonyms we can find: 'adumbrate, augur, forebode, forewarn, predict, presage, prophesy, vaticinate' (Knight, 1994: 444). In this regard, we should remember how delicate and subtle the reading of this *anunciada* is in the ST, since it has actually opened the way to different interpretations of the meaning of the whole novel, and is linked to the question of which role, if any, fate and destiny play in man's life. It cannot be denied, however, that the title chosen by Rabassa is both 'resonant and attractive', as Gordon comments (1985: 89); thus one tends to wonder what actually makes it so resonant. Apart from the already mentioned connotation that accompanies 'chronicle', the resonance of the other critical word 'foretold', with its 'hint of dark prophecy', is particularly amplified by the postponing of the past participle, which certainly makes the whole phrase more emphatic and *recherché*. This explains why Lois Parkinson Zamora finds this title so interesting and important for her own peculiar reading of the novel: according to her, even if the original title in Spanish is more direct in both syntax and diction, when translated by Rabassa it takes on a 'Biblical tone', thanks to the inverted word order and the 'apocalyptic ring' of 'foretold', which Zamora finds perfectly justified by what she defines 'the apocalyptic nature' of the text (1985: 106).

However, it is this apocalyptic and prophetic tone that is so debated by critics of García Márquez's novel, yet none of them seems to dislike the title as it sounds in the English text. Even those who find it 'misleading' cannot deny its value, as Gerald Martin explains in the following extract:

> *Chronicle of a Death Foretold* is another example of the irresistible mis-translation. Here the English is clearly 'better' than the very prosaic Spanish one, literally, 'chronicle of an announced death', contrasting with the way the rhythmical swing of *Cien años de soledad* finds little echo in the English version. Yet the effect is, first, to make the title again more literary in several ways, including word order; second, once more, to bespeak a Hispanic 'world' of destiny, superstition, and – yes – romance whose direction is the very opposite of García Márquez's intention in this superbly subtle and ambivalent work. The point of the word *anunciada* (announced) is to imply that the death is not unavoidable (or inevitable) whereas the primary meaning of 'foretold' tends to imply the opposite. That which is announced is by definition known; that which is foretold, much less so. Well, the whole point of the novel is to portray a death that everyone could have prevented and nobody did prevent and to inquire how and why this could have happened. To say that a death is foretold is to imply quite a different concept of destiny [...] Here the whole novel is, in one sense, lost. Would I have given another title? Probably not. (2002: 160)

The phrase 'una muerte anunciada' is repeated more than once in the ST, every time with slight additions, which are all meant to increase emphasis. When translating it, the TT always confirms both the choice of 'foretold' and the altering of the natural word order, even making the literary tone (or Biblical tone, to use Zamora's phrase) more relevant:

Nunca hubo una muerte más anunciada. (1981: 59)
There had never been a death more foretold. (1996: 50)[3]

---

3   All 1996 quotations are from Rabassa's translation in the Penguin edition.

[...] para que se cumpliera sin tropiezos una muerte tan anunciada.
(1981: 112)
[...] so that there should be the untrammelled fulfilment of a death so
clearly foretold. (1996: 100)

If in the first case the postponing of 'foretold' in the TT makes up for the
loss of the very effective and powerful beginning of the sentence in the ST,
which shows an emphatic inversion in word order (adv. + verb + subj.:
'nunca hubo una muerte'), in the second example the postponing of the past
participle 'foretold' in the TT conjoins with other subtle changes that strain
the natural flow of the English language, so as to make it sound really more
'Biblical' and dignified, and definitely less familiar and more 'foreignising'.
First of all, the choice of 'untrammelled' is to be noticed: a rather rare
term, uncommonly long and united to another long word, 'fulfilment', with
which it creates alliterative effects (*m*, *n*, and *t*); in its turn, 'fulfilment'
creates alliteration with the strategically postponed past participle 'foretold'.
Moreover, 'untrammelled fulfilment' renders, through an adjective + abstract
noun phrase, what in the ST is expressed very directly by a subjunctive verb
and a metaphor based on a familiar and colloquial phrase, 'sin tropiezos'
('tropezón' in standard Spanish), literally, 'without stumbles'. Thus the TT
opts for what could be described as a sort of inverted 'hypostatisation', which,
together with the postponing of 'foretold', has a 'displacing' effect.[4]

At this point, on leaving the evocative phrase of the title, with its recurring
echoes throughout the novel, and embarking on analysis proper, a guideline
for analysis becomes very useful: a dynamic 'tool', which favours, stimulates,
but also supports a systematic reading of the TT. Among other important
contributions, a particularly promising direction can be found in the writings
of Peèter Torop whose impressive work of research and systematisation gives
great prominence to the issue of the cultural and social implications of any
translation act. In particular his detailed table based on six translatability
parameters for cultural translation (the parameters of language, space, time,
text, work and socio-political commitment) offers considerable potential
(2000: 157). Thus, if we now read Rabassa's TT in the light of Torop's table,
beginning with the first parameter of language, and focus on grammar

---

4   For 'hypostatisation', the *Penguin Dictionary of Literary Terms and Literary Words*
provides the following definition: 'A form of personification in which an abstract
quality is spoken of as something human [...]. Not uncommon in everyday usage'
(Cuddon, 1988: 406). Therefore, the opposite rhetorical transformation (something
familiar and concrete is spoken of as an abstract concept: 'sin tropiezos' translated
as 'untrammelled fulfilment') goes in the direction of creating greater distance
from everyday language.

and syntax, what emerges immediately is that the differences between the
two languages, in grammar, clause and paragraph syntax, do not lead to
any prevailing strategy of 'denationalisation' (or 'neutralisation') in the TT,
nor to 'nationalisation' (or 'domestication'); this is no surprise, after all,
considering Rabassa's personal views and preoccupation with the cultural
value of grammar and syntax in a text. Obviously there are cases of necessary
linguistic adaptations, determined by the differences between the English
and the Spanish language, cases where the translator is not really left with
much of a choice. Nonetheless, it is interesting to observe how Rabassa's TT
tends to go beyond that, and pays great attention to syntax, often resorting
to inversion of normal word order (such as postponing the subject), or to
extended and protracted sentences, all of which contribute both to increase
emphasis and to strengthen the tone of oral story-telling as well as the 'Biblical
ring'. In this regard, therefore, the English of Rabassa's translation confirms
his idea that in order to preserve 'whatever slim shards of the culture may
be left lying about', it is necessary to skilfully and courageously work on
the language. From this point of view, the English of Rabassa's text actually
sounds 'acculturated', a language that has apparently been interacting with
the Spanish of the ST. Let us look at specific examples, which will help to
clarify the point:

> Era una costumbre sabia impuesta por su padre desde una mañana
> en que una sirvienta sacudió la almohada para quitarle la funda, y la
> pistola se disparó al chocar contra el suelo, y la bala desbarató el armario
> del cuarto, atravesó la pared de la sala, pasó con un estruendo de guerra
> por el comedor de la casa vecina y convirtió en polvo de yeso a un santo
> de tamaño natural en el altar mayor de la iglesia, al otro extremo de la
> plaza. (1981: 10)

> It was a wise custom established by his father ever since one morning
> when a servant girl had shaken the case to get the pillow out and the
> pistol went off as it hit the floor and the bullet wrecked the cupboard
> in the room, went through the living room wall, passed through the
> dining room of the house next door with the thunder of war, and turned
> a life-size saint on the main altar of the church on the opposite side of
> the square to plaster dust. (1996: 4)

The TT, apart from rendering the implicit clause 'al chocar' (on hitting) as
an explicit and more direct one, 'as it hit', does not split the prolonged
sentence, which would have made for easier reading, and even reproduces the *polysyndeton*, repeatedly linking the clauses with 'and'. Perhaps
even more remarkable is the repeated use of the postponing of the subject

(*hyperbaton*) and inversion of word order, which characterises these two other examples: '[...] desde la orilla opuesta llegaban canoas adornadas de flores' (1981: 26–27)/'from the opposite shore came canoes bedecked with flowers' (1996: 21); 'tampoco se supo con qué cartas jugó Santiago Nasar' (1981: 49)/'Nor was it known what cards Santiago Nasar was playing' (1996: 41), although in the latter example the TT, after reproducing the initial inversion, opts for a more normal syntax structure for the second clause, leaving out the *hyperbaton* of the ST.

Moreover, there are cases where the TT even strengthens the emphatic structure of the ST, perhaps helped by the linguistic differences of the languages, which therefore, far from being a hindrance, come to help the translator. It occurs, for example, in the following extract where the TT not only respects the fairly exceptional length of the sentence, but also introduces a word repetition in two consecutive clauses (*epiphora*), which is actually prolonged throughout the whole sentence. However, it must be observed that in this regard the TT is helped by the nature of the language: the repetition of the direct third person pronoun, 'him', is after all the exact rendering of the ST, with the only difference that the Spanish language has separate forms for the direct, indirect and prepositional object pronoun. Moreover, the omission of the subject in English is not possible, except in coordinate clauses, and the possessive adjective is needed when speaking of parts of the body or clothes; this leads to the insistent repetition of 'he' (*anaphora*) and 'his' in the TT. Finally, the TT profits from another 'happy coincidence': both Spanish verbs 'contestar' and 'responder' mean 'answer', which favours the introduction of another *anaphora* in the TT:

> *Lo* habían puesto ahí pensando quizás que era el sitio de honor, y los invitados tropezaban con *él*, *lo* confundían con otro, *lo* cambiaban de lugar para que no estorbara, y *él* movía la cabeza nevada hacia todos lados con una expresión errática de ciego demasiado reciente, contestando preguntas que no eran para *él* y respondiendo saludos fugaces que nadie *le* hacía, feliz en su cerco de olvido, con la camisa acartonada de engrudo y el bastón de guayacán que *le* habían comprado para la fiesta. (1981: 51–52; my emphasis)

> They had placed *him* there thinking perhaps that it was the seat of honor, and the guests stumbled over *him*, confused *him* with someone else, moved *him* so *he* wouldn't be in the way, and *he* nodded *his* snow-white head in all directions with the erratic expression of someone too recently blind, *answering* questions that weren't directed at *him* and *answering* fleeting waves of the hand that no one was making to *him*, happy in *his* circle of oblivion, *his* shirt cardboard-stiff with starch

and holding the lignum vitae cane they had bought *him* for the party.
(1996: 44; my emphasis)

Still within the parameter of language, a relevant component is that of
the so-called *realia*, which always represent a macroscopic cultural element
in a text; these are words that exist only in one given culture and refer to
specific objects and things that are typical of that culture. As such they are
one of the most obvious elements to be focused on by cultural translation
criticism. However, this by no means implies that they are automatically the
most important ones in a text, even from a cultural point of view; or, at
least, this clearly seems to be the way Rabassa considers them. We can say
that, meaningfully enough, his TT does not show innovative solutions in this
regard, and neither is there clear evidence of translational strategic coherence
in dealing with them, unlike what has emerged until now. Apart from
geographic proper names, which he simply transcribes (with the exception
of the phrase 'prófugo de Cayena' [1981: 39], where the TT opts for an
interpreting substitution to make it more explicit for the reader: 'had escaped
from Devil's island' [1996: 32]), he usually tends to translate cultural terms
literally, thus occasionally adhering to both domesticating and neutralising
strategies. This is the case, for example, with most names of institutions or
of public buildings (Club Social/social club, Banco del Estado/State Bank,
Casa Cural/parish house, Casa de Salud/Rest Home, and so on), with only
very few exceptions: if the name of Santiago's cattle farm, 'el Divino Rostro',
is translated as 'the Divine Face', 'el Hotel del Puerto' is simply transcribed
in the TT, even if a literal translation could be expected, given its similarity
to the previously mentioned cases.

With the other types of *realia*, specifically those referring to concrete objects
tied to the Northern Colombian culture of the ST, the solutions adopted vary
between two main options: either they are just transcribed (*repetition*), that
is, not translated, or they are translated, with varying degrees of precision
(*substitution*).[5] The first option, repetition, is adopted for both *realia* which
have by now become part of the general cultural knowledge of a Westerner,
such as 'merengue' (43) or 'fado' (21), as well as for *realia* which, instead, the
English/American reader of the TT is very unlikely to be acquainted with,
like 'cumbiamba', a traditional Columbian dance (45; italics in the TT), or
'papiamento', a local dialect (30), and which, at any rate, are not accompanied
by any type of commentary or notes. It is true that for this choice of avoiding
footnotes Rabassa is praised by García Márquez, who is definitely against

---

5   For *repetition* and *substitution* as translation strategies, see Delabastita (1993) cited
     by Torop (2000: 135).

any form of *metatranslation*,[6] and yet, if these *realia* are introduced by the TT without any cultural mediation, it cannot be denied that the two terms, 'cumbiamba' and 'papamiento', remain too obscure and distant to become an active cultural element for the reader. Moreover, in many other similar cases, substitution is the translation strategy adopted by the TT. Actually, it is not easy to detect any clear selective criterion to justify the difference in solutions, thus confirming the impression of lack of coherence in translation with regard to this particular issue. However, as already observed, this is rather to be interpreted as evidence of a different strategy of focalisation in Rabassa' s translation, with only marginal interest and attention paid to the issue of translating *realia*, and, instead, greater stress and care placed on other elements of the text.

With regard to the parameter of space, it should be observed that what greatly contributes to give García Márquez's narrative style its unique 'flavour' is certainly its being so anchored to the popular way of telling stories, being based on his grandmother's voice, as he himself has often explained. If this is true for his writing in general, it is even more the case for *Crónica de una muerte anunciada*, thanks to the active involvement in the story of almost a whole coastal town from Northern Colombia. With so many of its inhabitants acting as a classical Greek chorus through their continuous and direct comments, the language of the ST is socially and geographically strongly characterised. Let us first focus on those examples that seem to be preeminently connected to the sub-parameter of geographic space, with cultural implications that are usually most difficult to render fully and cor-rectly. The ST offers interesting occurrences of vocabulary that not only vary from Castilian Spanish, but denote a clearly local and regional voice to the point of not sounding completely familiar even to readers from other parts of Colombia. In this regard, we can see that the TT always provides accurate renderings, with great attention always paid to the popular register, but not to geographic connotations, which inevitably results in a certain degree of cultural neutralisation. Here are some interesting examples:

La mujer me dijo: 'Ella mastica a la topa tolondra, un poco al desgaire, un poco al desgarriate'. (1981: 89)

The woman said to me: 'She crunches like a nutty nuthatch, kind of sloppy, kind of slurpy'. (1996: 78)

---

6   'I have great admiration for translators except for the ones who use footnotes. They are always trying to explain to the reader something which the author probably did not mean [. . .]. A good translation is a re-creation in another language' (quoted by Plimpton, 2003: 147).

This is a really interesting example, which shows Rabassa's skills as a translator. Whereas the geographic dimension is lost, the core image of surrealistic craziness (the extract is from a dream) is accurately conveyed through a sophisticated mingling and intertwining of both interpretative translation and substitution with functional equivalent, supported by a secure handling of the language. 'Nutty nuthatch', which replaces the otherwise untranslatable 'topa tolondra' of the ST, is a carefully chosen simile: it is based on an image that, if not familiar and popular, is in any case taken from a natural context, and therefore is perfectly in line with the ST. The simile is also particularly appropriate for its sound effects, which produce an alliteration, exactly as the image of the ST does. Even more subtly, the TT increases the figurative effect, introducing a *diaphora*: 'nutty' means 'crazy', but it also contains the word 'nut', which is actually present in its literal meaning in the adjacent noun, 'nuthatch', a bird feeding on nuts.[7] Finally, it is to be noticed that similar care in the rendering is shown also in the second part of the saying, which recreates both the *anaphora* and the alliteration of the ST, 'kind of sloppy, kind of slurpy'. Here is another interesting case:

> Doce días después del crimen, el instructor del sumario se encontró con un pueblo en carne viva. (1981: 111)

> Twelve days after the crime, the investigating magistrate came upon a town that was an open wound. (1996: 99)

In this case, the TT, by working on the syntax of the clause, gives special relevance to the central metaphor: it is no longer expressed by a prepositional phrase ('un pueblo en carne viva') as in the ST, but is instead directly introduced by the copulative verb 'to be' ('a town that was an open wound'), thus making up for the slight loss of vividness that would occur because of the impossibility to render the ST phrase literally. 'En carne viva' is in itself a more direct and disquieting image than the more technical 'an open wound', but the TT counterbalances the diminishing effect through an increase in syntactical directness: copula + predicate noun.

We have already stressed that the distinctive feature of this narrative language remains its closeness to popular oral storytelling, which makes it so intimately rich in cultural connotations. It is not just a matter of vocabulary; it clearly influences the syntax of the text (explicit clauses preferred to implicit ones; abundance of emphatic structures; long sentences linked by *polysyndeton*), and it can be detected even in the unique taste for death and gruesome

---

7   *Diaphora* derives from the Greek word *diaphoros*, meaning 'different', and is there-fore a rhetorical figure activating a close interaction of sameness and difference.

elements, as well as in the love for strong contrasts, and for combinations of the macabre and the beautiful, or in the recurrence of taboo words, which are always introduced as a spontaneous way of talking, without any morbid connotation. With that, we are now clearly focusing on narration, and thus, referring again to Torop's table, we can say that the analysis is entering the parameter of text, although we have already had some glimpses of García Márquez's unique narrative style (and Rabassa's translation choices) even when working on the other parameters. But let us now take one more example, a passage from the very last pages of the novel, where finally the protagonist's repeatedly 'announced' death is fully narrated. Santiago has been stabbed several times and his entrails have even been exposed; however, although mortally wounded, he has the strength to walk into his home, a horrible and gruesome sight for everybody, even if he astonishingly manages to keep up his usual charm and elegance. The contrast could not be more appalling, and the novel actually indulges in stressing it, even 'foretelling' it through the vision that Divina Flor had had shortly before his killing:

> 'Fue una visión nítida', me contó Divina Flor. 'Llevaba el vestido blanco, y algo en la mano que no pude ver bien, pero me pareció un ramo de rosas'. [...] Se incorporó de medio lado, y se echó a andar en un estado de alucinación, sosteniendo con las manos las vísceras colgantes. [...] Empezaban a desayunar cuando vieron entrar a Santiago Nasar empapado de sangre llevando en las manos el racimo de sus entrañas. Poncho Lanao me dijo: 'Lo que nunca pude olvidar fue el terrible olor a mierda'. Pero Argénida Lanao, la hija mayor, contó que Santiago Nasar caminaba con la prestancia de siempre, midiendo bien los pasos, y que su rostro de sarraceno con los rizos alborotados estaba más bello que nunca. (1981: 130–134)

> 'It was a very clear vision', Divina Flor told me. 'He was wearing his white suit and carrying something that I couldn't make out well in his hand, but it looked like a bouquet of roses'. [...] He stood up, leaning to one side, and started to walk in a state of hallucination, holding his hanging intestines in his hands. [...] They were sitting down to breakfast when they saw Santiago Nasar enter, soaked in blood and carrying the roots of his entrails in his hands. Poncho Lanao told me: 'What I'll never forget was the terrible smell of shit'. But Argénida Lanao, the oldest daughter, said that Santiago Nasar walked with his usual good bearing, measuring his steps well, and that his Saracen face with its headstrong ringlets was handsomer than ever. (1996: 118–122).

On the one hand, we can observe how the insistence on the macabre detail of Santiago's bowels is slightly softened by the use of a more technical word like 'intestines' for 'vísceras' (incidentally, it should be observed that, in its obsessive reference to this part of Santiago's anatomy, the ST actually displays a striking range of synonyms, from the more aseptic 'intestinos' and 'vísceras', to 'entrañas', 'tripas', and even 'tripajo', which can hardly be matched in the English language), and how the ominous association between 'ramo de rosas' (bunch of roses) and 'racimo de sus entrañas' (bunch of entrails), is weakened in the TT ('bouquet of roses', 'roots of his entrails').[8] However, once again a countering strategy can be detected in Rabassa's translation. In describing Santiago's ringlets as 'headstrong', where the ST simply has 'alborotados' (rough, not in order), the TT fully develops the figurative potentialities of the text, introducing, thanks to the *hypallage*, a clear reference to Santiago's strenuous courage, which makes his beauty desperately greater and increases the already sharp contrast with the gruesome and ghastly scene: an interesting case of expressive substitution.

This last example integrates and thus also confirms what has emerged from the previous analysis. Rabassa's distinctive style is based on a view of translation as a creative force: according to him, a translator must be adventurous and original. After all, this is fundamentally a persisting Romantic view that, in fact, can find its roots in the nineteenth century, in particular in German literary and philosophical traditions (Friedrich Schleiermacher and Wilhelm von Humboldt – see Apel, 2008: 6; Venuti, 2000: 11). However, as Venuti repeatedly points out (2008: 250–264; 2009: 14), it is a line of thinking that has been revisited throughout the following century, from the Modernist movements (Yao, 2002: 2–7) to Henri Meschonnic's (2000: 11–24, 29–34) and Antoine Berman's contributions (2000: 285–297), but has also paved the way to further, more innovative and radical approaches in recent poststructuralist developments.

Applying his theoretical premises, and being aware of his responsibilities as a translator, Rabassa's TT strives not to 'hide' the ST. He laments that the act of translating, in itself, risks to divest 'the work of its most essential cultural aspect, which is the sound of its original language' (2002: 91). Since Rabassa is aware that this very aspect is particularly crucial in García Márquez's novel, he clearly endeavours to retain the 'original sound' of the language, trying not to silence it. We have noticed that his 'creativity' is not usually shown when dealing with the macroscopic cultural elements of the text, such as *realia* or terms referring to a specific geographic space; in these

---

8   About the ominous symmetry created in the ST by 'ramo' and 'racimo', see Zamora (1985: 107).

cases, his translation strategy can even be said to opt for a certain degree of neutralisation. However, he generally tries hard to keep the language as vivid as possible, and more importantly, the English of his TT is clearly the result of a sophisticated and carefully sought-after tension with the language of the ST, signs of which we have traced in a distinctively foreignising syntax, with its Biblical and apocalyptic echoes, starting from the rendering of the title. In this choice of the syntax as the fulcrum for the strategy 'to acculturate our English' in order to register, and not to hide, the 'foreignness' of the ST, Rabassa seems to revive Walter Benjamin's defence of 'a literal rendering of the syntax which proves words rather than sentences to be the primary element of the translator' (2000: 21).

When we started our analysis, Rabassa's ideas on the issue of rendering regional voices might have sounded as if suggesting more experimental approaches, like the provocative hypothesis of artfully created English dialects to suit the foreign characters of an ST. Instead, we can perceive now that it is literalism, and not experimentalism, the line actually followed by this translation. Berman says, referring to literalism:

> 'Literal' means: attached to the letter (of works). Labor on the letter in translation is more originary than restitution. It is through this labor that translation, on the one hand, restores the particular signifying process of works (which is more than meaning) and, on the other hand, transforms the translating language. Translation stimulated the fashioning and refashioning of the great western languages only because it labored on the letter and profoundly modified the translating language. As simple restitution of meaning, translation could never have played that formative role. (2000: 297)

Berman's words on 'literal translation' are particularly appropriate to conclude this reading of the target text which, as the theorist advocates, aims to be an evidence of 'the trial of the foreign' in the double sense of the phrase (2000: 285). Labouring on the letter, Rabassa's translation strives 'to open up the foreign work' to the receiving culture, without hiding its foreignness, while at the same time it 'uproots' García Márquez's text from its own 'language ground', putting it on trial and thus revealing 'buried' and 'distant' echoes (Berman, 2000: 285).

4

Claiming Ancestry and Lordship: Heraldic Language and Indigenous Identity in Post-Conquest Mexico

MÓNICA DOMÍNGUEZ TORRES

Por quanto yo soy señor natural y lo fue mi padre llamado Totoquiuaçi y mis agüelos, y a mí me llaman governador [...] demando en pago de lo que yo y mi padre sirvió en la conquista de México y después acá que siempre emos servido lealmente un escudo de armas, y que dentro entren éstas que nosotros antiguamente teníamos. (Pérez-Rocha and Tena, 2000: 161–162)

Since I am natural lord, and my father Totoquiuaçi and my grandfathers also were, and I am called governor, [...] I ask in payment for what my father and I served in the Conquest of Mexico and for what we have loyally served after that, a coat of arms with the arms that we had in ancient times. (My translation)

With these words Don Antonio Cortés Totoquihuaztli, governor of Tlacopan, addressed the Holy Roman Emperor Charles V in a letter written on 6 January 1552. Appealing to all the traditional European codes of courtesy, authority and lordship, the indigenous leader made sure to highlight the military assistance that he and his forefathers had provided to the Spanish Crown. He was aware that, despite all the differences that existed between European and Mesoamerican military practices in regards to equipment, strategies and protocol, there was a staggering common element: in both cultures, bravery and dexterity in warfare were valuable traits that ensured political and social privileges. In both the Spanish and the Aztec empires, rulers conferred badges and insignias to warriors with an outstanding military record, and these visual markers became conspicuous symbols of authority.

In the aftermath of the Conquest of Mexico, this commonality played an important role in the conformation of the new viceroyalty by securing political advancement to those who actively helped the Spanish Crown. Heraldry, in particular, became paramount in the first years of colonisation, when following a common practice among Spanish soldiers, indigenous leaders requested to the King of Spain his approval for their coats of arms, as part of the rewards they were entitled for their steadfast acceptance of Christianity and for their assiduous help to Hernán Cortés in the Conquest of Mexico. Within the negotiations between indigenous leaders and the Spanish Crown, requests for armorial bearings were crucial, not as superfluous acts of mimicry of metropolitan aristocratic conventions, but as deliberate attempts to preserve some of their ancient codes of authority and nobility.[1]

The area around Lake Texcoco, in particular, provides outstanding examples where the introduction of ancestral Mesoamerican codes of ancestry and lordship within the European vocabulary of heraldry exposes intricate negotiations meant to secure a political niche for the indigenous allies to the Spanish Crown.[2] Focusing on the particular case of Antonio Cortés Toto-quihuaztli's blazon, this chapter explores some of the resources the 'natural Lords' of New Spain used to legitimise their position within the new regime (Figure 1). Combining European and indigenous symbols, Don Antonio's coat of arms worked as a key instrument in the reconstruction of Tlacopan's past, and as such as a political symbol to negotiate its future.

According to Luis Weckmann, most of the armorial bearings granted by the Spanish king at this time were allusive arms, that is, coats of arms that briefly illustrated memorable deeds (1992: 146–147). Spanish veterans from the siege and capture of Mexico-Tenochtitlan, for instance, included among their arms Indian heads, indigenous temples, native shields and banners, in testimony of the communities and leaders they had defeated. In the case of the armorial bearings created by indigenous subjects, however, instead of merely appropriating foreign codes or inserting local motifs within a preconceived European format as most Spanish conquistadors did, indigenous élites used their own modelling systems to enrich the meaning and syntax of the formulaic models they were imitating.[3] What derives from this colonial practice is a new codification of ancestral symbols of lineage and worth, resorting to both Mesoamerican pictography and European emblematic codes.

---

1 Several compilations of New Spanish heraldic symbols published since the late nineteenth century include coats of arms conferred to indigenous nobles and warriors. See, for instance, Fernández de Recas (1961), Montoto de Sedas (1927?), Paz y Meliá (1892) and Villar Villamil (1933).
2 Few studies have exclusively focused on the indigenous heraldry of sixteenth-century Mexico. However, they all recognise the important role that Mesoamerican codes played within these idiosyncratic creations. See, for instance, Haskett (1996), Roskamp (2001), Luque Talaván and Castañeda de la Paz (2006) and Castañeda de la Paz (2009).
3 Jeanne Gillespie provides an explanation on how Mesoamerican modelling systems persisted in post-Conquest Mexico (1999: 1–25).

Figure 1.   Coat of arms granted to Don Antonio Cortés Totoquihuaztli in 1564. Archivo Ducal de Alba, Madrid (carpeta 238, legajo 2, documento 14, fol. 2v). Reproduced by permission of Fundación Casa de Alba, Madrid

A careful reading of the visual codes displayed in Don Antonio's idiosyncratic blazon makes clear that indigenous leaders assimilated the European language of heraldry and made it work for their own purposes. Located on the West shoreline of Lake Texcoco, Tlacopan was by the time of Cortés's arrival the smallest free city-state of the Aztec Triple Alliance, the confederation that ruled the central valley of Mexico. Having lost its important rank after the Conquest of Mexico-Tenochtitlan, from 1552 to 1564 several Tlacopan leaders tried to regain their former independent status and dynastic line, by appealing to the munificence of Charles V and Philip II (Pérez-Rocha and Tena, 2000: 50–51). Don Antonio Cortés Totoquihuaztli was successful in several accounts, and on 3 March 1564, a *real cédula* (royal decree) signed by Philip II granted his coat of arms.[4]

---

4   A copy of the *real cédula* granting the coat of arms to Don Antonio rests in the archive of the Fundación Casa de Alba in Madrid, and has been published in Villar

Don Antonio's coat of arms pays tribute to the high status that both his lineage and city enjoyed in pre-Conquest Mexico. As stated in his letters, Don Antonio belonged to the respected Totoquihuaztli lineage that had ruled Tlacopan for over half a century. His father Totoquihuaztli was the third ruler or *tlatoani* of Tlacopan by the time of the Spaniards' arrival. After his death in 1519, his son Tetepanquetzatzin, Don Antonio's half-brother, held the title of governor of Tlacopan until his sudden death in 1525 during an expedition with Hernán Cortés. Between 1525 and 1550, a number of individuals held the title of governor in Tlacopan, but in 1550 the succession devolved upon Don Antonio, the legitimate successor of Totoquihuaztli (Gibson, 1964: 171).

This dynastic reinstatement is celebrated in Don Antonio's blazon by means of the heraldic crest: crowing the overall device, this seemingly pure decorative element has been transformed into a lineage reference. Here the eagle that surmounts the European helmet carries in its beak a banderol that reads 'águila blanca pequeño' (small white eagle).[5] Although the eagle is a conventional element within European heraldry, in the New Spanish context the bird fulfils a totemic function by giving a Spanish interpretation to the name of the Totoquihuaztli lineage founder: Totoquihuatzin, an important Tepanec leader whose name alludes to a particular bird endemic to the Americas, often compared to a small eagle.[6] In 1428 Totoquihuatzin

---

Villamil (1933: cédula 140), and Paz y Meliá (1892: 253–255). In the same archive there is also a copy of the coat of arms granted to the city of Tlacopan, which is very similar to Don Antonio's blazon. María Castañeda de la Paz has published and discussed this civic symbol (2009: 135–138). Without being aware of each other's research, Castañeda de la Paz and I have reached similar conclusions regarding the common elements between the two coats of arms, except for the interpretation of the lion, the eagle and the calendrical symbols, in addition to the identity of the indigenous leader that appears in the shield.

5   Although the transcriptions by Paz y Meliá and Villar Villamil use the word 'pequeña', a personal inspection of the original document revealed that both the text and image of the *real cédula* say 'pequeño', thus indicating that the adjective does not refer to the bird (in Spanish, the correct adjective form for eagle is feminine), but to the man represented by the bird.

6   The name Totoquihuatzin can be translated as 'swift huatzin', i.e. 'swift Laughing Falcon'. According to the *Random House Webster's Unabridged Dictionary* the Nahuatl word *huāctzȋn, huāhtzȋn* was indiscriminately applied by early naturalists to several hen-sized birds of the Valley of Mexico (2001: 908). The *Florentine Codex*, in particular, refers in several instances to the *huactli* or *huacton* to identify various types of birds. Two of these references undoubtedly correspond to the Laughing Falcon (*Herpetotheres cachinnans*), a medium-sized bird of prey with a white head and a dark brown mask around the eyes. This bird was of great resonance in Aztec culture as a carrier of omens. See Sahagún (2000, vol. 1: 441–442; vol. 3: 1019). Hernando Ruiz de Alarcón, in his *Treatise on the Heathen Superstitions that Today*

joined forces with Mexico-Tenochtitlan and Texcoco against Azcapotzalco, becoming shortly after the first king of Tlacopan, now the capital city of the Tepanec kingdom.

In a similar way European kings filled the fields of their personal armorial bearings with the heraldic symbols of the different provinces they ruled over, Don Antonio used two of the blazon's six sections to present his particular community. The first and the fourth fields feature a lavish indigenous palace surmounted by three *copillis*, or pointed turquoise diadems that marked the authority of independent city-states in Aztec times.[7] By comparing this detail to folio 34r of the *Codex Osuna* (Figure 2), a contemporary document explaining the nature of the Aztec confederation, it becomes clear that the sequence of three native crowns represents an abbreviated reference to Tlacopan's independent status before the Spanish conquest. As Don Antonio clarifies in his letter to Charles V:

> [Los] señores de Tlacopan [...] nunca tributaron a México ni a otro señor ninguno con un tomín ni un grano de cacao, antes el señorío de Tlacopan, demás de muchos pueblos que aquí tenía subjetos y tributarios, tenía juntamente con México y Tezcuco parte de los tributos de CXXIII provincias y pueblos. (Pérez-Rocha and Tena, 2000: 161)

> [The] lords of Tlacopan [...] never paid tribute to Mexico or any other lord, not with a *tomín* [a grain measurement of twelve beans] or even with one cocoa bean. Formerly the kingdom of Tlacopan, in addition to many towns that were its subjects and tributaries, received along with Mexico and Tezcuco a part from the tributes of a hundred and twenty three towns and provinces. (My translation)

In addition, the blazon requested by Don Antonio Cortés confirms his adherence to the colonial system. The second and third fields feature interesting allusive scenes that point out to the role of the indigenous aristocracy in 'delivering' the New World to Christianity. In the second field, a tripartite orb missing a section stands on a body of water, while two arms hold a cross

---

Live Among the Indians Native to this New Spain published in 1629, describes the *huactzin* or *huacton* as 'a little bigger than an eaglet [aguilucho], with a very good bill and claws. It feeds on snakes and vipers killing them skillfully [...]. The calls of this eaglet are considered by the Indians to be an omen, and many times they stubbornly affirm that it calls them by their names' (1984: 68–69). I thank Pablo Escalante Gonzalbo for his invaluable help translating this name.

7   The colour and shape of these native crowns is explained with details in the *real cédula* (blue, with golden ends, red bow and yellow lace). See fn. 4.

Figure 2. *Pintura del Gobernador, Alcaldes y Regidores de México (Codex Osuna)*, 1565. Biblioteca Nacional de España, Madrid (Vitr. 26-8, fol. 34r). Reproduced by permission of Biblioteca Nacional de España

on top of it. The third field clarifies the identity of the person supporting the cross in the former field: an indigenous leader or *tlatoani* is now in the middle of the waters worshipping the cross on the orb. Creating a narrative sequence, these two scenes follow an established European pictorial convention: an orb topped with a cross was a symbol of the final triumph of Christ's reign over the world. A print by Hieronymus Wierix after Marteen de Vos, for instance, presents Christ handing a similar orb to both Philip II and Pope Gregory XIII as the champions of Christianity (Cuadriello, 1999: 65).

In sixteenth-century Mexico, moreover, the feats of the conquistadors were also allegorically represented as the act of offering the entire world to the Christian emperor. According to the *Codex Tlaxcala*, an indigenous manuscript produced around 1584 to complement Diego Muñoz Camargo's *Descripción de la ciudad y provincia de Tlaxcala* (*Description of the City and Province of Tlaxcala*) (Muñoz Camargo, 1981), a scene on display in Tlaxcala's City Hall presented a kneeling Christopher Columbus handing an orb to

Figure 3. Ms Hunter 242 f.249r *Christopher Columbus (1451–1506) Symbolically offers the 'New World' to Charles V (1500–08)*, from *Historia de Tlaxcala* by Diego Muñoz Camargo (1998), (pen and ink on paper) by Mexican School (16th century), © Glasgow University Library, Scotland/The Bridgeman Art Library. Reproduced by permission of Glasgow University Library

Charles V (Figure 3). The particular *tlatoani* who holds a cross on the orb and adores it in Don Antonio's coat of arms may very well be Totoquihuaztli, Don Antonio's father, who voluntarily accepted Christianity and unconditionally offered his help to Hernán Cortés. According to another letter Don Antonio addressed to the emperor in December 1552, his father:

> Al saber que habían llegado vuestros españoles con el Marqués del Valle mucho se holgó y les envió algunos regalos, y cuando se acercaban a

nuestro pueblo amenazados por los Manes, como a veces se dice, los acogió y les dio con abundancia lo que habían menester, y se dirigió al Marqués con las siguientes palabras: 'Ven enhorabuena con tu ejército, y sábete que nosotros estamos prestos a servirte a ti y a aquel en cuyo nombre vienes; al Dios que tú adoras, adoraré yo con todo mi pueblo; aquí tienes el cu de mis dioses, destrúyelo [. . .] y lo que allí encontrares y te agradare tómalo y úsalo'. (Pérez-Rocha and Tena, 2000: 175–176)

After learning that your Spaniards had arrived with the Marquis of the Valley [of Oaxaca], [he] was very pleased and he sent them some presents, and every time they [the Spaniards] approached our town, threatened by the Manes [Mexicas] as sometimes they are called, he welcomed them and gave them with abundance all what they needed, and he addressed the Marquis with the following words: 'At a good time you have come with your army. Know that we are ready to serve you and [the man] in whose name you have come; along with all my people, I will worship the God you worship; here you have the *cu* [temple] of our gods, destroy it [. . .] and whatever you find there that is of your liking take it and use it'. (My translation)

The two complementary scenes seem to confirm that the incorporation of this remote land to the Christian world was secured by indigenous leaders, with their labours in the *mundo menor* (or minor world – in the language of the period, the world of human action). Muñoz Camargo, for instance, claims that indigenous leaders helped the emperor 'ganar y conquistar toda la redondez y máquina de este Nuevo Mundo' (to win and conquer the whole roundness and machinery of this New World) (1981: 128; my translation). By presenting the orb with a missing section, moreover, Don Antonio is reminding the viewer that many lands of the new continent are still under pagan rule, and indigenous leaders like him are essential to continue the 'pacification' of the New World. Thus, Don Antonio is not only claiming the immediate acceptance of Christianity from the part of his forefathers, but also his own subsequent contribution to restore the integrity of the Christian world.

These two scenes also partake of the providential language that was used to narrate the Spanish Conquest of Mexico by the mid-sixteenth century. In particular, the prominent star to the left of these two scenes seems to refer to the omens received by the inhabitants of Anáhuac about the imminent end of the Aztec rule. Because of its size and important location, illuminating the cross according to the royal decree of 1564, this astral body more likely did not represent a star, but the planet Venus, which in ancient Mesoamerica was a force related to warfare and destruction. By the mid-sixteenth century, the codices created by mendicants and indigenous scribes in collaboration presented

Figure 4.   *Moctezuma sees a comet* from Diego Durán, *Historia de las Indias de Nueva España e islas de tierra firme*, 1579. Biblioteca Nacional de España, Madrid (Vitr. 26-11, fol. 182v). Reproduced by permission of Biblioteca Nacional de España

the Spanish Conquest as the natural consequence of a series of prophecies. Book XII of the *Florentine Codex* and the *Codex Durán* (Figure 4), for instance, explain how a 'smoking star', or comet appeared in the sky just before the arrival of the Spaniards foretelling the death of the Aztec ruler Moctezuma and the beginning of a new era (Magaloni-Kerpel, 2004: 182–190). Another Mesoamerican prophecy ensured that the self-exiled ruler Quetzalcoatl after his self-immolation transformed into Venus, and one day he would return to rule over Anáhuac (Nicholson, 2001: 251–252). Although there is controversy about the veracity of the misidentification story of Cortés with Quetzalcoatl, several sixteenth-century accounts do refer to the Quetzalcoatl myth as an omen for the coming of Christianity to Aztec territories.[8] The prominent star therefore could refer to this popular story that helped to construct the image of New Spain as a kingdom predestined to embrace Christian rule.

The last two partitions of the blazon, although smaller in size, present an interesting Mesoamerican complement to the hitherto Europeanised formulation. Two contrasting elements are presented next to each other: on the left, fire tongues in red and yellow stand on a dark background; to the right, the field is filled with a river of blue and white waters. This placement of fire and water side by side certainly alludes to the ancient Mesoamerican concept

---

8   For studies exploring the different versions of the Quetzalcoatl myth as well as its colonial reinterpretations, see Carrasco (2000) and Nicholson (2001).

Figure 5.   *Atl-tlachinolli* symbol (author's drawing)

of sacred war. Within Aztec visual culture, there was a particular image that perfectly illustrated the Mesoamerican understanding of the cosmos as a constant struggle of oppositional forces: the *atl-tlachinolli*, or burning water, which was pictographically represented by the intersection of two contrasting streams, one made of water (illustrated as a torrent made of bluish spirals ending in pearls and seashells) and the other of fire (depicted as a yellowish string of scales and dots finishing in flames) (Figure 5); or, as it is presented in folio 16v of the *Historia Tolteca-Chichimeca*, by the two elements contained within the same space (Figure 6).

This symbol embodied a very complex metaphor, in which two oppositional streams intertwined represented continuous cosmic regeneration. On the one hand, there is an equation between water as sustenance of human life and sacrificial blood from war captives as nurturing substance for the gods. On the other hand, fire represented victory over the enemy, since the conquest of an opposing settlement was expressed by burning its principal temple, as represented in several colonial documents, including the *Codex*

Figure 6.   *Historia tolteca-chichimeca*, 1540s–1550s. Bibliothèque Nationale de France, Paris (Manuscrit Mexicain 46–58, fol. 16v). Reproduced by permission of Bibliothèque Nationale de France

Mendoza (Figure 7). This binomial expression perfectly combined the two main elements that perpetuated divine balance – warfare was meant to procure captives, who will ensure with their blood the subsistence of the cosmos (Carrasco, 1990: 58–91).

   It would be logical to introduce martial references within the *tlatoani* of Tlacopan's coat of arms since this city joined the Aztec Triple Alliance

Figure 7. *The Conquests of Itzcoatl*, from the *Codex Mendoza*, early 1540s. Bodleian Library, University of Oxford, Oxford (Ms. Arch. Seld. A. 1, fol. 5v). Reproduced by permission of Bodleian Library

by means of a military coalition to overthrow the rival Tepanec city of Azcapotzalco. Moreover, in 1521, after being defeated by Cortés's troops, Tlacopan joined the Spanish Conquest, establishing an alliance with the Spaniards in the siege of Mexico-Tenochtitlan. Don Antonio was certainly aware that these series of military alliances were crucial for the survival of his community and, although Tlacopan had been severely affected by the territorial claims made by other indigenous leaders and Spanish *encomenderos* (colonists granted control of land and Indians to work for them), in his negotiations with Charles V, he is willing to reinstate his support to the Christian cause and to recognise the benefits of the Spanish Conquest:

> De allí que en V.M. podamos comprobar la verdad de lo que dijo el santo Job, a saber, que la vida del hombre sobre la tierra es una batalla; tal parece que el esfuerzo de V.M. está siempre empeñado en combatir a las naciones bárbaras, a los infieles, a los adoradores de los demonios, en fin, a los enemigos de Dios; en sacar a éstos de las tinieblas hacia la luz resplandeciente de los cristianos, es decir, hacia el mismo sol de justicia que es Cristo [. . .]; lo cual V.M. ha obrado felizmente entre nosotros, pues al combatir mediante vuestros españoles al horrendo ejército de los demonios e introducir el cristianismo, habéis colocado en suma quietud y paz a esta nuestra provincia, la cual aunque se duele por la matanza de nuestros mayores y la no pequeña pérdida de bienes temporales, sin embargo reconoce humildemente el inmortal beneficio de V.M. (Pérez Rocha and Tena, 2000: 167–168)

> In Your Majesty we can confirm the truth of what Job said, that is, that human life on earth is a battle; [. . .] your Majesty is always committed to fight barbarians, infidels, devils' worshippers, in sum, God's enemies, taking these nations out of the shadows, towards the shinning light of the Christians, that is, towards the Sun of Justice that is Christ [. . .]. All of which your Majesty has happily done among us, because by defeating through your Spaniards the horrendous army of demons and introducing Christianity, you have placed our province in great tranquillity and peace; and although we lament the slaughter of our forefathers and the not small loss of temporal goods, we humbly recognise the eternal benefit brought by your Majesty. (My translation)

Further references to the military character of Tlacopan appear in the blazon's bordure. Out of the eight sections in which this border is divided, five contain Mesoamerican military instruments: three arrows with flint points, five conch shell trumpets, a *macuahuitl* (or native sword made of wood and obsidian blades) and a *chimalli* (or indigenous shield). Given the ethnic specificity of these representations, these particular weapons seem to represent the arms of Don Antonio's forefathers (or according to Don Antonio's letter, 'las armas que nosotros antiguamente teníamos' [the arms that we used to have]). Most indigenous petitioners indeed claimed they wanted to display the weapons of their elders, equating thus the European tradition of heraldry to the ancient Mesoamerican practice of wearing tribal insignia.

In addition, the three upper sections of the bordure display more elements foreign to European conventions. The imagery in each of those three fields echoes Aztec toponyms: mounds with animals, plants and objects are standard features in the traditional grammar of Mesoamerican place names. A particular detail in the central field, moreover, seems to point out the crucial place that Don Antonio's home town plays on the whole coat of arms. According to the description in the royal decree, on top of the central heap there are 'dos ramas verdes con unas flores coloradas, á manera de clavellinas' (two green branches with some red flowers similar to carnations) (Paz y Meliá, 1892: 255; my translation), a codification that corresponds to Tlacopan's place name (see Figure 2, third pictogram). On the other hand, the left and right frames of the bordure feature two animals, an eagle and a jaguar, that had a profound military symbolism for Mesoamerican societies. Both of them condense the worth and bravery an Aztec warrior should display. According to Fray Diego Durán, ancient Mesoamerican warriors,

> flying like eagles in battle with invincible bravery and courage [. . .], were called Eagles or Jaguars. They were the men whom the sovereigns most loved and esteemed, the men who obtained most privileges and prerogatives. To them the kings granted most generous favors, adorning them with brilliant, splendid weapons and insignia. (Durán, 1971: 197)

Thus, these two animals indicate that the places they surmount were brave warrior communities. Beside each one of these emblematic animals, a miniature blue representation of the *atl-tlachinolli* emphasises this martial content (Figure 5). These scenes, however, do not seem to be mere indications of place but also of time. Floating on the right side of the lion, a small pictogram featuring a 'casa blanca principal' (a white élite house) with three dots in the centre seems to function as a calendrical sign, indicating the year 'three *calli*' (or 'three house'). The year of Tenochtitlan's (and Tlacopan's) fall, 1521, is a three-house year, and the building in flames at the left confirms the representation of a historical defeat. This section thus could be a commemoration of the Spanish Conquest of Mexico, and more specifically, the very subjugation of Tlacopan, which in some cases was represented as a castle with reeds, as in a scene about the siege of Mexico-Tenochtitlan from the *Lienzo de Tlaxcala* (Figure 8).

The opposite field in the extreme left presents similar Mesoamerican conventions to represent place, conquest and time. As I have already mentioned,

Figure 8.   Episode of the siege of Mexico-Tenochtitlan from the *Lienzo de Tlaxcala*, c. 1550. Published in Chavero, 1892: plate 42

close to the eagle of the left section we find a pictographic representation of the *atl-tlachinolli*, indicating some sort of military action. In addition, seven 'beads' with leaves below the eagle could refer to another calendrical sign, the year seven-reed. The fact that an eagle takes part of this scene could point to an event related to the Totoquihuaztli family, maybe their ascent to power. Unfortunately, given the scarcity of chronicles about Tlacopan, it is impossible to establish what crucial event in the history of this kingdom is represented here.

Further, the central frame of the bordure also presents a narrative emphasis, as the traditional place name for Tlacopan is complemented with additional foreign references. To the right of the carnations, there is a tree and 'un leon de oro, cercado de llamas de fuego, el cual esté abrazado con el tronco del dicho árbol' (a golden lion, surrounded by fire flames, is embracing the tree's trunk) (Paz y Meliá, 1892: 254; my translation). One of the infamous Conquest episodes that took place in Tlacopan (and is recorded in sixteenth-century chronicles) is the so-called the 'Noche Triste' (or the 'Night of Sorrows'). After fleeing Mexico-Tenochtitlan, harassed by Mexican warriors, Hernán Cortés rested in Tlacopan and lamented under an *ahuehuetl* tree the temporary loss of the city. According to some Tepanec sources, moreover, Cortés could only escape death that night thanks to the help offered by Tlacopan leaders. As Don Antonio claims in one of his letters to Charles V:

> Quando los españoles salieron de México heridos y desbaratados, que avían muerto más de la metad dellos, si como aquí los recebimos de paz y les dimos comida les diéramos guerra no quedara hombre dellos, y por este hecho los mexicanos fueron muy enojados contra nos. (Pérez-Rocha and Tena, 2000: 163)

> When the Spaniards left Mexico wounded and crushed, as more than half of them had died, if we had received them with war, instead of the peace and food we gave them, none of them would have survived; and because of that the Mexicans were very angry with us. (My translation)

Because the lion is the only non-American animal in this blazon and incidentally the one found in Hernán Cortés's coat of arms signalling his bravery, would it be too farfetched to think that this lion surrounded by fire is an allegorical reference to Cortés during the 'Noche Triste'? In a way similar to some Spanish conquistadors' coats of arms that refer to particular episodes in the Conquest of Mexico, this particular section of Don Antonio's blazon could allude to this specific event in which Tlacopan played a central role. There was indeed certain identification between the Marquis and the Totoquihuaztli dynasty, since the Tepanec family adopted the name of the insigne Conquistador as their own Castilian surname.

At any rate, it seems clear that Don Antonio chose to register in his coat of arms crucial moments in the incorporation of his city-state to the Christian empire, borrowing from an ancient Mesoamerican tradition of record keeping – the annals, books that recorded year by year the history of a specific settlement. These pre-Conquest and colonial documents presented important events in the history of a community arranged along vertical or horizontal bands containing a continuous account of year signs. For example, folio 5v of the *Codex Mendoza* presents to the right of a turquoise year count the conquests achieved by the pre-Conquest Aztec ruler Itzcoatl (Figure 7). In a similar manner, Don Antonio's coat of arms presents a strip of crucial events in the history of his community, even including in certain cases year markers. As opposed to European bordures that present decorative or secondary information about the person represented, in Don Antonio's coat of arms the bordure gains an unexpected historical importance.

Thus, Don Antonio Cortés Totoquihuaztli used the imagery of his armorial device to stress the legitimacy of his demands before the Spanish Crown. The indigenous leader expressed his claims of ancestry and lordship adapting heraldic conventions to Mesoamerican pictographic traditions. Instead of using one of the fields in the blazon to identify his hereditary symbols, Don Antonio chose the crest as the centre to outline his dynastic claims. Conversely, the blazon and bordure became narrative spaces to outline the support that he and his forefathers had given to the Spanish Crown. Inverting the grammar of heraldry and resorting to Mesoamerican narrative conventions, the idiosyncratic blazon of the Tepanec ruler thus became an ideal site to construct identity and worth.

5

The Role of Degeneration Theory in Spanish American Public Discourse at the *Fin de Siècle*: *Raza Latina* and Immigration in Chile and Argentina

MICHELA COLETTA

At the turn of the twentieth century, the heavy influx of European immigrants to the Southern Cone raised issues regarding both the social and the political implications of such a sharp and unprecedented increase in foreign population. Along economic considerations, the racial question became paramount, bringing about a flourishing of works based on the most recent European racialist theories. The 'social question' was strictly linked to the racial question, which 'preoccupied Argentine and Chilean thinkers no less than economic problems' (Solberg, 1970: 18). The impact of European immigration on the development of both racialist theories and social reforms has been widely discussed, especially in the case of Argentina. Considerable attention has been devoted to questions regarding the application of criminological theories to mechanisms of social control, to the impact of racial theories on the development of ethnic and national ideologies, or to processes of legalisation and medicalisation of social issues.[1] What I explore in this chapter is the relationship between perceptions of 'Latin' immigration and ideas of racial/national decadence, in an attempt to shed new light on the impact of European immigration on the discourse of the *raza latina* (or Latin race) in turn-of-the-century Spanish America.

The concept of *raza* did not have a well-defined meaning. It lent itself to a variety of interpretations that often involved ideas of national identity, carrying a variety of connotations that in some cases were more strictly biological, but in other cases were based on psychological or more generally cultural and historical assumptions.[2] In this context, the significance of the idea of degeneration was therefore not confined to the adoption of European and

---

1 See, in particular, Rodríguez (2006), Stepan (1991), Ruggiero (2004), Suriano (2000) and Zimmermann (1992).
2 See Zimmermann (1992: 24–25).

US racialist theories, but it was exploited within the more general discourse on the moral and political decadence of the *race* understood as a national or regional entity.[3] Especially from the last decade of the nineteenth century, European sociological theories of racial/national decadence – particularly French social theory, boosted by the consolidation of medical psychiatry in the second half of the century, and Italian social and political thought derived from the school of criminal anthropology – started to be incorporated into identity discourses. The category of degeneration thus came to play an important role in the relationship between tradition and modernity on the one hand, and conceptions of barbarism and civilisation on the other.

This chapter discusses the different ways in which, during the *fin-de-siècle* period, the concept of degeneration was woven into a variety of discourses that focused on ideas of racial identity and the representation of European immigration as a vehicle of civilisation. In both cases, I will argue, these narratives resulted in conflicting sets of representations revolving around the key idea of *Latinity*; their intrinsic ambivalence is precisely what allowed them to work successfully within the wider framework of the discourse of modernity. The adoption of the idea of Latinity that took place in the region at the turn of the twentieth century was strongly marked by notions of moral and racial degeneration.[4] The origin of the term *Latin America* as a geopolitical denomination has been traced back to the mid-nineteenth century, when Colombian diplomat and intellectual José María Torres Caicedo first used it to differentiate between the Spanish-speaking parts of the American continent

---

3   Degeneration as a scientific category was first used in the famous essay by French physician Bénédicte Auguste Morel entitled *Traité des dégénérescences physiques, intellectuelles et morales de l'espèce humaine* (*Treatise on the Physical, Intellectual and Moral Degeneracies of the Human Species*), published in 1857. After long study and research in both physical and mental pathology, Morel made a significant contribution to the inclusion into the medical sciences of the concepts of heredity and progressivity, which constitute the basis of degeneration theory. As is clear from the very title of Morel's study, degeneration theory was being applied not only to the study of the body, but also to the study of the mind and of the moral stamina of individuals. Research on behavioural and emotional disturbances was being applied increasingly often to the scientific branches of criminology and medical psychiatry, and from there to social theory. It is therefore clear how broadly applicable the category of degeneration was, and how it carried connotations of moral, social and racial condemnation.

4   Víctor Arreguine, *En qué consiste la superioridad de los latinos sobre los anglosajones* (1900); César Zumeta, *El continente enfermo* (1899); Rufino Blanco Fombona, *La americanización del mundo* (1902); Carlos Octavio Bunge, *Nuestra América* (1903), prefaced by Rafael Altamira; Agustín Álvarez, *¿Adónde vamos?* ([1904] 1915); Alcides Arguedas, *Pueblo enfermo* (1909); Salvador R. Merlos, *América Latina ante el peligro* (1914).

and the area that around the same time started to be referred to as Anglo-Saxon America. Uruguayan scholar Arturo Ardao, in his indispensable work on the subject, stresses both the oppositional value of the term with respect to North America and the intrinsic implications of the idea of *latinidad* in terms of political and cultural identity.[5] However, the incorporation of this idea into *fin-de-siècle* identity discourses was more problematic than has been traditionally assumed, mainly due to the connotations of political and moral degeneration that were attributed to the notion of 'Latin civilisation'.

Recent scholarship has called into question the ontological value of the term 'Latin America', raising issues regarding the colonialist and imperialist logic behind the 'invention' of the idea itself. Walter Mignolo has attempted to deconstruct – or 'decolonise' – a paradigm of modernity that according to him carried neocolonial values and displaced the intrinsic simultaneity of meanings and implications contained in the historical traditions of the Hispanic nations of America.[6] For Mignolo, 'white Creole and Mestizo/a elites, in South America and the Spanish Caribbean islands, after independence from Spain adopted "Latinidad" to create their own postcolonial identity. [. . .] Latin America is not so much a subcontinent as it is the political project of Creole-Mestizo/a elites' (2005: 59). Moreover, the inclusion of the previous Spanish and Portuguese colonies in the 'Latin race' implied the exclusion of both Blacks and Indians from the nation, i.e. those groups who represented traditions that would break the linear development of Western/European civilisation. By questioning the intrinsic validity of the idea itself and by putting forward new viable alternatives, this approach helps unveil the historicity of the 'idea of Latin America' against its supposedly ontological value. What it does not help to understand, however, is the context in which the term imposed itself and the specific function it served within that context.

The idea of Latinity was increasingly being associated with notions of racial degeneration, which, I argue, became instrumental to the wider discourse on modern civilisation. Mignolo states that after independence the history of Latin America was marked by a constant attempt by the local élites to embrace modernity (Mignolo, 2005: 57). It is part of my argument that (paradoxically) the idea of a decadent Latinity was in fact instrumental to shaping discourses of 'modernity' in the political and cultural context of late-nineteenth-century Spanish America, and that Old World values were also incorporated through perceptions of European immigration. This means that notions of moral and political decadence came hand-in-hand with the creation

---

5   See Ardao (1980). For a discussion of the Spanish debate on the origin of the term 'Latin America' mainly in the 1850s, see Ardao (1992).

6   See Mignolo's 'Preface' (2005: x–xx).

of national discourses. I will show that, far from being a univocal concept, the term 'América Latina' was characterised by ambiguous connotations that exploited the vagueness of the category of degeneration. I will argue that, on the one hand, the Chilean liberal élites incorporated the idea of a declining Latin race as a viable means to represent themselves as modern. On the other hand, in Argentina it was the immigrant who was represented as a vehicle of civilisation. Finally, in order to highlight the perception of modern civilisation as inherently incongruous, I will consider the symbolism of the 'death of the gaucho' not so much in the light of the nationalist tradition of the first decades of the twentieth century, but rather as a means to reinforce by opposition the incorporation of modern civilisation.

One trend of discourse that seemed to be especially popular among the liberal élites of turn-of-the-century Chile was based upon the concept of *latinidad*. The cultural, as well as political, implications of the term were at the centre of a heated debate in which a complex set of representations was built around the discourse of the decadence of the Latin race as opposed to the flourishing North-American civilisation. These discursive patterns assume special relevance in light of the intellectual production of the first decade of the twentieth century, when a number of works appeared that denounced the profound crisis that affected Chilean society, such as Nicolás Palacios's *Decadencia del espíritu de nacionalidad* (*Decadence of the Spirit of Nationality*) (1908), Alejandro Venegas's *Sinceridad: Chile íntimo* (*Sincerity: Intimate Chile*) (1910) and Francisco Encina's *Nuestra inferioridad económica* (*Our Economic Inferiority*) (1912). Yet some of the early 'essayists of the crisis',[7] like Liberal-Radicals Enrique Mac-Iver (1844–1922) and Emilio Rodríguez Mendoza (1873–1960), initiated a discourse of national decadence based on the idea of Latin decadence by incorporating, just at the turn of the century, French and Italian sociological theories about decadent Latinity well before the debate on immigration and racial identity became paramount around 1904.

The reception of the famous essay written by French pedagogist Edmond Demolins, *A quoi tient la supériorité des Anglo-Saxons* (*Anglo-Saxon Superiority: To What It Is Due*) ([1897] 1901), had immediate resonance in Chile. In the fifth issue of a major liberal publication of the time, the *Revista de Chile* (15 July 1898),[8] an article appeared by Alamiro Huidobro Valdés that presented Demolins's theory to the Chilean public. The Latin race, more than any other,

---

7   See Gazmuri (2001).
8   The *Revista de Chile*, published between 1898 and 1901 in Santiago, was a fortnightly publication run by exponents of the liberal élites during a period characterised by the continuous struggles for power between the Liberal-Radical and the more conservative elements of the Parliamentary Republic. Close to the

it was argued, was subject to a moral evil defined not so much as depending on the idea of race conceived in strictly biological terms, but rather on the grounds of a common inherited political culture. Those societies bound by the tie of Roman ancestry had not developed institutions, particularly educational institutions, that could compete with the logic of the survival of the fittest imposed by the 'natural' development of society. Huidobro Valdés defined a generic concept of Latin race, based on historical/cultural[9] rather than physical racialist concepts – as opposed to the tradition set by Arthur de Gobineau in his *Essai sur l'inégalité des races humaines* (*Essay on the Inequality of Human Races*) ([1853–1855] 1967) – , using it as the yardstick against which one could measure Chile's own state of decline.

The existence of a *raza latina* that unified the Southern peoples on both sides of the Atlantic was justified not necessarily in terms of racial inheritance, but rather in terms of institutional and cultural influence, which took on a historicist connotation. It has been argued that a more biological stream of racialism was something of an exception in European science of the late nineteenth century (see Todorov, 1993: 144). Similarly, this vague but, by virtue of its vagueness, very strong conception of *latinidad* – with all the inherent contradictions attached to it – was based in Chile upon a positivist tradition of historicist tendency and of liberal inclinations. This was a tradition that looked back at José Victorino Lastarria's conception of Positivism, which only used Auguste Comte's doctrine as a definition for the basis of social organisation without accepting the total submission of the individual to society. On this tradition was based the Instituto Nacional, where many liberal historians and politicians were formed, including Francisco Bilbao, Diego Barros Arana, Miguel Luis Amunátegui and positivist thinker Valentín Letelier (see Lipp, 1975: 53–55).

Ateneo de Santiago – a cultural and literary association that brought together the major intellectual figures of the time – the *Revista de Chile* was the expression of a liberal intelligentsia that was getting an increasingly stronger hold on the Universidad de Chile. Gustavo Adolfo Holley, one of the founders of the magazine, was among the main promoters of the European social sciences among his own generation; Domingo Amunátegui Solar was provost of the Universidad de Chile between the first and the second decade of the twentieth century, and son of the famous liberal historian Miguel Luis Amunátegui Aldunate. Among its regular contributors were also: Roberto Huneeus Gana, from one of the most distinct families in Santiago; Alberto Mackenna Subercaseaux, author of works of sociology and history, as well as of a memoir of his travels in Europe; historian Enrique Matta Vial, and many others.

9 See, in particular, Hippolyte Taine's critical works, especially his *Histoire de la littérature anglaise* (1864) and *Les origines de la France contemporaine* (6 volumes, 1876–1893).

The historical influence of the Roman legacy over the conquered populations was thought to be most apparent in the linguistic inheritance, seen as
the result of a profound sociological influence exercised by the conqueror
on the conquered. As Tzvetan Todorov shows in his discussion of Ernest
Renan's view of the link between race and nation,[10] the latter did not accept
the separation between the two concepts. Therefore, argues Todorov, Renan
used the term race with a new connotation: 'there is physical race and there
is cultural race; language plays a dominant role in the formation of a culture'
(1993: 142). Augustin Thierry's theory of the conflict of races as the basis of
the creation of a modern European civilisation[11] also seems to run through
the majority of these discourses, where the Latin race was said to coexist
to a certain extent with the conquered elements; after having succeeded in
exerting the strongest influence over time, the Latin legacy, it was argued,
never subsided completely under the subsequent barbaric invasions:

> Los romanos conquistaron el mundo entonces conocido, i fueron, a
> su turno, dominados por los bárbaros. Hubo pues, sucesivamente,
> la influencia latina sobre griegos, eslavos, jermanos e ibéricos, i la
> influencia de los bárbaros sobre los romanos. De aquí una pureza de
> raza que ha destruido la pureza de las razas primitivas. Producida esa
> mezcla, la calificación de cada raza no dependía sólo de su orijen: ha
> dependido también del grado de la influencia romana sobre ella. Así
> como la influencia de los bárbaros sobre los romanos, no llegó al punto
> de que la raza latina, propiamente dicha, se desnaturalizase i perdiese su
> nombre, de la misma manera la influencia de los romanos sobre algunas
> de las razas bárbaras no llegó al punto de qué estas se desnaturalizasen
> i perdiesen su nombre. (Huidobro Valdés, 1898: 298)

> After conquering the entire world that was known at the time, the
> Romans were dominated by the barbarians. So, first came the Latin
> influence over the Greeks, the Slavs, the Germans and the Iberians, and
> subsequently the influence of the barbarians over the Romans, hence a
> racial purity which destroyed the purity of the primitive races. After
> this mixture was produced, the quality of each race did not depend
> only on its origin, but also on the degree of Latin influence over it. The
> influence exerted by the barbarians over the Romans never led to the
> loss of either the nature or the name of the Latin race; similarly, the
> Roman influence over some of the barbarian races was never so deep as
> to cause them to lose either their nature or their names. (My translation)

---

10   *Qu'est-ce qu'une nation?* (Renan, 1882).
11   *Histoire de la conquête de l'Angleterre par les Normands* (Thierry, 1825).

What is worth pointing out is that while the notion of the mixing of races was justified as the foundation of modern European civilisation, the late nineteenth-century Chilean liberal élites exploited it as a discursive strategy for the legitimation of the *raza latina* as an entity that also comprised Latin America.

The authority of Thierry's theory was exploited both in Chile and Argentina, side by side with the more widely known racialist theories popularised by Hippolyte Taine, Ernest Renan and Gustave Le Bon[12] in particular. Argentine social scientist and criminologist José Ingenieros acknowledged the importance of Thierry's work for the subsequent development of European race theories in the introduction to his edition of Sarmiento's *Conflicto y armonías de las razas en América* (*Conflict and Harmony of Races in America*) (1883), published in 1915 in his series of popular editions of Argentine works called 'La Cultura Argentina' (Argentine Culture). Sarmiento stated that, while the formation of the European race was the result of the union between the Gauls and the Romans, the Saxons and the Normans, the Germanic and the Lombard peoples, etc., who all together created the Caucasian race, the same principle was not valid for races of different colour, as maintained by US-based Swiss scientist Jean Louis Rodolphe Agassiz,[13] whose authority Sarmiento acknowledged in the introductory statement to *Conflicto* (1883: 6). It was Carlos Octavio Bunge (1903), however, who linked the theory of the conflict of races with the idea of Spain's intrinsically degenerate character in his well-known work *Nuestra América* (*Our America*). First published in 1903 in Spain with an introduction by Spanish intellectual and academic Rafael Altamira, the essay was later revised and then republished by Ingenieros in 'La Cultura Argentina' in 1918.

While confirming the widely accepted ideas that Spain's decline was to be attributed to its culture of oppression and persecution dating back to the Habsburg monarchy, Bunge also highlighted the Iberian element as one which had never totally subsided to the Latin one. In other words, the process of *Latinisation* of Spain was never fully achieved, which had a catastrophic impact on the colonisation of what was to become Spanish America. The 'civilisation' that Spain and, consequently, Argentina, did not acquire through a sufficient dose of Latin heritage throughout the previous centuries, should be obtained through a massive wave of immigration coming from Europe at the end of the nineteenth century. It seems that what was in Chile a discursive strategy that used a notion of Latin culture as historical heritage became transposed in Argentina on to the level of the representation of the immigrant as a civilising factor. However, as I will show through an

---

12   *La Psychologie des foules* (Le Bon, [1895] 1905).
13   *An Essay on Classification* (Agassiz, 1859).

example of the reception of the figure of the immigrant in the pages of *Caras y Caretas*, a popular periodical publication of the period,[14] the term civilisation assumed ambivalent nuances related to the category of degeneration that make Sarmiento's traditional opposition between *civilización* and *barbarie* much less self-evident as one advances towards the turn of the century.

The concept of 'Europeanisation' reproduced the dynamics of the traditional dispute over the geographical and historical place of the New World with respect to Europe. As Antonello Gerbi shows in his classic book *La disputa del nuovo mondo* (*The Dispute of the New World*) (1983), the thesis of the weakness and immaturity of the American continent was scientifically explained in the second half of the eighteenth century by the works of Georges-Louis Leclerc, Comte de Buffon,[15] who justified on a scientific basis the need for Europeans to impose their own cultural and political models upon the Americans. The belief that the continent had only relatively recently emerged from the water had been widely endorsed so as to prove its physical – and, consequently, its moral – immaturity. These same ideas, however, were used from an opposite perspective by the defenders of the American continent, especially in North America, where a new theoretical tradition not void of political implications started to exploit the idea of America's primitivism in terms of freedom from the burden of a historical past and openness towards a forgeable future. It was Thomas Paine who, at the end of the eighteenth century, envisioned the possibility for America to create a new conception of itself precisely by exploiting its established opposition with respect to the Old World.[16]

At the beginning of the nineteenth century, the South Americans – who according to Gerbi had a much weaker autochthonous cultural tradition[17] – joined in by publishing Thomas Jefferson's defence of all the Americans as a strong and proud people,[18] depicting Europe as old and

---

14 Argentine magazine *Caras y Caretas* (1898–1938), a widespread publication popular among the middle and lower-middle classes, was sustained by the liberal political and intellectual élites of Buenos Aires. Supported by the Mitre family, who also owned the daily newspaper *La Nación,* it had among its most famous contributors José Ingenieros, Eduardo Ladislao Holmberg, Leopoldo Lugones, Francisco Grandmontagne, Alberto Gerchunoff, Manuel Ugarte and Juan José da Soiza Reilly.

15 *Histoire naturelle, générale et particulière* (Buffon, 1749–1788).

16 In a pamphlet published in 1776 entitled *Common Sense,* Paine advocated the independence of the American colonies, while in the following years he strongly supported the Revolution.

17 More recently, Jorge Cañizares-Esguerra (2001) has shed new light on Spanish American patriotic responses to the European side of the polemic.

18 See, for example, the *Gazeta de Buenos Ayres* (1810) edited by Mariano Moreno.

decadent in opposition to the intact Rousseauian primitivism of the New World (Gerbi, 1983: 442). However, from the second half of the nineteenth century, in the wake of a current of historicism, Agassiz (1859) found the American continent to be older than the European one. In Argentina, Florentino Ameghino ([1880] 1918), encouraged by Darwin's own findings in Argentina and other parts of South America, argued in his book *La antigüedad del hombre en el Plata* (*The Antiquity of Man in the River Plate Region*) (1880) that humanity had had its origin in the River Plate region. The terms of the dispute could therefore be easily inverted, thus creating the basis for a set of arguments that not only disclaimed the supposed primitivism of the Americas but set the foundations for a discursive pattern that could easily exploit this flexible dichotomy. Yet, as Leopoldo Lugones argued in a 1915 *folleto* written to celebrate Ameghino's contribution to Argentine scientific and intellectual life, his theories about the presence of prehistoric man in the Pampa could not put into question the derivation of Argentine historical development from Europe:

> La conexión étnica que puede existir entre aquellos hombres primitivos y los escasos indígenas de la época actual, carece de importancia conducente a la exaltación del patriotismo: la población argentina es europea, la civilización argentina también lo es, y todas estas reflexiones corresponden por igual a los Estados Unidos, donde la ingenuidad equivalente suele alcanzar exageraciones ridículas, sin excluir tampoco de su filosófica sensatez a aquellos sabios de Europa, que tienen por dogma de preeminencia nobiliaria el génesis del hombre en el mundo antiguo. (1915: 70)

> The ethnic connection that might exist between those primitive men and the few indigenous people of today lacks the kind of significance that leads to the exaltation of patriotism: the Argentine people are European, and so is Argentine civilisation. The same could be said about the United States, where a similar naivety often takes the form of ridiculous exaggerations, and whose philosophical soundness does not dismiss those European sages who hold as a dogma of aristocratic superiority the origin of man in the Old World. (My translation)

While describing Ameghino as a hero of the *patria* and his theories as a sort of second founding of Argentina, Lugones was also reaffirming his country's affiliation to European historical and anthropological traditions. His explicit critique of the United States' rejection of European values further remarked the profound difference between the 'two Americas'. If 'Europeanisation' in Argentina meant a process of 'Latinisation' based on the symbolic connections with the Old World, the impact of massive European immigration was crucial in the consolidation of a concept of modern civilisation founded on the idea of Latin decadence.

In many of his famous *Galerías de inmigrantes* (*Galleries of Immigrants*), which he started to write for *Caras y Caretas* in 1899, Francisco Grandmontagne, a Basque immigrant who made a name for himself both as a journalist and as a novelist in *fin-de-siècle* Buenos Aires, exploited the ambivalence of the old- versus new-world dichotomy in order to portray the American continent both as a land of opportunities for the European immigrant, and, paradoxically, as the civilising force in the life of the immigrant himself. In one of his *Galerías*, entitled 'El bachiller' ('The Bachelor') (1899), Grandmontagne portrayed the figure of a Southern European immigrant, described as being Spanish, Portuguese, French and Italian at the same time, having been fed on Latin milk. Born in a big European city, he was a sort of hidalgo descended from a decadent aristocratic family. So, the elements of education and civilisation that the 'Latin' immigrant intended to bring to these 'jóvenes países americanos' (young American countries) (1899: 7) consisted of nothing more than his *bachillerato:* it was only in Argentina that the *bachiller* learned how to become useful to society, in a country where his inclinations towards the vices of over-bureaucratisation remained frustrated. The old versus new opposition was used here as an interpretative category to respond to the waves of European immigration: the Europeans, says Grandmontagne in the text not without irony, have always been, and always will be, 'los roturadores de América' (the ploughmen of America) (1899: 7).

At the same time, however, this position denotes an important ambivalence: the immigrant himself becomes the bearer of old and decadent values that he brings with him to America. To what extent then could he be considered an agent of national regeneration? This ambiguity is quite consistent in Grandmontagne's depiction of European – in particular, Southern European – immigration between the last years of the nineteenth century and the beginning of the twentieth century. While the immigrant was described as a vehicle of civilisation, this concept took on ambiguous connotations that cannot always be related back to the traditional dichotomy *civilisation* versus *barbarism*. The following passage eloquently asserts the supposedly neat opposition between the two terms:

> Marking the struggle of a nation set on a course to modernity, the binary cluster separates the virtues of a civilized Europe from the savagery of American terrain. Generations of writers from Sarmiento to Borges have rehearsed this dualism in Argentine culture, as if to mark the achievement of the nation by proclaiming the triumph of the civilizing cause over the barbaric 'other'. (Masiello, 1992: 9)

Although Francine Masiello identifies a 'third position', which challenges this binary cluster, in the contribution of women writers to the debates on Argentine modernity, that opposition becomes already problematic in the light of Grandmontagne's manipulation of Sarmiento's dichotomy. If it is true that Europe, through its immigrants, was a civilising force in the American continent, it is also true that the nature of European civilisation, and of modern civilisation as a whole, could be quite problematic and even intrinsically contradictory. The immigrant was often perceived as the bearer of decadent values that had very little to do with the modernising thrust Argentina was thought to need at the end of the century. Interestingly enough, moreover, the figure of the immigrant of Latin descent, who is over-intellectualised and inclined to the allures of the *empleomanía* (i.e. an obsession with holding public office), echoes the Chilean intelligentsia's condemnation of a similarly dangerous attitude informing Chilean society. But while in the case of Argentina it was the immigrant who became the means through which the decadent values of an over-refined civilisation were brought over to America, in the discourse of the Chilean liberal élites an emphasis on the historical legacy of the Latin race was the central theme of the debate.

The insufficient acquisition of European blood turned into an increasingly common topic of debate in Chile from the turn of the twentieth century, particularly in relation to Argentina, whose vast empty lands were being filled with European labour force. Not all immigrants were equally welcome, however; interestingly enough, there were growing complaints about the poor immigration rates from Northern European countries. It is worth pointing out the extent to which Nicolás Palacios, in his best-selling book *Raza chilena: libro escrito por un chileno i para los chilenos* (*Chilean Race: A Book Written by a Chilean for the Chileans*), stressed the Northern European origins of the Spanish conquistadors:

> El descubridor i conquistador del nuevo mundo vino de España, pero su patria de origen era la costa del mar Báltico, especialmente el sur de Suecia, la Gotia actual. Eran los descendientes directos de aquellos bárbaros rubios, guerreros i conquistadores, que en su éxodo al sur del continente europeo destruyeron el imperio romano de occidente. [...] Por los numerosos retratos o descripciones que conozco de los conquistadores de Chile, puedo asegurar que a lo sumo el diez por ciento de ellos presentan signos de mestizaje con la raza autóctona de España, con la raza ibera; el resto es de pura sangre teutona. (1904: 4)

> Although those who discovered and conquered the New World came from Spain, their country of origin was on the shores of the Baltic Sea, especially Southern Sweden, now Gotland. They were the descendants

of those fair barbarians, warriors and conquerors, who during their diaspora through Southern Europe destroyed the Western Roman empire.
[...] Through the various portraits and descriptions of the conquerors
of Chile with which I am familiar, I can assure you that not more than
ten per cent of them show signs of racial mixing with the autochthonous
race of Spain, the Iberian race. The rest of them are of pure Teutonic
blood. (My translation)

Palacios's argument against the idea that Chile belonged to the Latin race – 'no
simpatizan pues con el chileno los pueblos latinos' (the Latin peoples have
nothing in common with the Chilean race) (1904: 7) – was based both on
contemporary Italian sociological theories about the dissolution of the Roman
Empire[19] and on Thierry's thesis about racial degeneration being attributed to
the extinction of the superior race. Palacios openly condemned the campaign
that some political figures together with a section of the press were conducting
in favour of the immigration of families of Latin race from Europe. Chile,
he stated, should only attract German immigrants, since these would adapt
easily to the characteristics of the Chilean people. According to Palacios, the
Latin tradition was alien to the Chilean race, so all efforts to absorb it and
adapt it would produce dangerous consequences. When considered first in
light of the discourse of Latin decadence and then in relation to the issue
of European immigration, Palacios's essay on the Chilean race reveals some
important nuances characterising the origin of Chilean nationalism in the
early twentieth century.

Also in Argentina, however, the Latin immigrant was not only said to
come to an equally old country where he was bound to find a modernising
civilisation, but was often represented as the exponent of a primitive culture.
Therefore he could only make his way into modern civilisation in the New
World. The over-refinement and the excesses of modern civilisation were
portrayed as the outcome of the modernising process in which the immigrant
himself lost his primitive innocence in the successive generations of his family.
But the 'shadow of the immigrant', as in another story by Grandmontagne,
is always looming over them, in an ambivalent relationship where Europe
incarnates the characteristics of Rousseauian primitivism through the image
of the 'uncivilised' Latin immigrant, while America becomes the cradle of a
new – but equally conflicting – kind of civilisation, once again inverting the
old versus new dichotomy. I argue that this is one aspect of a more general
attempt to represent Spanish America's entry into modernity, where the

---

19   Guglielmo Ferrero, *L'Europa giovane* (1897) and *Grandezza e decadenza di Roma* (5
      volumes, 1902–1906); Giuseppe Sergi, *La decadenza delle nazioni latine* (1900).

American nations incorporated the characteristics of European civilisation, thus taking on all the nuances of the Old World: over-refined, aristocratic, decadent, neurasthenic.

While modern civilisation was necessarily an urban phenomenon, the countryside, and more specifically the Pampa, gradually became the imaginable site of a past that was disappearing in order to give way to a modernity full of irresolvable contradictions. As with all nostalgic constructions, however, a feeling of – not so unconscious – relief over the loss of a barbaric past came hand-in-hand with the creation of ambiguous stereotypical figures that incarnated both the deeply rooted fears of a conquered past always looming over the uncertain present, and the need for balancing the contradictory nature of the modernising process with the certainties of an idyllic past. In the case of the Argentine Pampa, the – almost literal – incarnation of the conquered past was the figure of the gaucho, the symbol of a barbaric legacy that was increasingly present in the world of popular literature.

What I would like to discuss briefly now is the representation of the figure of the gaucho, particularly in *Caras y Caretas*, in relation to the perception of the implications of modern civilisation. What I will try to show is that the image of the gaucho, even before becoming an instrument of national revival, was used right at the turn of the twentieth century as a symbolic antidote to the degenerative tendencies of modern civilisation, thus once again making the clear-cut dichotomy between civilisation and barbarism problematic. As the one who had been sacrificed to the demands of progress, the gaucho took on the qualities of the strong and energetic ranchero, becoming antithetical to the refined and decadent civilisation of the urban space. It has been argued that it is paradoxical that the gaucho should become a national hero after having been eliminated in the late nineteenth century.[20] In fact, I argue that it was by virtue of his disappearance from the scene of history that he became a symbolic counterweight to the fears and contradictions of modern urban civilisation.

What is important to point out straight away is that the representation of the gaucho in the pages of *Caras y Caretas* was always set in the open spaces of the Pampa through which modernity had not yet made its way – and

---

20 'Also targeted for extermination were the gauchos, who were independent of large landowners and had often sided with the natives or with local strongmen, known throughout Latin America as caudillos. Roughriding cattlemen, many gauchos were of mixed race, a few were Jewish immigrants. The Buenos Aires elite regarded all gauchos and caudillos with contempt. They considered the gauchos to be unmodern and racially and culturally barbaric. Ironically, once the gauchos had been eliminated, they began to be romanticized by poets and writers and, eventually, came to symbolize the new nationalist idea of the "true" Argentine national character' (Rodríguez, 2006: 17–18).

when that happened, it did so with catastrophic consequences. Moreover, as Adolfo Prieto fully shows in his study of *criollismo* in the popular *folletos*, '[s]i en la década del 90, con la difusión masiva de folletos impresos, el concepto de literatura "criollista" tendió a asimilarse, sin más, al de literatura "popular", en la primera década de este siglo el de "moreirismo" tendió a asimilarse al de "conducta antisocial"' (while in the 1890s, due to the massive circulation of printed *feuilletons*, the concept of *criollista* literature became fully assimilated into that of popular literature, in the first decade of the twentieth century the concept of *moreirismo* started to be associated with the idea of 'antisocial behaviour') (1988: 186; my translation).[21] In other words, the 'death of the gaucho' sparked a process of mythologisation of the countryside, setting the premise for the creation of a perfect symbolic rural innocence that counterweighted the degenerative tendency of urban civilisation, of which *moreirismo* was a vivid example. So, the intellectual and political élites were able to further reaffirm themselves as part of the process of modern civilisation as an utterly urban phenomenon. Paradoxically, during this time, the idea of an over-refined and, therefore, decaying civilisation was used by the Argentine élites to identify with modern values in opposition to an unadulterated rural past. The denotative field associated with the idea of degeneration was therefore turned into a useful discursive strategy for the incorporation of modern Western values.

It was a gaucho, and not an immigrant, who was portrayed by Grandmontagne in the 15 February 1902 issue of *Caras y Caretas*. Set in the vastness of a Pampa untouched by modern civilisation, the story portrays the figure of the gaucho Lecica, 'semisalvaje aún, que en aquellos campos abiertos no había caído todavía bajo los progresos pecuarios, en enervante domesticidad' (who, still living like a half-savage in the open fields, had not yet fallen into a state of enervating domesticity subject to the constraints of the farming industry) ('La máscara en el desierto' ['The Mask in the Desert'], 1902: 14; my translation). From the very beginning of the story, Grandmontagne highlights the fixedness of rural life, free from the enervating ties of the modern metropolis where one cannot escape the pains of the psychological process of the 'análisis sujetivo' (or self-analysis). And here once again comes to the fore the intrinsic contradiction of modern civilisation: 'el fenómeno esencial de la civilización es que la existencia vale menos' (the essential fact of civilisation is that life is of lesser value) (1902: 15; my translation). It is precisely when the gaucho Lecica has his first encounter with modern civilisation that his primitive innocence

---

21   *Moreirismo* is a literary and cultural strand celebrating the gaucho Juan Moreira, whose story was popularised by Eduardo Gutiérrez in a series of *feuilletons* published between 1879 and 1880.

comes, quite literally, to an end. Lecica does not know about Christianity, and when a bunch of gentlemen from the city tell him about the devil, he cannot resist the temptation to dress up in red and ride through the plains among his own bulls, with lethal consequences. The death of Lecica – the death of the gaucho – has been caused by civilisation itself, of which he is an innocent, but necessary, victim. After his death, the neighbouring landowners are able to make profit from the division of his property, and civilisation advances even more into the Pampa.

Even though Grandmontagne's story is tinged with a touch of nostalgia for a past that is forever lost, the sacrifice of the gaucho is nevertheless necessary for modern civilisation to progress. While Lecica remains a positive symbol of an innocent primitivism that conjures up a timeless picture of careless happiness devoid of any incongruity, it must also be pointed out that it is precisely because of his death that the gaucho can fulfil this role. This reflects a strand in the representation of the gaucho that was quite common in turn-of-the-century Argentina, where even his most convinced defenders not only recognised but conjured his extinction for the sake of the country's modernisation. Or, in other words, they were only able to turn him into a national symbol precisely because of his 'death'. In his essay *De cepa criolla (Our Creole Origins)* (1908), Martiniano Leguizamón, who was one of the strongest defenders of the *criollista* tradition in early twentieth-century Argentina, says:

> Existen temas de estudio útil para la reconstrucción del medio ambiente y el perfil auténtico de los rudos protagonistas ya casi esfumados en la vaga leyenda. No todo es áspero, instintivo y brutal en las pasiones que agitaron el alma tempestuosa del hombre agreste; ni fue su tosco rancho aduar de barbarie donde vivió 'la edad del cuero crudo', como se ha dicho recientemente con ligereza – sin asomos de duda – y con un total desconocimiento de las tradiciones del país. [...] Y espero que no se verá transparentada en las siguientes páginas una apología tendenciosa del criollismo, sino la contribución en la medida modesta de mis fuerzas al estudio de un tipo tan genuinamente nuestro – *cuya desaparición no lamento* – pero que reclama con justicia un homenaje severo y de consciente información de las letras argentinas. (1908: viii-ix; my emphasis)

> There are useful topics that can be studied to reconstruct both the natural environment and the authentic features of those rough characters who have become blurred through legend. Not all is raw, instinctual and brutal in the passions that moved the stormy soul of the rural man; nor was his shabby ranch a barbarous dwelling where he lived during 'the age of raw leather'. This is what some have recently argued, no doubt

lightly and in total ignorance of the traditions of our country. [...] And I hope that the following pages will not be seen as a biased apology of *criollismo*, but rather as a modest contribution on my part to the study of a human type that is so genuinely ours – *whose disappearance I do not lament* –, but which justly claims a serious and well-informed homage by the Argentine letters. (My translation)

Leguizamón explicitly sets the terms of his argument by stating in the very first pages of his essay that he does not mourn the disappearance of the gaucho, confirming a position also expressed by Ernesto Quesada in his famous essay of 1902 entitled *El criollismo en la literatura argentina* (*Criollismo in Argentine Literature*). It is necessary, states Leguizamón, to defend our autochthonous national type, especially in a time when Argentina is facing a foreign invasion that risks to obliterate its true national character (1908: x). But what is most interesting is that, while the gaucho is set against the background of the wave of European immigration, he is also defined in opposition to the degenerative tendencies of modern civilisation.

In a chapter from the same book entitled 'El suicidio entre los gauchos' ('Suicide Among the Gauchos'), Leguizamón sets out to prove that it is impossible for the gaucho to commit suicide. He is not afraid of dying – in fact, he will throw himself into any great deed careless of death; but he will never commit suicide, simply because he is not civilised enough: 'el hombre refinado por todas las culturas de la educación y la fortuna pone fin al hastío de su inútil existencia' (only when refined by fortune, culture and education does man put an end to the melancholy of his worthless existence) (1908: 246; my translation). Once again the gaucho is used as an antidote to modernity, as the symbol of a lost innocence; at the same time, the disappearance of the values he represents is the most tangible proof of Argentina's advancement towards modern civilisation.

Leguizamón had already celebrated the 'death of the gaucho' in a piece written for *Caras y Caretas* in 1900, which betrayed a certain ambiguity towards the expansion of the civilising process. The old gaucho is portrayed as the last representative of an almost extinct race, which has degenerated into a half-civilised rural population that has lost the vehemence of the original inhabitants of the Pampa. The new gaucho is described as a 'semi-civilised man' ('hombre semicivilizado'); this hybrid of the Pampa is the result of the 'invading wave' ('ola invasora') that has destroyed Argentina's original character. Again, the civilising power of the immigrant acquired an ambivalent value with respect to the gaucho, in a moment when, just at the turn of the century, the debate on immigration policies in the country was at its peak while the alternative to Argentina's historical savage had yet to be assimilated. The power of civilisation in the rural areas was in fact put into question, particularly with respect to the new settlements of European immigrants, who were perceived to be the cause of degeneration of the original rancheros.

While the gaucho was described as the last representative of a *raza vencida* (or vanquished race), having succumbed as a consequence of the principle of the survival of the fittest in the process of *civilización*, another savage was thought to be menacing the Argentine nation. Specifically, in a piece written by Alberto Ghiraldo in 1904 for *Caras y Caretas*, the death of the gaucho is portrayed as the outcome of his forced encounter with Jewish settlers in the Pampa. They are the new *savages*, who symbolically cause the end of Argentina's lost barbaric past in the name of civilisation. In this double-edged representation of the country's process of modernisation, the discursive exploitation of the category of degeneration is two-fold: on the one hand, the immigrant is both a civilising element and a bearer of decadent values, while, on the other hand, the process of civilisation is intrinsically contradictory and at odds with itself.

The flexibility of the category of degeneration comes fully to the fore in these discourses, which exploit its intrinsic vagueness in order to adapt it to different socio-political contexts. Both in the case of Chile and in the case of Argentina, this intrinsic ambivalence constitutes the basis of the discourse of tradition as well as of that of modernity. While the *raza latina* was deemed to be the cradle of a superior form of civilisation, it was also described as the bearer of a degenerative tendency that impinged upon the meaning of civilisation itself; at the same time, the 'Latin' immigrant was represented as an ambiguous carrier of modern values, which had a significant effect on the representation of Argentine modern identity, while causing in Chile a heated debate on the national character in the early twentieth century. Ultimately, in both cases the category of degeneration was turned into a discursive tool, acquiring the flexibility of a discursive metaphor, which allowed it to be as pervasive and adaptable as we have seen.[22] Michael Aronna, in his study of the *fin-de-siècle* Hispanic canonical essay, maintains that the end of the nineteenth century 'was the juncture where optimistic positivism was transformed into pessimistic degeneracy theory' (1999: 27). Moving from this interpretation, I would argue that in *fin-de-siècle* public discourse the category of degeneration was applied as a discursive strategy in order to represent Spanish American modernity; or, in other words, degeneration was not used as a sign of resistance to modernity, but rather as part of a way of constructing a specific Latin American modernity.

---

22   For a theoretical discussion of these issues, see Ricœur (2003).

6

(Mis)appropriating Europe: the Argentine Gaze in Ricardo Piglia's *Artificial Respiration*

EMILSE HIDALGO

The cultural crossings between Argentina and Europe, or simply 'the West', inform the way history, politics and cultural memory are symbolically repre-sented in Ricardo Piglia's 1980 novel, *Respiración artificial* (*Artificial Respiration*) (Piglia, 2001/1994), through the use of voice, translation, quotation and the proper name. However, these textual strategies do not mean much by themselves unless they are examined in conjunction with the historical and socio-political contexts fictionalised in the novel. As is well known, much of the novel's overall structure revolves around an antagonism or tension between two recurrent ideologemes in Argentine culture, namely civilisa-tion and barbarism, where civilisation is historically bound to the European model of progress, modernisation and high culture, and barbarism to what has historically stood in opposition to those goals as they were understood by an oligarchic political élite (i.e. the 'darker' interior provinces, the caudillos, the Amerindians, the gauchos, the workers). To understand the importance of these conceptual tropes in Argentine culture, I would like to invoke Fredric Jameson's notion of the ideologeme as 'the smallest intelligible unit of the essentially antagonistic collective discourses of social classes' (1994: 76). Jame-son's emphasis on the social and polemical dimensions of the ideologeme is useful to understand why the notions of civilisation and barbarism, so central to the nineteenth-century cultural and political debates in Argentina, became revitalised and recoded 100 years later in Piglia's novel.

The characters in *Artificial Respiration* overtly polemicise with the Euro-peanised high culture pretensions of Domingo Faustino Sarmiento, Esteban Echeverría, Bartolomé Mitre, Juan Bautista Alberdi and other political and cultural thinkers, who were exiled during Juan Manuel de Rosas's dicta-torship in the first half of the nineteenth century. Piglia works with these ideologemes, setting them in dialectical tension following Walter Benjamin's notion that there is no document of civilisation that is not at one and the same time a document of barbarism (1999: 248). Through the use of a double-coded narrative, the political and cultural debates of the exiled Generation of 1837 and the Generation of the 1880s provide the allegorical coordinates in which to decipher Argentina's cycles of violence, particularly the brutal and systematic repression of the last military dictatorship (also known as 'Proceso de Reorganización Nacional' [National Reorganisation Process]) from 1976 to 1983.

Thus, the dichotomy introduced by the Generation of 1837, who opposed the barbarism of the gaucho and the Indians to the refinement of the literary salons of Buenos Aires and the European models they admired (especially French literature and culture, and liberal politics), served as an ideological basis for the liberal governing élite of the Generation of the 1880s (represented by Julio Roca, Miguel Juárez Celman, Carlos Pellegrini, Roque Sáenz Peña and José Evaristo Uriburu). The connection between both Generations is their advocacy for European liberalism and free trade. For William H. Katra, the Generation of 1837 'defended a program advocating republicanism in government, free trade, individual freedoms of speech and assembly and, above all, material progress' (1996: 9). As heirs of the country's May Revolution, 'they promoted a government headed by a social and intellectual elite that would protect civil order and property while combatting (what they believed was) a retrograde traditionalism and accelerating the development of the country's social and material potentialities' (1996: 9). So, when Rosas and his 'barbarians' fell from power in 1852, the young militants of this Generation, who had been exiled in Chile and Uruguay, returned to contribute to the construction of Argentina as a modern, liberal state.

The Generation of the 1880s, however, opposed other 'barbarians', namely the immigrant anarchist and socialist groups of workers who came to Argentina between 1880 and 1916. Anarchism and socialism were antagonistic ideologies to the liberal economic tendencies of the Generation of the 1880s. Social unrest prompted by workers' strikes and demands were deemed to be detrimental to the image of stability that this Generation wanted to project in order to attract foreign investment. Keeping the workers under control, and fostering an economy based on the production of primary food products and the import of manufactured goods was part of the project this generation of politicians called 'Proceso de Organización Nacional' (National Organisation Process). For David William Foster, the liberal ideology of the period of 1880 to 1900 'provided [. . .] a basic national and sociocultural identity that [. . .] continues to characterize that nation's abiding self-image (at least from the optic of Buenos Aires) as a progressive, sophisticated, and essentially European people' (1990: 7). However, the underside of this Europeanising project was the crushing of any organised opposition coming from workers, the peasantry and left-wing or non-liberal political dissidents.

In 1976, the military junta (headed by the three commanding officers of the Army: Jorge R. Videla, Orlando R. Agosti and Emilio E. Massera), who took power to fight the guerrillas and the dissidence coming from the labour sector and left-wing Peronism in general, embarked on what they termed the Process of National *Re*organisation, thereby explicitly positioning themselves as the ideological, political and cultural heirs of the Generation of the 1880s (Heinz and Frühling, 1999: 645). The 'barbarians' they repressed were union leaders, workers, leftist intellectuals, members of the Movement of Priests for the Third World and the armed groups of the left, such as Montoneros, FAR (Fuerzas Armadas Revolucionarias [Revolutionary Armed Forces]) and the ERP (Ejército Revolucionario del Pueblo [People's Revolutionary Army]), and eventually any form of social, political or cultural dissent to their neoliberal economic plan (Heinz and Frühling, 1999: 640–645).

In addition to the continuities that Piglia sees between the political struggles of the nineteenth century and those of the 'present' of the junta's dictatorship in the 1970s, *Artificial Respiration* also discusses the tensions that arise when European culture is 'transposed', 'grafted' or 'translated' into the social and political coordinates of a peripheral country. Historically, and unlike other postcolonial cases, this transposition did not entail an 'erasure' of or a palimpsestuous 'juxtaposition' with a previous archaic or premodern culture, but created a field of cultural forces that had to be contested without making reference to a legitimating 'indigenous' past. It is this artificially-created gap or void at the centre of Argentine culture that came to be filled in by European culture, giving rise to the notion that an Argentine tradition had to be created 'from scratch'. Thus, the conscious adoption and propagandising of European cultural values that Sarmiento carries out in his essay *Facundo: civilización y barbarie* (*Facundo: Civilisation and Barbarism*) [1845] (2001) aimed not simply at indoctrinating the masses of 'barbarians' but at establishing this élite's cultural and political legitimacy within the Argentine civil society. In contrast, what Piglia attempts to do in his novel is to unsettle any reductive cultural and political opposition by confronting the positive term of the Self/Other antithesis with its own internal contradiction. In the process of establishing this dialectical tension, Argentine culture, politics and identity are read 'against the grain', proving that all political and cultural hegemonies are liable to be irreverently challenged.

The following excerpts from Piglia's *Artificial Respiration* engage in a debate over the construction of Argentine identity based on the crossings between national and foreign cultural sources.[1] The first passage reproduces a

---

1　All quotations in Spanish are from Ricardo Piglia's *Respiración artificial* (2001). All quotations in English are from Daniel Balderston's translation of Piglia's novel published as *Artificial Respiration* (1994).

discussion on literature and history between Renzi, the novel's main narrator who is on his way to meet his 'disappeared' uncle,[2] variously named in the novel as Maggi or the Professor, and Tardewsky, the Professor's Polish friend:

> Esos europeos, decía el profesor, habían logrado crear el mayor complejo de inferioridad que ninguna cultura nacional hubiera sufrido nunca [...]. Pedro de Angelis era el primero, decía el profesor, le digo a Renzi [...]. Frente a él Echeverría, Alberdi, Sarmiento, parecían copistas desesperados, diletantes corroídos por un saber de segunda mano. Yo era, según Maggi, el último eslabón de esta cadena: un intelectual polaco que había estudiado filosofía en Cambridge con Wittgenstein y que terminaba en Concordia, Entre Ríos, dando clases privadas. En este sentido, le digo, mi situación le parecía al profesor la metáfora más pura del desarrollo y la evolución subterránea del europeísmo como elemento básico en la cultura argentina desde su origen. (2001: 102–103)

> Those Europeans, the Professor said, had managed to create the greatest inferiority complex that any national culture has ever suffered [...]. Pedro de Angelis was the first one, the Professor would say, I tell Renzi [...]. In comparison to him Echeverría, Alberdi, Sarmiento all seemed like desperate copyists, dilettantes consumed by second-hand knowledge. I was, according to Maggi, the last link in that chain: a Polish intellectual who had studied philosophy in Cambridge with Wittgenstein and who ended up in Concordia, Entre Ríos, giving private lessons. In this sense, I tell him, my situation seemed to the Professor like the purest metaphor of the development and secret evolution of Eurocentrism as the cornerstone of Argentine culture since its inception. (1994: 110–111)

The proper names mentioned in the passage (Pedro de Angelis, Rosas, Echeverría, Alberdi and Sarmiento) form a network of cultural referents not

---

2 The term 'disappeared' ('desaparecido') has a literal meaning here in the sense that during the last military dictatorship over 15,000 people were illegally kidnapped and taken to clandestine detention centres where they were tortured and killed. Many intellectuals and social activists also became exiled, which was another, more figurative form of disappearance that created a social, political and cultural gap in Argentina. In a report transcribed and published by *Clarín* newspaper on 14 December 1979, Videla claimed that 'the disappeared' 'no puede tener ningún tratamiento especial, es una incógnita, es un desaparecido, no tiene identidad, no está, ni muerto ni vivo, está desaparecido' (cannot have any special treatment, they are a question mark, they disappeared. They are people without identity, neither dead nor alive. They have disappeared) (my translation).

only of the Argentine political and intellectual tradition of the nineteenth century but also of those Europeans that were incorporated into the social fabric of the country through immigration after the 1880s. The excerpt illustrates the thesis that the European intellectual (a synecdoche for European and Western culture at large), once installed in Argentina, came to incarnate universal, revered knowledge, and to be used politically as an ostentatious mechanism of self-legitimation. This positioning of European culture and modernity at the centre of a national cultural and political debate in a peripheral country like Argentina is what Tardewsky comes to identify as the genealogy of Argentine culture.

In terms of form, the use of indirect speech quotation, as in 'the Professor would say, I tell Renzi' and 'according to Maggi', entails a very clear rejection of any notions of originality and origin (and thereby of legitimating authority) as the speaking voice is constantly recycled by a proliferation of enunciators. As Idelber Avelar has argued, Piglia's novels tend to this anonymity of the voice through a constant recycling of speech because 'all anonymity has something utopian about it' (1999: 101). As the citation of 'absent' voices reintroduces a collective or social dimension into the narrative, previous literary and cultural referents are recuperated as part of a collective palimpsest of social discourses that is also the site of socio-political debate. What is utopian about this discursive strategy is the notion that the *act* of enunciating (in all its historical and spatial specificity) changes the message itself; that is, a change in the context of enunciation can turn a previously conservative message into a radically subversive one. The past, then, in Karl Marx's words, is no longer seen as a burden weighing like a nightmare on the brain of the living, but as offering a reservoir, an archive, or a site of potential subversive activity.

Furthermore, the bridging or spanning function of the quotation thus employed to subvert tradition raises the related question of how national identity and history can be interpreted from the context of the present. In short, what does it mean to recreate history – and with it a nation's cultural heritage and identity – in the same, but at the same time, *other* words? According to Mary Orr, when considering the function of the quotation, 'it is not what is repeated, or indeed who repeats, that is intrinsic to quotation, but the how and why of its repetition' (2003: 132), that is to say, the quotation does not merely replicate a message through another person's or entity's voice but draws out 'the relative paucities of both the old and new quoting contexts' (2003: 133). This has the effect of shifting the focus not to the verbatim reproduction of the message itself but to the contrast in the context of (re)production of the message (in the sense of producing again, or repeating or quoting), that is to say, it pays attention not to the intertextual relation *per se*, in which one message is transposed or grafted from one text to another, but to the social dimension or context of utterance in which one speaker communicates with another, establishing a dialogue *across* time.

Orr, in fact, compares this political and social use of quotation to a time capsule in which a message is passed on across epochs and that, in the transmission, becomes enriched – or problematised – by the new contexts and conditions of reception. The message is repeated but with a difference, specifically, the repetition or quotation entails sameness (the message) and difference (the new context), adding along the way new or accumulated socio-political meanings. Throughout the novel, the different quotations through which a character's speech is passed on (by word of mouth, by the reproduction of letter fragments, by gossip and rumour, and so on) enact in form a process of 'translation' or slippage in meaning. As in Jorge Luis Borges's 'Pierre Menard', the context of production and reception radically alters the message. Piglia reinscribes Borges's paradox by making it, together with double coding, the basis or *method of composition* of *Artificial Respiration*. Therefore this stylistic or formal method works in tandem with a subversive critique of the past and present.

Citation constitutes a central postmodernist 'homeopathic' strategy (Jameson, 1989: 59) as it turns against itself the monologic appropriation of the discourse of the cultural élite and of the repressive state at different times in Argentine history. In fact, this form of oppositional politics finds its correlate in what Raymond Williams has theorised as 'alternative' or 'oppositional' initiatives 'made *within* or against a specific hegemony' (1977: 114; my emphasis). These concepts help explain how politically dissident or 'oppositional' initiatives such as Piglia's novel take on the reservoirs of knowledge and cultural referents of the dominant culture and of a political hegemony in order to create with those same materials a form of counter-culture or counter-narrative. As Piglia's novel illustrates, the most important implication of Williams's distinction is that these different tendencies are seen to co-exist within a single cultural formation or text and are always made against a dominant ideology.

In a second passage from the novel, Renzi, Marconi and Tardewsky elaborate their thesis on the origins of Eurocentrism in Argentine culture. The discussion illustrates Sarmiento's pretentious cultural Europeanism, which is undermined through an antagonistic reading:

El europeísmo, dijo Renzi [. . .] empieza ya con la primera página del *Facundo* [. . .], texto fundador de la literatura argentina. ¿Qué hay ahí? dice Renzi. Una frase en francés, así empieza [. . .]. El gesto político no está en el contenido de la frase, o no está solamente ahí. Está sobre todo, en el hecho de escribirla en francés. Los bárbaros llegan, miran esas letras extranjeras escritas por Sarmiento, no las entienden: necesitan que venga alguien y se las traduzca. ¿Y entonces? dijo Renzi. Está claro, dijo, que el corte entre civilización y barbarie pasa por ahí. (2001: 119)

Europeanism, said Renzi [...] starts with the first page of *Facundo* [...], [the] foundational text of Argentine literature. What does it consist of? asked Renzi. A phrase in French: that's how it starts [...]. The political gesture is not in the content of the phrase, or not only in that content. It is, above all, in the fact of writing it in French. The barbarians arrive, look at those foreign words written by Sarmiento, fail to understand them: they have to get someone to come and translate them. And then? asked Renzi. It's clear, he said, that the line between civilization and savagery runs right there. (1994: 128)

The passage illustrates a vision of Argentine culture as one that is from its very inception fractured and torn by cultural difference but, at the same time, in permanent dialogue with a dominant tradition of a European high culture from which the Argentine political élite attempts to borrow its legitimacy. Sarmiento's *Facundo* is thus exposed as repressing its own ideological role in shaping social distinction, and class legitimation, between the barbarians who cannot read French and the educated, 'lettered' élite who can. The unsettling of the ideologeme of civilisation makes manifest the cracks and fissures of what before presented itself as homogeneous and whole, and shatters any notion of a singular or pure national identity through ironic intervention. As Homi K. Bhabha puts it, 'the problem [of postcolonial identity] is not simply the "selfhood" of the nation as opposed to the otherness of other nations. We are confronted with the nation split within itself, articulating the heterogeneity of its population' (1994: 148). Clearly enough, this implies not only the ethnic and cultural heterogeneity of immigration and of a culturally hybrid society, but also the heterogeneous histories of contending political factions *within* the nation itself. But this is not all. Piglia also wants to foreground the barbarism inside Sarmiento's own quote:

Pero resulta que esa frase escrita por Sarmiento (*Las ideas no se matan*, en la escuela) y que ya es de él para nosotros, no es de él, es una cita. Sarmiento escribe entonces en francés una cita que atribuye a Fourtol, si bien Groussac se apresura [...] a hacer notar que Sarmiento se equivoca. La frase no es de Fourtol, es de Volney. O sea, dice Renzi, que la literatura argentina se inicia con una frase escrita en francés, que es una cita falsa, equivocada. Sarmiento cita mal. En el momento en que quiere exhibir y alardear con su manejo fluido de la cultura europea todo se le viene abajo, corroído por la incultura y la barbarie. A partir de ahí podríamos ver cómo proliferan, en Sarmiento pero también en los que vienen después [...] esa erudición ostentosa y fraudulenta, esa enciclopedia falsificada y bilingüe. (2001: 120)

But it turns out that that phrase written by Sarmiento ('Ideas can't be killed', in the school version), and which for us is his own isn't his at all but a quotation. So Sarmiento writes a quotation in French, attributing it to Fourtol, although Groussac hastens to clarify [...] that Sarmiento is mistaken. The phrase is not by Fourtol but by Volney. So, Renzi says, Argentine literature begins with a phrase written in French, which is a false, mistaken quotation. Sarmiento misquotes. At the moment he wants to show off, to call attention to his familiarity with European culture, everything collapses, undermined by savagery and a lack of culture. And from that moment we could see the proliferation, in Sarmiento but also in those who follow him [...] of an ostentatious fraudulent erudition, a forged bilingual encyclopaedia. (1994: 128–129)

The plagiarism and misquotation of Sarmiento's text stands as an allegorical homology to the fraudulent mechanisms of political hegemony often used by the Argentine élite to perpetuate their grip on power. In this way, irony works as a powerful destabilising force to the imposition of a dominant tradition of Europeanised high culture, and as a form of counter-politics in as much as Sarmiento's misquotation points to whatever is shameful, embarrassing and illicit within a cultural tradition that thinks of itself as the highest truth and the peak of high culture. If, as Piglia reiterates, Sarmiento can be said to have founded the metaphorical field of forces of the Argentine dominant class in the nineteenth century, then displacing Sarmiento out of this central position through paradox and irony amounts to vindicating the tradition of those who were defeated, silenced and subjected by this hegemony. Therefore, if civilisation and barbarism are the two coordinates that define the map of Argentine reality, the gesture of finding a dialectical tension *within* the ideologeme of civilisation itself (that is, of acknowledging the suppressed or repressed Other(s) within the Self) amounts to making possible the utopian gesture of creating spaces of opposition, dissidence and resistance within a given dominant reality.

In both passages, Piglia carried out a clever disruption of the Argentine cultural heritage and, together with it, of a geographically displaced high European culture. In so far as the literary canon is the equivalent of the art museum, Piglia's cultural critique exposes, on the one hand, the violence upon which the literary archive, as a cultural institution, is formed, and, on the other, the impossibility of literature as a detached or neutral cultural practice. A nation's foundational fictions are as implicated in that country's social reality and politics as are other non-cultural spheres like the legal and political systems. Along the same lines, Piglia's textual ironies also underscore the importance of a materialist critique of canonicity, best summed up in Benjamin's seventh thesis of history: 'Whoever has emerged victorious participates to this day in the triumphal procession in which the present rulers step over those who are lying prostrate. According to traditional practice, the spoils are carried along in the procession. They are called cultural treasures, and a historical materialist views them with cautious detachment' (1999: 248).

No doubt Piglia follows Benjamin's thesis as a *method* of writing: at the same time that it 'preserves' the literary treasures of the past, it critically views them with a 'cautious detachment' that seeks not only to open up a space (or enunciation site) for a transformation of national identity and politics, but also for a renewed reading or radically subversive hermeneutic of its cultural heritage. In this sense, Bertolt Brecht's influence on Piglia is undeniable since both cultural producers favour literary forms that challenge the dominant ideology (Brecht through epic theatre; Piglia through quotation, allegory and double coding), and seek a 'combative' stance in culture intended to move the receiver from 'general passive acceptance to a corresponding state of suspicious inquiry' (Brecht, 1964: 192). The *interrogative* and at the same time *pedagogic* function of Piglia's ironic rereading of the cultural heritage discourages the reader's identification with a unified subject of enunciation and an unproblematic and homogeneous account of the nation's history and politics. Piglia, like Brecht before him, employs these textual techniques in a potentially politically progressive manner, rather than as just a formal (or formally evolutionary) textual strategy.

However, there is another issue that such a method needs to address: to what extent does this 'combative' position bring together, in a synthesis, the fields of culture and politics *today*? In other words: what sort of affirmative or constructive programme can be derived today from a radically confrontational cultural programme? One suggestive answer is that provided by E. L. Doctorow, for whom 'a book can affect consciousness – affect the way people think and therefore the way they act'. For Doctorow, books create 'constituencies that have their own effect on history' (in Trenner, 1983: 43). Thus, changing consciousness, denouncing past oppression and repression, raising awareness of how power legitimates itself through its cultural institutions, and creating an affective relationship between the reader and the text can change the way people think and act; they can, in a word, lead to active political action through the transformation of consciousness.

Unlike the socio-political context in which *Artificial Respiration* was written and published (that of the censorship and repression of the Junta), the context in which Piglia's novel is read today is that of the social and political changes of post-default Argentina. Does this change in socio-political context change our reception of Piglia's novel? Up until the 2001 crisis, Piglia's texts and other similar works were read as part of the canon of the literature of mourning, memory and defeat (see Sarlo, 1987; Avelar, 1999; and García Canclini, 2004). In 'Política, ideología y figuración literaria' ('Politics, Ideology and Literary Figuration'), Beatriz Sarlo argued that fictions like Piglia's *Respiración artificial*, Andrés Rivera's *En esta dulce tierra* (*In this Sweet Earth*, 1984) and David Viñas's *Cuerpo a cuerpo* (*Body to Body*, 1979) could be grouped together in so far as they contain many coded references to the junta's dictatorship, despite having a plot that many times revolves around well-known figures and events of the nineteenth century. Those corpora could be read as a critique of 'the present' even in those cases where the specific referent is located in the past (1987: 31–34). As Sarlo argued, those fictions filled in a void in discourse during the 'Proceso', as the collective means of communication of the public sphere were cut off by repression and censorship:

> Al mismo tiempo que las fuerzas armadas ocupaban el estado, la trama de vínculos entre diferentes sectores sociales se disolvía o era obturada por la represión. Intelectuales y sectores populares permanecen durante este período casi completamente incomunicados [...] y esta clausura en la circulación de los discursos [...] es uno de los rasgos más estables de lo que Guillermo O'Donnell ha descripto como la 'cultura del miedo'. [...] Obturadas las vías de relación entre los diferentes actores sociales, se clausuraron también los canales de transmisión de experiencias comunes y se bloquearon las redes de la memoria colectiva. La experiencia de la vida cotidiana se alteró profundamente y las fantasías de persecución, muerte y pérdida marcaron el tono general del período. (1987: 32)

> At the same time as the army took control of the state, the networks among the different social sectors became increasingly sealed off by the repression. The intellectual and popular spheres remained for most of the period almost totally cut off from each other [...] and it is precisely this closure in the circulation of discourses [...] that Guillermo O'Donnell has termed 'the culture of fear' [...]. Once communication among the different social actors was sealed off, the means of relaying shared experience and collective memory were blocked. The experience of daily life was utterly affected and the fantasies of persecution, loss and death set the general tone of the period. (My translation)

In the crevices left by the repression of state terror, literature often served as the last stronghold of dissidence, and allegory became the safest form in which to break with imposed silence. Sarlo argued that these novels had 'coded' the present of the 'past ten years of Argentine history' (1987: 31). However, Sarlo wrote her essay in 1987 and so the 'present' to which she referred included roughly the period 1977–1987. From the perspective of a more recent present (from the 1990s onwards), Argentina's post-dictatorship novels have resorted not only to euphemisms and allegories – like Martín Kohan's *Ciencias morales* (*Moral Sciences*) (2007) – but to more direct or explicit modes, like narratives focalised in the perpetrators – as in Kohan's *Dos veces junio* (*Twice in June*) (2002) – or fictions that discuss the legacy of the 1970s in its connections to the present – such as Kohan's *Museo de la revolución* (*Museum of the Revolution*) (2006), Guillermo Saccomanno's *77* (2008) and Martín Caparrós's *A quien corresponda* (*To Whom It May Concern*) (2008) – or those that discuss the violence of Montoneros from a critical perspective – like Daniel Guebel's *La vida por Perón* (*My Life for Peron*) (2004). Unlike Piglia's novel, none of these fictions go back into the past any further than the last military dictatorship and the leftist movements of the late 1960s and 1970s. Therefore the continuities suggested by Piglia are absent from more recent postdictatorial fictions.

These considerations of changes in the postdictatorial canon aim at historicising not only the reception of Piglia's novel at the time when it was written, published and circulated (in and around the 1980s), but also now, in more contemporary times. This begs the question, too, of whether the post-dictatorship period becomes a different reality or a different historical context after the 2001 default and political crisis, and after the derogation of the pardon and impunity laws?[3] And if so, what relevance do Piglia's strategies of displacement, ironic quotation and utopian reading 'against the grain' hold for readers today? My guiding assumption is that each of the historical moments mentioned above may favour a certain reading of these fictions. During the repression, as Sarlo explains, fictions like those of Piglia provided the representational means for a 'coded' *denunciation* of the horror, whereas on returning to democracy, fiction moved to the period of *mourning* and defeat, and the focus for the reader was on reconstructing

---

3   The Full Stop and Due Obedience laws, promulgated by President Raúl Alfonsín in 1986 and 1987, and the pardons to military officials, granted by President Carlos Menem between 1989 and 1990, were all derogated by Congress in 2005 after the Argentine judicial system declared them null and unconstitutional. These laws had been promoted by the aforementioned ex-presidents in order to grant impunity to the ex-military repressors, and to stop them from being tried in court and sent to prison on charges of gross human rights violations. (For the legal argumentation provided by the judicial system on the unconstitutionality of these laws, see Hauser, 2005).

memory (however fragmentary and provisional) and on understanding what had happened and *reflecting* upon it (1987: 31–34). After the crisis of 2001, and with the annulment of the pardon laws, mourning may have given way to another, perhaps more *(re)constructive*, less mournful moment. I am not here suggesting that we have passed from one period to another in clean cuts or breaks from the past, but that, on the contrary, even as these reading functions still overlap, some of them may have become more prominent or *active*, while others may have receded and become more residual.

In the specific case of Argentina, such reconstruction may be seen as necessary after the intellectual driving force behind oppositional or dissi-dent political factions was physically exterminated in clandestine repression camps, or else forced into exile or self-imposed silence, while its organ-isational basis (trade unions and political parties) were undermined not only through repression but also through the very suspension of democracy itself during the *de facto* government. Moreover, on returning to democ-racy, any surviving or residual distinction between Left and Right soon became neutralised for most of the 1990s in the Menemist style of politics and through blind compliance with the IMF and World Bank neoliberal economic mandates. Even after democracy was restored, the silence about what had happened during the dictatorship remained as deafening as ever, with none of the oppressors being brought to justice. The Truth Commis-sion in charge of writing the report on 'the disappeared' (the *Nunca Más*, or *Never Again*) regrettably provided little more than 'a talking cure' or national therapy. For these reasons, fictions like Piglia's may come to revi-talise collective memory without becoming unbearably didactic or utterly anachronistic.

Emphasising the importance of discursive re-articulation may in future prove a very effective way of bringing back (or 'resuscitating' as if after a cardiac arrest, as Piglia would say) the memory of a culture or tradition of dissidence and of oppositional politics in a country like Argentina where those very discourses were sealed off by repression and later on suffocated by neoliberalism and the process of national reconciliation. In fact, an ideological reconstruction of an alternative politics is an urgent precondition if the corpus of books Sarlo examines as well as new instances written after 1987 can be put to more affirmative uses than the traumatic recollection of the past.

What I am proposing here is a form of reading suggested by Piglia himself, when he claimed that 'la corrección es una lectura utópica' (rectifying a text is a utopian reading act) (2000: 18; my translation). And this is so for various reasons: first, because it entails exposing the text to the new field of social forces of the present in which the narrative is received and so 'corregir un texto es socializarlo, hacerlo entrar en cierto sistema de normas, ideologías, estilísticas, formales, las que usted quiera, que son sociales' (to rectify a text is to socialise it, to make it enter a system of norms, ideologies, styles, formalisms, what have you, which are socially-conditioned) (2000: 18; my translation); secondly, because, in this sense, Piglia may be seen as continuing the tradition of the vanguard understood not only as a mode of writing that is innovative, eclectic and experimental, but as a mode of reading precursor texts. By offering innovative readings of Argentine history, of its main and most controversial political figures, and by 'rectifying' or debunking the high pretensions of Argentine culture through the 'mistakes' made by the literary tradition, such as that of Sarmiento's quotation, he renews the kinds of arguments that are incorporated into the public sphere (and so do we as intellectuals and literary critics). Reinterpreting tradition, that is, creating alternative or controversial canons, amounts to reading the social context in which those traditions and canons emerged in a different light. What is utopian about it is that it opens a door to questioning that tradition through irony, and by reversing the dichotomy civilised/barbarian, Piglia makes the voices of the defeated be heard from a position of legitimacy and power. It is not 'barbarians' who are to be despised or laughed at, but the liberal élite who built up a false notion of superiority based on the sham imitation of European values and culture.

Artificial Respiration may thus also be read from this utopian perspective since it presents itself as an allegory of the importance of cultural texts as articulations of a desire for a better world. As Piglia argues, 'coding is the work of fiction in any context. I don't believe that the ellipsis of political material performed by fiction depends on authoritarian situations [. . . .]. I believe that fiction always codes and constructs hieroglyphs out of social reality. Literature is never direct [. . .]. What I do believe is that *political contexts define ways of reading*' (Piglia quoted in Balderston, 1994: 2; my emphasis). In any case, his reading of the Argentine political tradition suggests that the 'Proceso' was not the only act of massive violence in Argentine history but only one of its most brutal and systematic cases. This is why it would be deceptive to interpret his novels exclusively as allegories of the 'Proceso' since they are ultimately concerned not only with the deaths of 'the disappeared', but of all those who since the nineteenth century have configured the 'graveyard map' of Argentine history (the indigenous populations, the peasants, the gauchos, the immigrants, and so on).

Thus, to conclude, what kind of gaze is that which Piglia casts over the Argentine and European cultures? It is clearly a double gaze since, on the one hand, it acknowledges the European cultural heritage as the cornerstone of Argentine cultural identity and, on the other, as Borges famously said in 'The Argentine Writer and Tradition', it irreverently operates within and against the Argentine misreadings and misappropriations of that culture for its own political interests (1999a: 420–427). Piglia's use of European culture is therefore more a provocation or oppositional strategy than an aim in itself; that is to say, it is the excuse that allows him to carry out a renewed, 'ex-centric' reading of Argentine politics and culture, and of their usual suspects. In the context of 'the disappeared', of periodic financial bankruptcies, brutal state-sanctioned violence and repression, as well as of the market's abuses of memory through its recycling of the past as nostalgia, Piglia's subversive gaze is primarily about enabling a utopian and reconstructive rather than mournful reading of the Argentine tradition.

7

Transatlantic Crossings: Don Álvaro as a Threshold

CHRISTINA KARAGEORGOU-BASTEA

Any society that hopes to be imperishable must carve out of itself a piece of space and a period of time in which it can look honestly at itself. This honesty is not that of the scientist, who exchanges the honesty of his ego for the objectivity of his gaze. It is, rather, akin to the supreme honesty of the creative artist who [. . .] reserves to himself the privilege of seeing straight what all cultures build crooked. (Turner, 1984: 40)

Romanticism, with its obsession about feelings, opens the textual space to representations of violence, and the play *Don Álvaro o la fuerza del sino* (*Don Álvaro and the Force of Fate*) (Rivas, [1835] 1990, 2005) is a perfect example of this. It has all the ingredients of human passion: an accidental murder, two fatal duels, a fratricide, a suicide, a conflict among several swordsmen, the roar of war, escapes through gun fights, all accompanied by constant verbal violence. In this chapter, I analyse the reasons of this violence through looking at *Don Álvaro* as a *social drama*. According to Victor Turner, social dramas are literal or symbolic manifestations of conflict between social fractions and ideological tendencies regarding institutions, values and social practices that affect the life of a community (1984: 20–24). The play by Ángel de Saavedra, best known as Duque de Rivas, is often thought of as disjunctive between the works of fate and free will – both leading to the annihilation of its protagonists – that corresponds to the clash of institutions, forces and values, intelligible only in the political context of Spain at the beginning of the nineteenth century, namely within the framework of (post)colonialism, imperialism and modernity (Iarocci, 2006: 123–138).

Violence is manifested in an initial displacement: the location of the play in eighteenth-century Spain.[1] Inscribed on this basic inadequacy and in the

---

1 Indicative of the unease awaken by the historical moment represented in the play is the proliferation of articles that intend to draw the time frame of action. George Mansur (1989) confronts David Quinn (1975), and John Dowling (1989) praises

form of a painful palimpsest, the protagonists carry out and suffer their transformations located on geographical, national, racial and gender borders. The memory of the French invasion, the disappointment from living under a weak regime, the momentary faith in liberalism, the ominous decade, exile and, more than anything else, the independence of the Americas resurface, extrapolated and evanescent, despite the setting of the text in the eighteenth century, creating the first in a series of ideological contingencies and avatars handled throughout the play on a symbolic level.[2] Michael Iarocci very perspicaciously observes that silencing the painful processes of dealing with the imperial past seemed to affect not only critics who deal with Rivas's play, but also the entire scholarship of the Romantic Spain (2006: 125).

The features of an *indiano* – a Spanish immigrant to Latin America who returns to his country years later – do not change significantly since its first appearance in the theatre of the Golden Age: he is an arriviste loaded with money earned in obscure circumstances, a displaced figure with regard to the centre of the Empire, of an uncertain origin and a suitor of an aristocrat. For different reasons such as a special talent in verbal expression (Mariscal, 2001: 59), the insinuation of social ascension due to merit (Walde Moheno, 1993: 153–154; Mariscal, 2001: 55), the skin colour that announces *mestizaje* and alerts all prejudices related to blood purity (Mariscal, 2001: 57), and even a perverted sexuality sometimes (2001: 56–57), the *indiano* represents danger to the status quo. Literature takes up the task of rendering legible the elusive constitution of this *other* who escapes easy classification and upsets established categories: 'Because he was figured as the embodiment of multiple vices, he was a corruption of "nobility" itself and in a variety of writings was figuratively removed from the symbolic space of culture' (Mariscal, 2001: 59). Fear towards the *indiano* is caused, according to Lillian von der Walde Moheno, by the fact that the character embodies ambitions and modalities proper to middle-class Spaniards, while he or she is different

---

the precision with which Ángel de Saavedra makes his drama evolve throughout a historical period; while Loreto Busquets affirms that the ideological values on which the play is built belong typically to eighteenth-century Enlightenment and not to Romanticism (1996: 62–64).

2   It is worth noting that the apparent obliteration of historical contexts did not fool Rivas's contemporary public. Ermanno Caldera observes that for the audience in 1835 the conflict between different political parties – liberals, moderates, Carlists – is evident in the reviews of the play in the press (1995: 26–27). Before Michael Iarocci's *Properties of Modernity* (2006), contemporary criticism had flagrantly overlooked Spanish colonialism as the context in which the play becomes the arena of political issues at stake. The only critics before Iarocci that very briefly had mentioned without interpreting these circumstances are Linda Materna (1994: 18) and Busquets (1996: 63).

from them.[3] Thus, for the middle-class Spaniard, the *indiano* evokes and reflects issues painfully related to the Self: doubts regarding blood purity – a reason for rejection – , and excess of wealth – a proper foundation for desire.

Interpreting the representation of these men and women that come from across the Atlantic to Spain, Barbara Simerka affirms that

> the most prominent trend [. . .] is the liminality by which the *indiano* characters are marked [. . .]. They are marginalized as subaltern, Americanized figures, yet they are incorporated into the dominant culture through conflation with stock characters. [. . .]. The conflation of new forms of alterity with extant literary models of marginalized, exotic, or alien identities, as deployed by Lope and Tirso, is a common cultural practice through which dominant groups delineate the border between insider and outsider, subject and subaltern. (2003: 44–45, and *passim*)

Straddling between two worlds accounts for the menace recognised as a particular feature of the *indiano*, a presence that stirs insecurity, obscure desires, resentment and even hatred. Between the characters of Lope and Tirso and that of the Duke of Rivas there is a lot of common ground: don Álvaro brings wealth from America, he comes from an illustrious yet unclear lineage, he is the suitor of a noble woman, and is in trouble with the law for honour duels. However, unlike other *indianos*, before or after, don Álvaro fails terribly in all his purposes.

The play offers a variety of perspectives on a crippled empire, and these approaches spring out of the polyphonic construction of its characters.[4]

---

3   In her article on the *Entremés del indiano*, this scholar sustains: 'El hombre que vuelve o visita a la Madre Patria, que es español, que habla el mismo idioma, que profesa y defiende la fe católica, que es, en una palabra, tan cercano, es subversivo en cuanto que ha alcanzado un rápido ascenso económico debido a su inscripción en una economía mercantil, y poco o nada debe a "heredades" ni a linajes. Además, y para colmo, produce interés e incluso reconocimiento en los estratos medios y bajos de la sociedad, que ven en él el espejo de la propia posibilidad de progreso' (The man who returns or visits the Mother Land, who is a Spaniard, who speaks the same language, who professes and defends the Catholic faith, who is in other words so familiar, is subversive to the extent that he has achieved a quick financial climb due to his participation in a trade economy, and he owes very little or nothing to inheritance or lineage. In addition, what is worse is that he triggers the interest of and is recognised by middle and lower classes of the society, since they see in him a reflection of their own possibility to progress) (1993: 153; my translation).

4   For Simerka, the dialogic structure is integral to the *indiano* characters since their debut in the theatre of the Golden Age. This feature, according to Simerka, allows for the defence of dissident political positions (2003: 76).

Contrary to what Iarocci maintains, namely the 'persecutory' quality of prose and social polyphony (2006: 115–118), I claim that it is precisely the encounter and debate of the social voices through the *costumbrista* scenes that allow for alternative ways of thinking history, and thus relate the play inexorably to ideology. Multiple voices, representative of an array of social convictions and tendencies, compose the legend of don Álvaro and his conflict with the decadent Andalusian nobility (Cedeño, 1997: 439–441). In addition, each one of the antagonists originates in what the community considers to be his or her transcendence in other characters' lives. In general, the protagonists are born for the audience, refracted and seen through the prism of dialogues that convey evaluation and judgement. Through a series of axiological utterances both the object of the discourse – don Álvaro, doña Leonor, etc. – and its subject – the society around them – take shape.

In 'Act 1', don Álvaro and the Marquis of Calatrava are created by an exchange of opinions in which the point of view of the lower class opposes that of the priest. The *populacho* (populace) is in favour of the *indiano*, which does not mean that he is not the victim of their mockery. Nevertheless, for Preciosilla, the Majo, the Military Officer and Uncle Paco, don Álvaro is 'el mejor torero que tiene España' ('Spain's best bullfighter'), 'todo un hombre, muy duro con el ganado y muy echado adelante' ('every inch a man, very hard on the brutes and utterly fearless'), 'muy buen mozo' ('handsome'), 'un hombre riquísimo cuyos modales están pregonando que es un caballero' ('a very rich man whose manners proclaim that he's a gentleman'), 'digno marido de una emperadora' ('worthy of marrying an empress'), 'gallardo' ('gallant'), 'formal y generoso' ('correct and generous'), 'un hombre valiente' ('a gentleman') (1990: 54–55).[5] Certainly, everybody comments on his origin, but for the canon the uncertainty of it suffices to make him unworthy of doña Leonor, whereas Uncle Paco believes that 'cada uno es hijo de sus obras' ('we are what we do') (1990: 56). On the other hand, the Marquis of Calatrava is presented through the same people as owner of 'mucho copete y sobrada vanidad' ('much too upper-crust and much too vain'), like the rest of Seville's noblemen characterised by 'vanidad y pobreza todo en una pieza' ('vanity and poverty [. . .] two sides of the same coin'), 'un viejo tan ruin' ('a stingy and doddering old fool'), worthy of a 'buena paliza' ('good thrashing') for not letting his daughter get married to don Álvaro. The latter opinion makes the priest take the side of the absent Marquis and claim the paternal authority on his behalf (1990: 54–55).

---

5 Quotations in English come from Robert M. Fedorchek's 2005 translation of *Don Álvaro* (Rivas, 2005). Page numbers correspond to the Spanish edition (Rivas, [1835] 1990) – no page numbers are given in the case of English quotations to avoid overloading the text with numerical symbols.

The task of the modern chorus, according to scholarship, is to push forward the plot (Zaragoza et al., 2002: 96). However, the convergent voices also offer a map of social forces that evaluate the conflict in the kernel of the play. The echo of this quarrel reported through embodied social voices affects the audience for it converts a symbolic duel between passion and obedience to an ethical quest. In addition to the typical attitude of Romantic literature to make public what is private, namely feelings, the various choruses in the water stand outside Seville, on the edge of the battlefield, and in the monastery entrance propose that individuals and their actions cease to be private by means of public critical comment and debate.[6]

Chorus and character, public and private, nobility and bourgeoisie, America and Spain, the violence of thresholds crossed is at the core of the play, and art's work here is to capture the historical turbulence of the moment and express social qualms. During the first years of the 1830s, part of the Spanish people supported monarchy, while another part endorsed the need for change as it was shaped by the French invasion. In Rivas's work this opposition is presented symbolically in the protagonists' defiance of paternal authority. However, this analogy is quite disturbed and complicated by don Álvaro's identity. Although being a *mestizo* – as is don Álvaro, born to a Spanish father and an Inca mother – is in itself a source of concern for the peninsular context of the play, Rivas's protagonist is more than that: his father has usurped imperial authority and proclaimed the independence of Peru; his mother, an Inca princess represents the glory and defeat of an indigenous past, purported both with pride and resentment by don Álvaro. Through these features, Rivas depicts the perplexity with which liberals in Spain viewed Spanish America and the citizens of the new nations. In this sense, what in Spain was a matter of sovereignty was insurgence across the Atlantic. The mestizo evokes the broken bond between homeland and colony, and for some Spaniards this translates automatically into rebellion and violence. Therefore the hero is seen with bitterness. The words that the author puts in don Carlos's mouth depict forcefully this relation: 'Ruge entre los dos un mar/de sangre. . .' ('A sea of blood roars between us. . .') (1990: 132; ellipsis in the original). For the short moment of the enjambment, the frontier

---

6   Jo Labanyi maintains that 'one of the major political effects of Romanticism would be its alignment of individual and political sentiment, since it conceives of both as the rebellion of the individual against authority' (2004: 238). Beyond the problem of the alleged rebellion that don Álvaro carries out, questionable in as much as he surrenders to the will of the marquis, what needs to be underlined in this quote is the transformation of the private space of feelings into public. In the case of *Don Álvaro*, this is made possible through evaluation and debate of the characters by the surrounding community.

of blood becomes the Atlantic Ocean, the limit that unites and separates the Spaniard from the *indiano*.

While the social contexts where don Álvaro is received – secular society, nobility, the army, the church – are hostile towards his otherness, he himself appears also to be at odds with his origin and fate:

> Para engalanar mi frente,
> allá en la abrasada zona
> con la espléndida corona
> del imperio de Occidente,
> amor y ambición ardiente
> me engendraron de concierto,
> pero con tal desacierto,
> con tan poca fortuna,
> que una cárcel fue mi cuna
> y fue mi escuela el desierto. (1990: 106)

> To adorn my head with the
> splendid crown of the Empire of the
> West, far away in the torrid zone, love
> and burning ambition begot me in
> concert, but so misguidedly, with such
> adverse fortune, that a jail was my
> cradle and the wilderness my school.

The hero encapsulates himself in the pride of his lineage and the shame that comes from it, in reason and confusion, in benign intention and disastrous outcome. Moreover, the mere idea of destiny goes against the vigorous existence of the one whose mission is to restore his parents' honour for which he has to submit himself to royal authority and ask for pardon. The bearer of rebellion is placed by the author in the position of repentance and submission, which on a bigger scale implies a symbolic restoration of authority to the Spanish crown over the American colonies. Opposite to the mestizo, displaced in the context of the eighteenth century, a moment in which the animosity between colonies and the metropolis seems to decrease (Minguet, 1989: 34–36), the author launches his ideological endeavour from the standpoint of the moderate liberal, wounded by domestic political vicissitudes and the Independence movements overseas. The plot that Rivas weaves against the *indiano* echoes the agony of the Spaniards faced with their fallen empire and the incapacity of their rulers. Thus, the discourse that draws the contours of don Álvaro shares with the protagonist, although from the opposite shore of the ocean, a radical historical liminality: the belief that sovereignty lies with the nation and the people. Spain will base on this assumption its transformation into a modern state, but this same political principle will be fought against in the name of colonialism.

In 'Act 2', doña Leonor is the object of curiosity for the group in Monipodio's inn. Her presence is mysterious and provokes speculations: 'Estudiante. – Quisiéramos saber, tío Trabuco, si esa personilla de alfeñique que ha venido con usted y que se ha escondido de nosotros, viene a ganar el jubileo [. . .] ¿es gallo o gallina? [. . .] ¿por qué no ha venido a cenar el caballerito? [. . .] ¿es hembra o varón? [. . .] con que es pecador [. . .] ¿cómo viene en el mulo, a mujeriegas o a horcajadas?' ('Tío Trabuco, we were wondering if that delicate person who arrived with you, and who has hidden from us, came for the jubilee indulgence [. . .] do we have a goose or a gander? [. . .] why hasn't this young gentleman come to eat supper? [. . .] But is it a man or a woman? [. . .] So he's a sinner [. . .] how did that person ride the mule, sidesaddle or astride?') (1990: 79–80). Suspended between unresolved disjunctions that put emphasis on gender confusion, in transit with no clear origin or destiny (80), without a name, and isolated, the heroine becomes an alien to such an extent that the text is unable to define her: 'A mí me parece que es persona muy. . .' ('I think this person is very. . .') (80; ellipsis in the original), says the Mesonera, the same who affirms a bit later to her husband what defines the fugitive: 'una mujer afligida' ('a/woman in distress') (83). Don Álvaro's identity is established, in the same unstable terms: 'el mejor torero que tiene España' ('Spain's best bullfighter') (54), a pirate, the son of a nobleman and a moor princess (55), 'la prez de España' ('the glory of Spain') (108), the good father Rafael, loved by the poor, according to Melitón (150); but also a violent character (150), whose skin colour and wild countenance make comparable both to a *mulato* and a fierce *indio* (151).

Doña Leonor disguises herself in order to travel to a safe place, covering underneath her change of identity an ethical claim, revealed in her monologue in 'Act 2':

> [. . .] Dios de bondades,
> con penitencia austera,
> lejos del mundo en estas soledades,
> el furor expiaré de mis pasiones. (1990: 86)

> God of goodness, I will atone for
> the frenzy of my passions through

austere penance, in the wilderness far
from the world.

The same kind of imperative necessity makes don Álvaro turn into a soldier:

sin nombre en extraña tierra,
empeñado en una guerra
por ganar mi sepultura.
¿Qué me importa, por ventura,
que triunfe Carlos o no?
[...]
Si el mundo colma de honores
al que mata a su enemigo,
el que lo lleva consigo,
¿Por qué no puede...? (1990: 107–108; ellipsis in the original)

[...] nameless, in a foreign
land, involved in a war to earn my
grave. What does it matter to me
whether or not Carlos triumphs?
[...]
If the world showers honors
upon the man who kills his enemy,
then why cannot the one who has
his enemy inside him...?

Both protagonists feel appalled by themselves, doña Leonor because she is in love with the murderer of her father, and don Álvaro due to his false identity and the ethical ambiguities to which it eventually leads, namely deceit, betrayal and lack of loyalty. This self-loathing will lead the heroine to isolation, while suicide will be the destiny of the *indiano*. The need to invent an identity, thus, has its reason in the hate towards one's own self. Here instability of border subjectivity does not produce cracks from where to launch against the establishment, in pursuit of change. Don Álvaro and doña Leonor loathe themselves because they are despised by others, because they internalise hatred and dwell in self abjection, without being able to head to a new system of values voiced by the people. The spaces opened for the protagonists through change of identity, namely the possibility of heroism and fame won in the war by don Fadrique, the goodness of father Rafael and the sanctity of the hermit, turn to feeble opportunism, whose only purpose is self preservation. Personal guilt and social hatred are the reasons for the characters' abject liminality.[7] Rejection of one's self goes together with the abomination one's identity provokes to others. Hence don Álvaro's words on himself, after deadly wounding don Carlos: 'Que soy un monstruo, una fiera,/que a la obligación más santa/he faltado' ('That I am a/monster, a wild beast; that/I failed the most sacred/of obligations') (1990: 138).

The fact that don Álvaro is originally from Peru is not an insignificant detail. Since Gonzalo Pizarro and Lope de Aguirre, a model and discourse of rebellion have been launched from this region of the Latin American continent against the Empire, one that puts in doubt the legitimacy of the Spanish crown rule in the colonies, and vindicates the territory for the soldiers who actually fought and conquered the New World (Jos, 1927: 49–52; Pastor, 1983: 282–287). Don Álvaro comes from this same region. During early colonial times, Peru was the focus of violent insurgencies – triggered by disappointment of the myths that accompanied America in the European imagination – and struggles against inclement and powerful nature. The discomfort of this memory, transparent in the overlapping of chronology and the confusion regarding the hero's identity, is enacted by the historical conditions of the early nineteenth century, namely the final independence of Latin American countries as remembrance and epitome of previous rebellions.

The play is a new verdict: it sentences don Álvaro, first, to cruel expiation by obliging him to serve the two pillars of imperial power, the church and the army, and then to death. Destroying the memory of rebellion is a sign of the same imperial discourse that condemned Lope de Aguirre in 1561:

> y porque de todo lo susodicho hasta agora no se avya fecho proçeso contra la memoria y fama del dicho lope de aguirre como de derecho se deuia fazer; dixo; que mandava y mando; hazer [*sic*] cabeça de proceso contra la memoria del dicho aguirre por ser difunto [...] y condeno a la dicha memoria e bienes. (Jos, 1927: 203–204)

> and since against all the aforementioned there was no trial as it should have happened against the memory and fame of the above said Lope de

---

7   Donald Schurlknight points out this attitude of the *indiano* towards himself as a necessity to retrieve 'from his "being", from the way he is' (1995: 345). Similarly, Materna concludes her psychoanalytical reading of the play affirming that 'the plot of *Don Álvaro* is dominated, in fact by remorse and guilt [...]. His remorse immediately gains ascendancy in Don Álvaro's passive surrender to the Marqués [...]. The fate or destiny that destroys Don Álvaro is not only, not primarily, a force external to him, but one that originates in the interiority of his divided self' (1998: 613).

Aguirre, I declare that I ordered and I order to start the process against the memory of this Aguirre because he is deceased [. . .] and I sentence this memory and properties. (My translation)

According to Mark Kingwell, 'the function of the threshold [. . .] is not to *be wide* but to *separate*, and thus to *be crossed*. Every limit is also its own negation. Drawing the limit-line is coeval with the desire, we might even say the demand, that the line be crossed. Once established, boundaries "ask for breaching" – traditionally, a task for heroes' (2006: 93). It is apparent that Rivas's play proves true what Kingwell theorises, but with a final coda: crossing the limits can also be the task of villains, and on this tenuous line that separates a villain from a hero, doña Leonor and don Álvaro are constructed through social dialogue of praise and admonition, memory and oblivion. On the threshold of circumstances created against their will, on the edge of themselves, about to escape at every moment until their death, don Álvaro and doña Leonor move the emotion of audiences who have to be in charge of the terrible ending, a culmination of constant violence, a visceral reaction to what because of its diffused limits makes it impossible for a clear discernment between good and evil, justice and iniquity, logic and madness. The play is filled with abject heroes whose attitude and discourse do not provide for an easy empathy or immediate identification. Criticism has seen in this uncertainty the seal of Romanticism or the crisis that the Duke of Rivas goes through at the moment he writes the play (Lovett, 1977: 80). In my reading, the questions put forward by the text belong to Spain's historical context of the first three decades of the nineteenth century, and make patent its political consequences in society and individuals. Unable to solve the conundrum of citizenship, sovereignty and authority, the play refuses to offer an easy way out. It annihilates the present, and ultimately offers a wiped-off space for literary tradition, ridding itself of pain, and declaring its impossibility to stop violence and reconcile differences in a dialectical movement.

8

Transatlantic Deficits; or, Alberto Vilar at the Royal Opera House

ROBERTO IGNACIO DÍAZ

Because the tale of Alberto Vilar, the elusive Cuban-American investor and philanthropist, is such a strange pairing of truth and fiction, of facts and simulation, one is easily tempted to look for parallels to his story or search for character elucidation in the realm of the novel. Indeed, a possible key to understanding Vilar's role as a transatlantic cultural player can perhaps be found in *The American*, by Henry James. First published in serial form in the *Atlantic Monthly* between June 1876 and May 1877, this early novel, the author's third, is set in Europe and, like other works by the American-born master, thematises transatlantic cultural relations. In many ways, it is the classic Jamesian story, one in which the protagonist, the symbolically named Christopher Newman, succumbs to the pleasures and perils of the Old World – a new world for him, really, and one whose various intrigues he slowly discovers. The plot seems to exemplify what William Spengemann calls 'America's perennial love-hate relationship with Europe' – that is, 'feelings of cultural inferiority and moral superiority, of parricidal guilt and newborn innocence, of nostalgia for the old home and the urge to destroy it' (1981: 9). One may debate whether the plot of *The American* is fully persuasive, and James himself had his doubts, as the heavily revised New York edition of 1907 testifies.[1] Yet the figure of Newman as the 'cosmopolitan capitalist' (2003: 205), to use John Carlos Rowe's phrase, may well offer an insight into the nature of Vilar's deeds – or misdeeds, as many would deem his fervent, if flawed, performance of the international theme, in the globalised realm of opera at the turn of the twenty-first century, to have been. Like Newman and so many other characters in James's fiction, Vilar is a rich American traveller who confidently engages in the happy pursuit

---

1   As James states in the preface to the 1907 edition, 'what I have recognised then in *The American*, much to my surprise and after long years, is that the experience here represented is the disconnected and uncontrolled experience – uncontrolled by our general sense of "the way things happen" – which romance alone more or less successfully palms off on us' (1978: 11).

of culture, which is often not to be found in the United States, but on the other, purportedly more refined, side of the Atlantic. Consider, for instance, Newman's radiant self-assurance in the European setting at the opening of *The American:*

> On a brilliant day in May, in the year 1868, a gentleman was reclining at his ease on the great circular divan which at that period occupied the centre of the Salon Carré, in the Museum of the Louvre. This commodious ottoman has since been removed, to the extreme regret of all weak-kneed lovers of the fine arts; but the gentleman in question had taken serene possession of its softest spot, and, with his head thrown back and his legs outstretched, was staring at Murillo's beautiful moon-borne Madonna in profound enjoyment of his posture. He had removed his hat, and flung down beside him a little red guide-book and an opera-glass. (1981: 33)

Armed with the inevitable Baedeker, the classical travel guidebook, and an artefact, the purpose of which is to see more and better, Newman hails from a distant nation, and has made his fortune in a particularly remote city, San Francisco. But now, a rich man, he finds himself in what readers may view as the very centre of the world – not only Paris, but the Louvre; and, within that noble edifice, the loftiest of spaces, the brilliant Salon Carré. Beyond the fact that his posture seems to give him more pleasure than the Murillo on the wall, Newman's movement from geographical periphery to the heart of Europe is a journey to the centre of the arts, as he now stands in close proximity to some of the masterpieces of Western civilisation, the absence of which in America will be at least partially mitigated, with time, by the efforts of its great art collectors, from J. P. Morgan and Isabella Stewart Gardner to Andrew W. Mellon and J. Paul Getty. The story of transporting artworks across the Atlantic is, of course, as much about the emotional wish to possess rare, beautiful things as it is about the display of financial might – the fact that Americans, through their wealth, have been able to purchase, for instance, important European paintings, many of which now reside in the great museums of America.[2] An entry in the diary of Jack Gardner, husband of Isabella Stewart, records their activities in the course of one day in Paris in 1892: 'Lunched at Café de Paris. Had Ralph. Went to sale at Hotel Drouot. Mrs G. bought the vander Meer picture for fcs. 29,000. Went to reception at Mrs. Coolidge's – Lydia Eustis dined and went with us

---

2   On the links that bind money, art collectors and museums in the United States, see Duncan (1995: especially Chapters 3 and 4).

to the Opera – Samson and Dalila' (Chong et al., 2003: 149). Social gatherings, a night at the opera, and the purchase of Vermeer's *The Concert*–these are some of the activities in the life of these Americans in Paris. Four hundred years after Columbus's first landfall, the descendants of Europeans voyage across the ocean in search of purchasable treasures. One can understand the fears of Hugh Crimble, a young Englishman in *The Outcry*, James's final novel, when faced with Breckenridge Bender, a rich American reminiscent of J. P. Morgan who travels in England in search of as many Old Master pictures as possible; Crimble gloomily foreshadows 'the certainty – if we don't do something energetic – of more and more Benders to come: such a conquering horde as invaded the old civilisation, only armed now with huge cheque-books instead of with spears and battle-axes' (2002: 99). When Christopher Newman is said to take 'serene possession' of the ottoman in the Salon Carré, it is not just a story of physical comfort that is told, but one that invokes, unwittingly and *avant la lettre*, the long and often controversial history of American acquisition of, or influence in, the real and symbolic spaces of European cultural life.[3]

But the act of possession that interests me here does not concern museums – paintings or broken golden bowls, to invoke again James's fictions about collectors – but opera houses, and it is not simply about the United States but, more specifically, about one man of Latin American background living in that country, a man publicly defined most often as a Cuban-American – a liminal, hyphenated persona.[4] It is, if nothing else, an operatic story, variously grand and tragic and, at times, arguably grotesque. On a day in November, in the year 1999, in the centre of London, the Queen Mother

---

3   As is well known, the American pursuit of European masterpieces continues to this day, and its discourse is often marked by a rhetoric of ardour. In November 2002, Carol Vogel wrote in *The New York Times*: 'A passionate tug of war is being waged by the super-rich J. Paul Getty Museum in Los Angeles and the National Gallery of Art [*sic*] in London over Raphael's *Madonna of the Pinks*' (2002: np). In February 2004, after the Getty is denied an export permit and the *Madonna* finally purchased by the London museum, Maev Kennedy reported in *The Guardian*: 'Jubilation in the National Gallery over deal to retain Raphael masterpiece' (2004: np). Not everyone in Britain, though, viewed the transaction with such zeal, including Sir Nicholas Serota, director of the Tate museums: 'He claimed that such fire-brigade appeals to chauvinism and national pride had "skewed" the way galleries were spending their tiny and shrinking acquisitions budgets' (Gibbons, 2003: np).

4   On the meanings of hyphenation in Cuban-American culture, see Pérez Firmat, who posits the bicultural condition of Cuban-Americans: 'Unlike acculturation or transculturation, biculturation implies an equilibrium, however tense or precarious, between the two contributing cultures. Cuban-American culture is a balancing act' (1994: 6).

renamed the iron and glass atrium at Covent Garden's Royal Opera House as the Vilar Floral Hall, in gratitude to Alberto Vilar, the Cuban-American investor who, in the last years of the twentieth century, became known as the most generous philanthropist in the history of opera, with colossal and highly publicised donations to various companies on both sides of the Atlantic, from St Petersburg and Vienna to Los Angeles and New York. Indeed, one of Vilar's most visible gifts was his pledge of ten million pounds to Covent Garden, which resulted in the naming of the Vilar Floral Hall, a splendid architectural space that serves as the Royal Opera's foyer and bar area, and as the ideal place, before performances and during intermissions, for the social aspects of opera going, eating and drinking as well as meeting friends and acquaintances, all in opulent surroundings seemingly designed for viewing others and displaying oneself.[5] After Vilar's financial collapse and subsequent failure to complete payment on his pledge, his name was removed – 'reluctantly', according to the press release – from the Floral Hall, as well as from the Vilar Young Artists Programme, which the investor had previously funded.[6] (This lapse from grace, of course, may well have been the least of Vilar's problems; in February 2010, he was sentenced to nine years in prison for his role in a fraud scheme).[7] My focus here is the short-lived visibility of Vilar's name in Covent Garden, not just as an episode in the history of arts philanthropy, or a rather operatic case-study in vanity and excess, but as an exemplary tale in the transatlantic yarn of European and North and Latin American cultural relations – a story in which the New World seems to compensate for its self-perceived cultural periphery, especially in the very European realm of opera, through a highly visible display of wealth. It is

---

5 On the Royal Opera House renovation project, in which the Floral Hall, the old Covent Garden floral market, occupies a central position, see Powell (2001: 112–113).

6 As reported on the BBC website ('Opera House Drops Benefactor Name', 20 September 2005), the press release from the Royal Opera House read: 'We will cease to use Mr Vilar's name on printed material and programmes, and the signage in the public areas will be altered over the next few months in no particular order or time-scale. However, in recognition of his generous donation of approximately £4.4 m to the Royal Opera House since 1999, he will remain listed on the Donor and Benefactors Board'.

7 Reporting for *The New York Times*, Colin Moynihan described Vilar's sentencing in operatic terms: 'In his years as a prominent patron of the arts, Alberto W. Vilar sat in red velvet seats in the first row at the Metropolitan Opera, where he watched performances he had helped finance. But on Friday, Mr. Vilar himself was at center stage, standing in front of a packed wood-paneled courtroom in Lower Manhattan as a judge sentenced him to nine years in prison for his role in a $22 million fraud scheme' (2010: np).

easy to imagine Vilar, who proudly comes from Havana via New York, as a new Christopher Newman with a large chequebook and no opera glasses. There was no need of opera glasses, really, for at Covent Garden, like at the Metropolitan Opera House, he would usually sit in the first row, in order to have the closest view of the orchestra and singers, and so that everyone would know where to find him – performing, as it were, his role as the loftiest Maecenas of the art form, at his ease and in serene possession of the hallowed spaces of opera. As he told Allan Kozinn of *The New York Times* in 2000: 'I adore the Met, there's no question about that. [...] I go into that place, and I get goose pimples. Wow, this is the Met! My rich friends laugh at me, because I sit in the same seat every night, in the first row. A101, that's my seat. I want to watch the conductor, the pit, the stage. Not only that, I hold court. My friends come up. They know where I am' (2000: np). If the Queen Mother looked a bit diminutive in the picture with Vilar that graced an intimate corner of the Floral Hall, it may well have been due less to her physical stature than to the donor's own majestic self-esteem.

According to Norman Lebrecht in his rather polemical history of the Royal Opera House, the story of Britain's premier company mirrors that of the nation in whose capital it resides:

> In manners and morals, habits and hobbies, attitudes and ambitions, England changed fundamentally in the second half of the twentieth century. The upheavals were most visible in demographics and wealth distribution. In 1946, any non-white face at Covent Garden would certainly have belonged to a North American soldier or a Latin American diplomat. By 1996, opera appealed to Londoners of Asian and Caribbean descent. (2000: 4)

Although one would be hard-pressed to view the naming of the Vilar Floral Hall after a rich Cuban-American philanthropist as part and parcel of the history of race and ethnicity in Britain, one may still read the uncanny presence of Vilar's name throughout the house as a significant, albeit mostly symbolic, development in the globalisation of operatic culture, a realm in which Europe still plays a leading role – most of the performed repertoire, for instance, remains firmly European – but in which other parts of the world exert a growing influence. Indeed, Vilar's tacitly performed politics of identity concern the entire globe, or at least those parts thereof, especially Europe and North America, or elements therein – general managers, stage directors, performers, audiences – that still compete for the ultimate possession of opera. In this, Latin America plays a minor role, though one may recall the brilliant history of Buenos Aires's Teatro Colón in the past century, or the growing importance of composers such as Daniel Catán and Osvaldo Gólijov in the United States, or even the uses of Latin American literature and themes in the works of John Adams. But if composers are esteemed figures, a man like Vilar, through his monetary power and the possibility that it might afford him undue influence over artistic decisions, raised the eyebrows of many. As Robert Hilferty reported in *New York* magazine,

> the British press treated the billionaire as if he'd scrawled graffiti on a national monument. One journalist characterised him as a 'one-man globalisation merchant' whose 'tentacles stretch from St. Petersburg to Los Angeles by way of Salzburg, Glyndebourne and Washington, and wherever else opera is a ritzy, glamorous affair'. Another acknowledged, grudgingly, that 'the future of international opera and ballet now depends to a startling extent on Alberto Vilar'. (2002: np)

Indeed, reporting on the Salzburg Festival for the *Times* of London in 2000, Rodney Milnes had referred to large donations by the 'ubiquitous Alberto Vilar' while declaring, 'it's starting to look as though the future of opera will depend on the whim of a Cuban-American stock market investor with a love of music' (quoted in Kozinn, 2000: np). And in 2006, as Vilar's legal troubles began, John Allison would write an article in *The Telegraph* entitled 'Opera Moneybags Faces the Music', in which Vilar is depicted as an infantile fool as well as a social and artistic climber of sorts: 'Money – or, rather, the promise of money – was the only thing Vilar had to offer. As I remember from sitting next to him at a Covent Garden lunch I attended reluctantly some years ago, there can be few more boring men on this planet. Supporting an art form he loved in an unsophisticated, childlike fashion gave him entrée into a world of excitement' (2006: np).[8]

If Allison diminishes Vilar's generosity when he calls him a 'would-be opera philanthropist' – after all, Vilar did contribute more than £4 million to the Royal Opera alone – the truth remains that Vilar's prominence and pro-nouncements often resounded with a certain measure of New World moral superiority, as when he chastised European, including British, millionaires for not donating enough to the arts, or when he complained that governments did not acknowledge his bequests with sufficient enthusiasm. Thus, speaking to Hilferty, he deplored the fact that, in Salzburg, the president of Austria failed to recognise him after a performance of *Ariadne auf Naxos* for which he had paid: 'He did not even say, "We have the biggest donor of this place

---

8   The article's deck exaggerates Vilar's shortcomings even as it seems to rejoice at the reported events: 'John Allison examines how false opera benefactor, Alberto Vilar, finally got his comeuppance'.

in our midst. We thank him. Wouldn't it be nice if everyone followed his example?" Didn't say a word [. . .] That's a mistake. That is an *absolute mistake'* (Hilferty, 2002: np; emphasis in the original). Speaking to the *Times* in 2003 before addressing the Association of British Orchestras in Liverpool, Vilar expressed his opinion that the British élite were less generous with their wealth than their American counterparts; the article was entitled 'Rich told, get your hand in your pocket', a phrase mirrored by *The Guardian* in its own article on the interview, by Sarah Gaines: 'Britain's super-rich are miserly, says philanthropist' (2002: np). If Lord Joffe, chair of The Giving Campaign, defended Vilar in a letter to the *Times* editor by stating, 'Sir, Alberto Vilar is to be congratulated not only on his generosity, but on opening up a debate which needs to take place' (2003: np), others replied by pointing out important examples of British philanthropy as well as different taxation laws in the United Kingdom and the United States.[9]

The convoluted story of Vilar's actual and putative philanthropy has been analysed in greatest detail by James B. Stewart in 'The Opera Lover', a profile for *The New Yorker* that appeared in February 2006, several months after the removal of Vilar's name from the Floral Hall. The term *opera lover* to describe Vilar is fitting, for his is a story of passion, that of a man who, at the height of his wealth and fame, was said to attend as many as 100 performances of opera every year – some 50 at New York's Met, and the rest at other venues on both sides of the Atlantic – and whose ardent devotion to the genre resulted in phenomenal displays of promised wealth. Among his numerous gifts and pledges one finds items not related to the arts, and these include – only in 2001, which happened to be the worst year in the history of Amerindo, his investment company – $23 million to New York University; $10 million to Columbia University's medical school; $4 million to the Hospital for Special Surgery, also in New York; and $25 million to a Denver hospital (Stewart, 2006: 117). But if these amounts alone are impressive, the pledges to opera companies and music festivals are nothing short of spectacular. In his article, 'Alberto Vilar: On Money and Opera', published in May 2001, Lebrecht reports the following bequests: $50 million to the Kennedy Centre, in Washington; $45 million to the Metropolitan Opera, in New York; a commitment of $20 million to the Kirov Opera, in St Petersburg; a pledge of £20 million to Covent Garden; $14 million to the Los Angeles Opera; more than $6 million to produce two operas at the Salzburg

---

9   In May 2007, in a denouement of sorts that seems to belie Vilar's claims about European millionaires, the Royal Opera House announced the renaming of its atrium as the Paul Hamlyn Hall, in recognition of the many contributions of the foundation created by the German-born British publisher and philanthropist.

Festival; $14.5 million to an arts centre in Beaver Creek, Colorado; $2 million to celebrate the Verdi centennial at Milan's La Scala; the unknown cost of a new production of *Tannhäuser* at the Bayreuth Festival; and the cost of three artistic residencies in Berlin (2001: np). Stewart recounts how Vilar himself told *The New York Times* in 2000 that his donations made him 'the largest supporter of classical music, opera and ballet in the world', and how *Forbes* magazine reported that his donations between 1996 and 1999 amounted to $300 million – 'a largess', in the words of Stewart, 'reminiscent of the projects of the mad King Ludwig II of Bavaria' (2006: 108).

Indeed, the comparison with an extravagant European monarch is fitting. Much has been written on Vilar's operatic ego, specifically, his desire to see his name and person acknowledged everywhere he contributed money, as if his donations were intrinsically a kind of artistic spectacle. In Salzburg and St Petersburg, his colour photograph appeared in programmes, while in Los Angeles and Washington he was recognised on stage, like a performer, for his donations. He told *The New Yorker*, 'You look [. . .] at the program for, say, *The Marriage of Figaro* and it starts with "Libretto by. . ." Well, who cares who wrote the libretto? How about the guy who wrote the cheque?' (Remnick, 1999: 104). He complained to Johanna Fiedler about the treatment of donors by the Met as 'second-class citizens': 'What makes me less important than Plácido Domingo? Why shouldn't I take curtain calls?' (2003: 337). For Vilar, then, philanthropy was not an anonymous avocation but rather a public performance as well as an instrument for the achievement of personal glory in the annals of opera – and in the operatic history of other countries. If, to a large extent, his gifts focused on New York and other cities in the United States, he often proclaimed his own elective affinities for Europe, as he tells Lebrecht: 'I happen to be a Cuban refugee, [. . .] I landed in the States and I didn't like it. I came to Europe as a student, and it was one of those infatuations. London in the late 1960s and '70s had some of the best music. So I have been coming to Covent Garden all my life. Plus, I used to take tours from here to Russia and discovered the quality of their art' (2001: np). This devotion to European cultural forms becomes visible in the spaces of his New York apartment through a series of artefacts that invoke Mozart and Austria. Hilferty enumerates these objects:

> It's the life-size statue of a young violin-toting Mozart, his back turned defiantly to Donald Trump's 90-story Trump Tower across the ether. And the imposing bronze of Don Ottavio, from Wolfgang-Amadeus's *Don Giovanni*. And the miniature facsimiles of the Metropolitan Opera's Austrian crystal chandeliers glittering above the dining-room table. Oh, and the frescoes overhead, copies of the rococo paintings in Salzburg's famed Mozarteum concert hall (2002: np).

Significantly, what seems to prevail in Vilar's self-fashioning, besides his multiple declarations of love for European musical culture, is the proud reiteration of his Cuban background, a leitmotif that runs through his own public retellings of his biography as well as in what others write about him. A long-time resident of New York, Vilar appears first and foremost as a Cuban-American. Fiedler, for instance, relates what one may now read as the standard version of Vilar's life, the origins of which are tinged with the relative exoticism and ancien-régime ambiance of his childhood in pre-revolutionary Havana, redolent of old money, lost after Castro and regained in the United States:

> Vilar's father had owned a sugar plantation in Cuba, and the family had fled the Cuban revolution as penniless refugees. The young Alberto had come to New York because he believed that the United States would not tolerate Castro's regime in its own backyard. While he waited out Castro, he joined Citibank as a trainee in their overseas division. About the time he realizes that Cuba was not going to change, he became sick of banking, and moved to London, where he began his career as an investor. (2003: 334)

The other side of the Cuban story concerns Vilar's father's refusal to support his son's interest in music and the arts. When young Alberto wanted a violin, his father said no, which, according to Vilar, stemmed from cultural prejudices about gender roles. Hilferty tells the story of how Vilar tried to share his enthusiasm for music by playing a recording of Beethoven's *Emperor Concerto*, an invitation rejected by the father; later, when the boy expressed his wish to play the violin, his father replied: 'Cuban men do not play the violin' (2002: np). The father, however, was overstating the culture's machismo. For many decades before the son's birth, men of wealth had played an important role in promoting classical music, including opera, in Cuba. It is a tale of cosmopolitan capitalism in which both men and women enthusiastically participated, one in which Vilar's passionate spectacle is not altogether exceptional.

Opera arrived on the island as early as 1776, when a setting of Metastasio's *Didone abbandonata* by an unnamed composer was first sung at Havana's Teatro Coliseo (González and Pitt, 1992: 1022). During the 1811–1812 season, nine operas were staged in the city by a company from Madrid, and, in 1818, Mozart's *Don Giovanni* was performed for the first time in the Americas (Stevenson, 1992: 669). Other milestones would soon follow, most importantly the New World premieres of five of Verdi's early operas, including *I Lombardi alla prima crociata* in 1846; *I due Foscari* in 1847, *Nabucco*, also in 1847; *Attila* in 1848, and the first version of *Macbeth* in 1849 – all of them within two to five years after their world premieres in Italy (Río Prado, 2001: 163–166). Indeed, Havana's well-established Italian opera companies not only afforded the city vigorous operatic seasons, they also travelled, under the general rubric of Havana Opera Company, to the United States in a series of important tours that, as we shall see, music historians credit for transforming the face of opera in America. In *Pasión cubana por Giuseppe Verdi*, Enrique Río Prado analyses Cuba's fervour for opera, which he describes as 'un desenfrenado fanatismo' (a frenzied fanaticism) (2001: 10), and that seems to have had at its core the works of Verdi, as reviews in Havana's newspapers, collected by Río Prado, suggest. After the first performance of Verdi's *Ernani* on 20 November 1846, for instance, the reviewer for the *Faro Industrial de la Habana* notes with a certain measure of drama the extent to which the city's Gran Teatro was completely filled by an audience paradoxically described as both *inmensa* and *selecta* (Río Prado, 2001: 19). As it turns out, a hurricane had passed through Havana not long before the arrival of *Ernani*, so this first night at the opera constitutes a return to a kind of public spectacle where the audience, men and women, are as much a part of the show as the opera itself. The same reviewer of the *Faro Industrial* writes:

> A la plateada luz del gas se veían lucir los semblantes de nuestras aristocráticas bellezas que retraídas hace tiempo del bullicio del mundo por la poca galantería de los huracanes, y la falta de espectáculos atrayentes, no encantaban con su presencia nuestros ojos. (Quoted in Río Prado, 2001: 19)

> In the silvery gaslight one could see the faces of our aristocratic beauties who, having been kept away from the bustle of the world by the little gallantry of hurricanes and the absence of interesting shows, had not charmed our eyes with their presence until now. (My translation)

Another reviewer, writing for the *Diario de la Habana*, adds:

> El público ansiaba la salida de la prima-donna, las miradas se fijaban hacia la parte por donde debía salir: llegó el momento, viósela sobre la escena; el auditorio la saludó con un estrepitoso aplauso y guardó silencio para no perder el más pequeño acento de la emocionada Elvira. (Quoted in Río Prado, 2001: 19)

> The audience anxiously awaited the prima donna's entrance, and all eyes were focused on the section from which she was supposed to come out. The moment finally arrived, and she was seen on stage; the audience greeted her with boisterous applause, but then kept silent lest they miss the slightest sound of the shaken Elvira. (My translation)

One is struck by these rhetorical flourishes whereby the citizens of Havana share the limelight – or 'the silvery gaslight' – with the singers and musicians: the adoring standing-room audience; the elegant young women, who are there to see and be seen; the ardent opera lovers, who applaud with rapture and then become silent upon the soprano's apparition on stage; and, last but not least, the members of the press, who take it all in and then represent it for their readers, among whom we may surely count those who attended the opera themselves. These are bodies that, by standing or sitting, applauding or being quiet, listening or watching, function as key performers in the operatic event. Like their European counterparts, audiences in nineteenth-century Havana, in what appears to be an altogether modern gesture, seem to seek their own elevation through the ostentatious spectacle of opera. The women in the audience are described as *aristocráticas*, and there might have been a countess or two in the audience, but their large numbers suggest instead the rise of a bourgeois class happy to flaunt its perceived majesty. One is reminded of the words of Theodor Adorno in 'Bourgeois Opera': 'It would be appropriate to consider opera as the specifically bourgeois genre which, in the midst and with the means of a world bereft of magic, paradoxically endeavours to preserve the magical element of art' (1994: 29).

Colonial, ostentatious Havana imported the magic of opera, thereby situating itself, if only through the fleeting ravishments of performance, on a par with the metropolitan centres of the Old World. Rich, entrepreneurial Havana exported opera to the United States, and in so doing asserted a cultural superiority of sorts – an affiliation with one of Europe's signature art forms that achieved a level of excellence in Havana before doing so in the cities of the much bigger republic to the north. If the operas that travelled to the United States from Cuba were Italian operas, and if the singers who performed in them came also from Italy, the fact remains that the show was announced under the somewhat uncanny sign of Havana. A playbill for a performance of Pacini's *Saffo* at Boston's Howard Atheneaum in 1847 reads: 'Italian opera company from Havana', and the troupes, in their various configurations, were often simply known as Havana Opera Company. In her impeccably researched book, *Opera on the Road*, which examines travelling troupes in the United States from 1825 to the start of the Civil War, Katherine K. Preston (1993) recounts in detail the itineraries of the various companies that originated in Cuba. The first tour took place in 1837, when a Havana-based company presented a two-month season in New Orleans, the only American city at the time that, because of its cultural ties to France, boasted a non-English operatic tradition. After the opera season ended in Havana, Francesco Brichta took his company to New Orleans, performing four US premieres, including Rossini's *Semiramide* and Bellini's *I Capuleti e i Montecchi*. This was followed in 1842 by a second season in New Orleans, where four more works, again, were premiered. This time the troupe was managed by Francisco (Pancho) Martí y Torrens – an unsavoury character, to say the least, who was rumoured to have been a pirate and was involved in the slave trade (Sublette, 2004: 129–130), but who distinguished himself as an impresario. In an appendix to her book, Preston lists the names and occupations of various people employed by the company; besides the many Italian singers, there is one A. Beckerim, identified as *apuntador* (prompter), while one Ester Mencer is described as director of *sastreria* (costumes), Spanish words that signal the company's Cuban management (1993: 320). The third tour took place in 1843, beginning in New Orleans, but this time the company travelled through much of the country – to Cincinnati, Pittsburgh, Philadelphia, Baltimore, New York, Washington, and back to New Orleans before returning to Havana. Again, important premieres took place, like those of *Lucia di Lammermoor* and *Norma*, sung for the first time in Italian in New York. Preston quotes a number of reviews that show the high regard in which the Havana Opera Company was held. More than once wealth is credited for the unusually high artistic standards. A reporter for the *New York Evening Star* writes: 'The Havana Company is one of the best that has ever crossed the Atlantic [...] because operatic singers have been always well paid by the rich and music-loving Spaniards' (Preston, 1993: 115). Indeed, not only was Martí y Torrens a wealthy individual; he also seems to have counted on the support of numerous subscribers in Havana as well as a government subvention (1993: 155). By 1847, when Martí y Torrens returned with his company to New York, the costumes alone were supposedly worth $30,000 (Dizikes, 1993: 123). John Dizikes quotes a writer for the *New York Herald*, who describes the Havana Opera Company as 'the most finished and excellent company that has ever visited this city [...], the largest and most completely appointed and equipped' (1993: 123). In 1850, the Havana Opera Company returned to the United States once again, and Max Maretzek, a newly arrived impresario who had worked in various European cities with such people as Berlioz, described it as 'the greatest troupe which had ever been heard in America' (quoted in Preston, 1993: 153). In a letter to a friend back in Europe, Maretzek writes that the Havana Opera Company 'has seldom been excelled in any part of the Old World' (1993: 153), and then adds: 'It would be useless, my old friend, to attempt to indicate the excellence of this Company. You have long since known their names, or been aware of their standing as artists, in the World of Music. The greater portion of them enjoy a well-deserved European reputation, and their re-union, anywhere, would form an almost incomparable Operatic *troupe*' (1993: 153–154). Indeed, as both Dizikes and Preston observe, the various ensembles of the Havana Opera Company that toured America left an amazingly rich legacy for the future of opera in the United States. By the twentieth century, however, the north–south operatic axis was reverted, and in 1919, Enrico Caruso travelled from the United States to Havana to sing the role of Radamès in *Aida*, an event remembered for an explosion that interrupted the performance as well as for the elevated fees the tenor commanded – the highest in his career and a clear sign of the wealth, pretensions and (why not?) real passion for opera of Havana's bourgeoisie.[10]

Since that explosion, Cuba's best known connection with the realm of opera has been, arguably, the now infamous philanthropy of Alberto Vilar and his New York-based wealth. But as befits a personage in whose life story fiction simulation has been as powerful as reality, the link with Cuba may be more tenuous than previously thought. Perhaps coincidentally, yet placed at the heart of the story, an upshot of Vilar's downfall from the hallowed spaces of opera has been the strange twilight of his Cuban origins. Stewart writes in *The New Yorker* about the discovery by Vilar's fiancée, Karen Painter, that the philanthropist was born not in Havana, but in East Orange, New Jersey. In Stewart's account, Vilar's alluring background unravels as dramatically as his finances: 'According to others who have known him well, most of the life story Vilar had laid claim to was fiction. Although his father was indeed Cuban, his mother was Irish-American, and he never lived in Cuba. The father worked for a sugar company with offices in Havana' (2006: 120). When confronted with the apparent embellishments in his biography, Vilar backs off 'the more colourful aspects, including the claim that he lived in Cuba and that the family had fled the Castro revolution' (2006: 120). Allison puts it more bluntly in *The Telegraph*: 'All that can be said with any certainty is that Vilar is a fantasist of the first order, with stories of a childhood in Cuba and an early flight from Castro's revolution. It now appears that he was born "Albert" in New Jersey' (2006: np). Even as the name of Vilar, the cosmopolitan capitalist, disappears from the operatic centres of the world, Cuba vanishes from his biography, and the elegant and rather old-fashioned figure of the Cuban-American philanthropist seems to morph in the public eye into an ungraceful character from an unglamorous corner of the United States. His newly dehyphenated persona becomes yet another element in a story of unfulfilled promises and glaring untruths; as Vilar exits the stage, Cuba fades away too, as if only American money could buy the kind of love that the Cuban-American opera lover once possessed.

---

10   On Caruso's visit to Havana in 1919 and its subsequent uses in fiction, see Díaz (2004).

9

A European Enclave in an Alien Continent? Enduring Fictions of European Civilisation and Indigenous Barbarism in Argentina Today*

LESLIE RAY

It is not uncommon for the élites in a society to harbour a grudging respect for other cultures; in certain historical moments, this respect can even reach the point of adoration, as in the case of Czarist Russia's love of France and the French language, or the English Romantics' attraction to all things Italian. Yet these two examples do not even come close to matching the level of centrality that Europe has had and continues to have for the dominant class in Argentina, and consequently for those subject to the latter's influence.

The Argentina – the Buenos Aires, that is – as advertised to itself and the world has a white face; it wants to be European. To find confirmation of this, it is sufficient to leaf through any of the glossy lifestyle magazines, such as *Gente* or *Caras*, and count the disproportionate number of 'European' faces in the photographic images. A concrete example: in one specific edition of *Viva*, the Sunday colour supplement of *Clarín* (2005), Argentina's leading newspaper, leaving aside the celebrities, there were a total of 16 advertisements and articles using 39 models: 15 were blond and 'Nordic', all female (2 children); 15 had 'Mediterranean' features (7 male, 8 female, all adults); and 9, all children, had 'indigenous' features. The 'indigenous' presence of 9 children (23 percent) might not seem so bad, were it not for the fact that 8 featured in an ad asking for charitable contributions to support rural schools and the other one, Lautaro (a Mapuche name), was a figure of fun, as he appeared in a comic section in which a humorous anecdote was told at his expense. So in this I believe not atypical example, while European-looking women and children are desirable, indigenous children evoke a sense of pity and/or humour, and are only allowed into the space of magazines in such terms. The story on the national TV is similar. As regards entertainment, on variety programmes,

---

* This chapter is based on previous research (Ray, 2007).

the glamorous 'vedettes' are almost invariably leggy blondes. Indigenous faces play little part in that world; in contrast, they appear in close-up on news programmes, as angry faces during *cortes de ruta* (road blocks) or as distraught faces following acts of theft or violence. In other words, they are associated with *inseguridad* (literally, insecurity), that catch-all term that groups together every middle-class angst from graffiti to terrorism. In short, those of European ancestry stroll in the sunlight, while the indigenous people lurk in the shadows. The Europeans hold the centre ground, leaving the 'other' on the margins. Examples of this are Calle Florida, one of Buenos Aires's main tourist streets, where artisan street vendors attempting to sell their wares are regularly rounded up and removed by the police. Or the army of *cartoneros* (waste-paper scavengers) who collect the waste paper, metal and glass from the streets of Buenos Aires in the hours of darkness.

In the nineteenth century, the campaign known as the 'Conquest of the Desert' was conducted by the Argentine state over a period of 50 years to gain control of the highly desirable lands in central, southern and northern Argentina occupied by the indigenous peoples: Mapuches, Tehuelches, Tobas, and a number of others. Following the campaign, Argentina's surviving original peoples were presented as being as good as wiped out, and were pushed to the margins of society. Though the indigenous origins of Argentina's neighbour Chile have not been glorified as much as those of, say, Mexico, it is interesting that – in contrast with Argentina – Chile has found it possible to incorporate the heroes of the Mapuche resistance against the Spaniards, such as Lautaro, Caupolicán and Galvarino, into the composite Chilean identity. Chileans, generally speaking, are proud of the brave heritage of Mapuche resistance, and have adopted it as their own. Images of strong, heroic Caupolicán and Lautaro are often to be found in places such as Chilean children's books. In contrast, a similar process has never occurred with the great indigenous leaders in Argentina, such as Kalfukurá, the so-called 'Lord of the Salt-flats', who, according to Argentine historian Carlos Martínez Sarasola, was 'el más poderoso cacique en la historia argentina' (the most powerful indigenous leader in Argentine history) (1992: 110).[1]

---

1   In around 1818 many groups of Boroans came to settle in the Salinas Grandes area in Patagonia, near the laguna of Masallé, west of the Salinas Grandes; their leader was Mariano Rondeau. One morning in 1834 around 200 Mapuches arrived from across the Andes to trade, which was not unusual. Their leader was Kalfukurá (or Blue Stone), and they came from the Llaima, or possibly from Collico. The unsuspecting Boroans were taken by surprise and massacred, and Rondeau was killed. So it was that Kalfukurá established his power base in the Salinas Grandes, the beginning of a domination of the Pampa that was to continue for 40 years, first by Kalfukurá and then by his descendants. Kalfukurá created an indigenous

Though the 'Conquest of the Desert' is long since over, Argentina's squares and public places continue to offer reminders of the military victory, such as the 'Monolito en Memoria a los Héroes Expedicionarios de la Campaña al Desierto' (Monolith in Memory of the Expeditionary Heroes of the Campaign of the Desert) on the banks of the Río Neuquén. The monuments and signage in the towns and cities of Patagonia and elsewhere continually reinforce the association between conquest and subsequent development, such as the sign outside Bahía Blanca station that highlights the way the conquest was rapidly followed by the arrival of the railway (Figure 1). There are a large number of historical museums in Patagonia, as most of the towns of any size have one. They all seem to follow the same basic pattern, or rather, the same route-map through time:

> 1st: the handiwork of pre-contact indigenous cultures, such as weapons, ceramics and textiles (Figure 2)
> 2nd: artefacts of the arrival of the military, models of forts, uniforms and Remington rifles
> 3rd: photos and maps denoting the coming of the railways
> 4th: memorabilia from the sitting-rooms of the arrivals from Europe, clothing, furniture, gramophones, etc. (Figure 3)

The subtext is clear: the rifle and the railway brushed aside the 'natives' to make way for European civilisation.

While the country's indigenous peoples occupy the shanty towns and poor barrios, the high-rise apartments in the town centres tend to be inhabited by people of European ancestry. Similarly, it is the politicians who extolled Europe's virtues that look down from their pedestals in the town squares. Take any given central square, and you will be almost guaranteed to find a statue of one of Argentina's statesmen or intellectuals, many of whom contributed to the formation of the guiding fiction of European cultural superiority, and the idealising and denigrating assumptions that underpin them. Here are a few brief profiles: The statue of Bernardino Rivadavia stands proudly in the main square of Bahía Blanca, gazing down benignly over the city (Figure 4). He travelled extensively in Europe, and greatly admired the British political system and the utilitarianism of Jeremy Bentham. Briefly President of Argentina in the 1820s, Rivadavia planned to induce industrious European peasants to migrate to Argentina, to turn the Pampa into a tapestry

---

confederation, by persuasion or force, unifying dozens of caciques and their tribes, and making his capital in the strategic centre of salt extraction. He was so bold and astute that the Mapuche oral tradition sometimes even credits him with magical powers.

Figure 1.   Bahía Blanca Railway Station. The text of the sign reads: 'Historical reference 1884–1984. Once the Conquest of the Desert had been secured, the first train arrived in Bahía Blanca on 25 April 1884. It marks a fundamental milestone in the development of the region and Patagonia'. © Leslie Ray

of small holdings. Bartolomé Mitre was another Europhile, but more a lover of their swords than their ploughshares, as he idealised European military power, capacities and virtues. It was his idea to bring over Italian combatants, fresh from their own Independence struggles, to garrison the new towns of La Pampa and Patagonia, such as Bahía Blanca.

Figure 2.   The Museum in Carmen de Patagones: The Barbarians – Handiwork of Pre-contact Indigenous Cultures. © Leslie Ray

The process of nation-building in nineteenth-century Argentina went hand-in-hand with fomenting immigration and settlement. Juan Bautista Alberdi, of the so-called 'Generation of 1837', condensed their reform philosophy in the phrase that formed the underlying spirit of the Argentine Constitution of 1853 – 'gobernar es poblar' (to govern is to populate). Alberdi had no doubts as to who the purveyors of civilisation were, despite his clear awareness of the consequences of this 'civilisation' for the subjugated peoples:

> Hoy mismo, bajo la independencia, el indígena no figura ni compone mundo en nuestra sociedad política y civil. Nosotros, los que nos llamamos americanos, no somos otra cosa que europeos nacidos en América. Cráneo, sangre, color, todo es de afuera. [. . .] No conozco persona distinguida de nuestras sociedades que lleve apellido pehuenche o araucano. El idioma que hablamos es de Europa. [. . .] El salvaje está vencido: en América no tiene dominio ni señorío. Nosotros, europeos de raza y de civilización somos los dueños de América. (Terán, 1996: 122 and 57–58)

> Today under independence, the native does not appear or constitute a world in our political and civil society. We, who call ourselves

Figure 3.   The Museum in Carmen de Patagones: Civilisation – Memorabilia from the Sitting-Rooms of the Arrivals from Europe. © Leslie Ray

American, are none other than Europeans born in America. Skull, blood, colour, everything is from outside. [...] I do not know of one distinguished person of our societies who has a Pehuenche or Araucanian surname. The language that we speak is from Europe. [...] The savage is conquered: in America he has neither domain nor dominion. We, Europeans of race and of civilisation, are the owners of America.[2]

However, the arch-Europhile of Argentine history was undoubtedly Domingo Faustino Sarmiento, whose admiration for Northern European countries was only exceeded by that for the United States (Figure 5). He saw the future of his country as a battle between civilisation – enlightened European culture – and barbarism – represented by the gaucho and the 'indio'. Sarmiento saw the environment as having a key influence on society, and so saw the product of the desert – 'el vacío' (emptiness) – as barbarism. Though Sarmiento did not know the Pampa, in his view, the effect of this environment could be

---

2   The translations are mine.

Figure 4.   Under the protective Gaze of Bernardino Rivadavia in the Main Square of Bahía Blanca. © Leslie Ray

countered by culture and education. While he believed the barbarian gaucho could be saved, the 'savages' were beyond salvation. He declared his repugnance for the 'savage' in this famous quote:

> Sobretodo quisiéramos apartar de toda cuestión social americana a los salvajes, por quienes sentimos, sin poderla remediar, una invencible repugnancia, y para nosotros Colocolo, Lautaro y Caupolicán [. . .] no son más que unos indios asquerosos, a quienes habríamos hecho colgar [. . .]. (Sarmiento, 1948: 220)

Figure 5.   Bust of Sarmiento in Neuquén. In the Background, the Equine Statue of San Martín Indicates another Way. © Leslie Ray

Above all, we would like to remove the savages from all American social questions, for whom we feel, without being able to remedy it, an unconquerable loathing, and for us Colocolo, Lautaro and Caupolicán [...] are no more than disgusting Indians, whom we would have had hanged [...].

The Indians were an anathema to Sarmiento and what 'we' – the 'civilised' – stand for. They lie outside of 'our' history and should be excluded from it, as has indeed happened.

The prominent explorer and academic Francisco P. Moreno (also known as Perito Moreno) was very committed to the national project of extending the geography of the new Argentinean state, to 'naming and claiming', as it were, but he also had mutually respectful encounters with the great cacique Sayhueque, and befriended Mapuche leaders such as Inakayal and Foyel. That is why his reaction to the slaughter that was soon to come appears troubled and contradictory:

> Tengo la seguridad de que bien en esa ocasión pudo evitarse el sacrificio de miles de vida [*sic*], por supuesto muchas más de indios que de cristianos. [...] Durante esa lucha se realizaron matanzas inútiles de seres que, creyéndose dueños de la tierra, la defendían de la civilización invasora. (1994: 99)

> I am certain that on that occasion the sacrifice of thousands of lives could have been avoided, of course of many more Indians than Christians. [...] During that struggle useless slaughters took place of human beings that, believing themselves to be the owners of the land, defended it from the invading civilisation.

Moreno was clearly saddened by the killing, but I cannot detect any irony in his use of the expression 'invading civilisation'. Such views as the above did not emerge in a vacuum, but were in accord with the requirements of a new state founded on immigration. The Museum of Immigration in the port area of Buenos Aires presents the immigrant as heroic (Figure 6). However, with the dawning of the twentieth century, immigrants were becoming increasingly scapegoated for the country's problems, and so the heroic figure of the gaucho emerged. José Hernández wrote the epic poem *Martín Fierro* between 1872 and 1879; it was a lament in defence of the gaucho, the intention of which, in Hernández's words, was to highlight 'todos los abusos y todas las desgracias de que es víctima esa clase desheredada de nuestro país' (all the abuses and misfortunes of which this disinherited class of our country is the victim) (2004: 1). It seems odd today to hear of the gaucho being disinherited, when it appears that the figure is placed on a pedestal as the quintessential Argentinean. Yet this is the result of a revival in the gaucho's fortunes in 1913, when Leopoldo Lugones 'rediscovered' *Martín Fierro* and claimed the book was the essence of 'argentinidad' (Argentineness) in a series of essays entitled

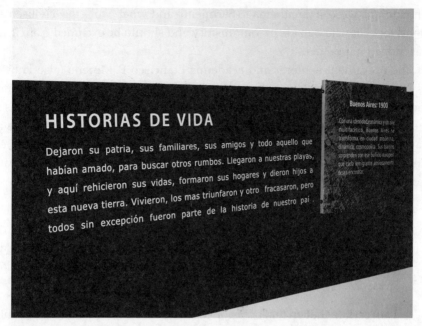

HISTORIAS DE VIDA

Dejaron su patria, sus familiares, sus amigos y todo aquello que habían amado, para buscar otros rumbos. Llegaron a nuestras playas, y aquí rehicieron sus vidas, formaron sus hogares y dieron hijos a esta nueva tierra. Vivieron, los mas triunfaron y otro fracasaron, pero todos sin excepción fueron parte de la historia de nuestro paí .

Buenos Aires: 1900

Con una identidad dinámica y un aire multifacético, Buenos Aires se transforma en ciudad moderna, dinámica, cosmopolita. Sus barrios sorprenden con ese bullicio europeo que cada inmigrante ansiosamente deseba encontrar.

Figure 6.   Museum of Immigration, Buenos Aires. The text reads: 'LIFE STORIES. They left their mother country, their relatives, their friends and everything they had loved, to seek other destinations. They arrived on our beaches, and here they remade their lives, formed their homes and gave children to this new land. They lived, most succeeded and others failed, but all without exception were part of the history of our country'. © Leslie Ray

El Payador (*The Gaucho Minstrel*).[3] By that time the tide had turned, and the immigrant was now coming to be seen as grafting and corrupt, whereas the gaucho, reviled in Hernández's time as lazy, uncivilised and outmoded, was to represent the pure essence of all that was good and noble about the Argentinean.

During the period that Hipólito Yrigoyen presided over (1916–1922), the Argentine élite became ever more fearful that the working-class immigrants arriving in the country from Europe were bringing dangerous elements with them, with subversive ideas such as anarchism and communism. They came to be associated with delinquency and disorder, and it is in this context that the nostalgic image of the noble gaucho, with his stoicism and simple, honest values, came to flourish. Despite this nostalgia for the noble gaucho, Europhile Sarmiento still has his heirs in modern Argentina. Many of today's Argentines have internalised his ideas. For instance, the Italians of Argentina, like their British counterparts, never completely separated from their mother country,

---

3   *El payador* (published in 1916) contained a series of lectures on *Martín Fierro* which were given in 1913.

and indeed in recent decades many thousands have taken advantage of their right to Italian passports to seek a better life in Italy in a return migration. Many Italians feel a particular affinity for Argentina, no doubt because of their close blood ties. My attention was drawn to this by an article in one of Italy's leading newspapers, *La Repubblica*, on the crisis of December 2001, specifically the following paragraph:

> E' una tragedia che ci tocca da vicino per ragioni che vanno ben oltre gli interessi economici. Quel paese sconvolto fa parte del nostro album di famiglia, non solo perché è popolato dai nostri emigrati ma perché i suoi cittadini leggono gli stessi libri, credono negli stessi valori, sono una parte vitale della storia e della cultura occidentale. (Rampini, 2001: np)

> This crisis is a tragedy that touches us closely for reasons that go well beyond economic interests. That disrupted country is part of our family photo album, not only because it is populated by our emigrants, but because its citizens read the same books, believe in the same values, are a vital part of Western history and culture.

So, according to Rampini, whose views I have not found to be uncommon, we Europeans – or at least the Italians among us – care about Argentina more than other Latin American countries because we have more in common with them.

Argentina's most famous and revered writer, Jorge Luis Borges, was also an incurable Europhile, but more specifically a champion of northern Europeans. His disdain for the Spanish was only exceeded by his utter contempt for the Mapuche. The following is an extract from an interview with Borges, originally published in Buenos Aires magazine *7 Días* in April 1973:

> Periodista: ¿Y usted justifica el exterminio de los indios? ¿La forma en que procedió su abuelo?
> Borges: Bueno, creo que nosotros hicimos bien en librarnos de los españoles. España era un país en decadencia y las invasiones inglesas demostraron que podíamos gobernarnos solos: por lo tanto, la guerra de la independencia se justifica. Algo parecido sucedió con los indios. Asaltaban las estancias y había que defenderse. [...] La guerra contra los indios fue muy cruel de ambos lados. Pero los españoles primero y los que conquistaron el desierto después, representaban la cultura.
> Periodista: ¿Y usted cree que los conquistadores trataron de transmitir a los indios esa cultura?
> Borges: No, puesto que ellos mismos tenían poca cultura. Pero de cualquier manera tenían más que los indios, que no tenían ninguna.

Periodista: ¿Entonces usted plantea el problema en términos de cultura
e incultura?
Borges: Sí, creo que sí. Como dijo Sarmiento: civilización y barbarie
[. . .]. (Quoted in Mateo, 1997: 56)

Journalist: And do you justify the extermination of the Indians? The
way your grandfather acted?
Borges: Well, I believe we did the right thing to get rid of the Spaniards.
Spain was a decadent country and the English invasions demonstrated
that we could govern ourselves: the War of Independence is therefore
justified. Something similar happened with the Indians. They attacked
the ranches and these needed to be defended. [. . .] The war against the
Indians was very cruel on both sides. But the Spaniards first and those
who conquered the desert later, represented culture.
Journalist: And do you believe that the conquerors tried to transmit that
culture to the Indians?
Borges: No, since they themselves had little culture. But in some way
they had more than the Indians, who didn't have any.
Journalist: So you pose the problem in terms of culture and lack of
culture?
Borges: Yes, I believe so. As Sarmiento said: civilisation and barbarism
[. . .].

Nelly Arrieta de Blaquier is the owner of the Ledesma Sugar Refinery in
Jujuy, North West Argentina. The refineries had been established in Jujuy
by the English company Leach's Argentine Estate, back in 1830. In the sugar
refineries, where most of the employees were and are indigenous, working
practices used to be as close to slave labour as it was possible to be without
the actual use of whips and chains. Yet Nelly Arrieta de Blaquier is on record
as saying that Argentina would prosper more if indigenous people did not
lack a 'desire to work' ('deseo de trabajar').[4]
We have seen how monuments and museums work to consolidate the
notion of Argentina as a European country. The same function is also
performed by the many historical re-enactments that take place, such as the re-
enactment of the defeat of the British in 1806 and 1807, during the Napoleonic
Wars, when the citizens of Buenos Aires, then still a Spanish colony, twice
defeated the invading British expeditions commanded by Generals William
Carr Beresford and John Whitelocke respectively. In much the same way as

---

4   This comment appears in Fernando Krichmar's documentary film *Diablo, familia y
propiedad* (*Devil, Family and Property*) (1999).

the festival of Thanksgiving is used in the USA to consolidate the myth of a peaceful coexistence between the pilgrims and the local indigenous people, in Chubut in Patagonia the notion is propagated of peaceful coexistence between the Tehuelche indigenous people and the Welsh who colonised the region in the mid-nineteenth century. Every year on 28 July in Puerto Madryn re-enactments are held of the coming together of two cultures. 'El monumento al Indio Tehuelche' (The Monument to the Tehuelche Indian) (Figure 7) is a statue sculpted by Luis Perlotti that stands in Puerto Madryn, on the east coast of Chubut. He gazes out to sea from on high, seemingly awaiting the arrival of his new brothers.

Not far from Puerto Madryn is Gaiman. Welsh tea houses have provided the best opportunity for the Welsh community of Gaiman to benefit from the influx of tourists in recent decades caused by the attractions of the marine wildlife of the Valdés Peninsula. Diana, Princess of Wales, visited Gaiman the year before she died. The appropriation or creation of a 'tradition' enables the descendants of the Welsh settlers to benefit from the new tourism. For the region's indigenous peoples this is not so easy. In San Carlos de Bariloche, which advertises itself as a Swiss-style chocolate-box ski resort, it is hard for a tourist to contact Mapuche communities. While visiting Bariloche in 2000, I called in at the tourism office in the main square. I asked for a leaflet with information on the local Mapuche communities, and was told by the member of staff that 'they cannot be visited'. When asked why, I was told that 'they do not take kindly to visits by tourists'. Those who control tourism do not take kindly to fair competition, would be closer to the truth. I was able to contact the Mapuche Centre, and in fact found a very approachable group of activists keen to teach the Mapuche language, history and traditions to the youngsters who go to classes there (Figure 8).

Reality for these Mapuche youngsters is life in the city; for them, as 'people of the land' (in the Mapudungun language, *mapu* means 'land' and *che* means 'people'), this urban identity represents a double alienation, a sense of distance from both the Western ideal of prosperity and the Mapuche one of life in harmony with the land. For these young urban Mapuches the sensation must be that of being stuck in the small aperture in an hourglass. When the dream of the glistening white-toothed freedom that consumerism can buy beckons, their poverty and dark skins prevent them from slipping through; yet when the hourglass is turned over and the dream of a return to a more noble, idealised, 'authentic' Mapuche existence in the communities is posited as the goal, their lack of knowledge of their language and roots, the 'corruption' of their urban ways, denies them access. They are truly stuck. Stanton Wortham et al. have referred to the liminality of Latino children in the Unites States, but could equally well be considering the urban Mapuche experience: 'Hostility in the community, and the resulting internalized message that they were

Figure 7.   Monument to the Tehuelche Indian, Puerto Madryn. He Awaits the Arrival of his Welsh Brothers. © Leslie Ray

deficient/undeserving, left many of the children in a position of liminality, "betwixt and between" two unknown cultures – the natal culture of Mexico or Central America and that of the school and the dominant culture it represented' (2001: 164). According to José Ancán Jara, 'the urban Mapuche defines his or her existence on the triple discrimination for being Mapuche, poor, and urban. Only the recuperation of subtle fragments of ethnicity adapted to the new frontier environment will allow for the recreation of a solid identity' (1997: np).

Figure 8. The Mapuche Centre, San Carlos de Bariloche. Visitors Welcome. © Leslie Ray

Figure 9. Mapunkies in Bariloche. Reproduced by permission of IWGIA

In my view, young urban Mapuches do not simply seek to recover 'subtle fragments of ethnicity', but rather a new composite identity that is the amalgamation of ethnic and urban elements mixed and matched. And for Mapuche teenagers, what better way to respond to this sense of being marginalised, to vent your anger at not being understood, than punk? So, borrowing the language, clothes and attitude of late seventies London and New York, the young urban Mapuches of Argentine Patagonia, from Bariloche, Neuquén and Bahía Blanca, like those from Santiago in Chile, now identify themselves as Warriache (*warria* + *che:* people of the city), or even as 'Mapunkies' (Figure 9). Seventeen-year-old Fakundo Wala from Bariloche explains: 'Of course we are rebels against the system that our parents were forced to enter, where they were forced to be workers, to leave the countryside when they were kids. So we're not going to be happy and contented, and we identify with the attitude of punk. In the city, what else is there to do?'. Oskar Moreno, aged 22, also from Bariloche, runs a radio programme, 'Grito Suburbano' (Suburban Shout), on a community radio in Bariloche, Gente de Radio:

> Many people don't see us as an expression of the Mapuche People, but these days we are another form of expression of our people. These are processes that are under way, realities, however much they deny them. We are here, we are the product of living in the city and not wanting the way of life the city offers. Many Mapuches reject us, discriminate against us or overlook us because we think this way, because we dress this way. Because we reflect what we think in our clothes, in what we say, constantly questioning.

So in adversity, young urban Mapuches are finding a sense of pride and self-worth. Thankfully, some things seem to be changing for the better.

There are manifestations of this change elsewhere too. After my initial visit to Carmen de Patagones in 2000, in which I discovered the presentation of the official view of the history of the region as civilisation overcoming barbarism, I returned to the same museum in April 2007, to find the first section completely transformed. What had previously been a rather shoddy assembly presenting the Tehuelche in the early nineteenth century as solely engaged in war and hunting activities, soon to be overwhelmed by a supposedly superior culture, has now been revamped, with a series of new displays, attempting to explain the complexity of the commercial exchanges that took place in that period in the Pampa and Northern Patagonia between indigenous peoples and European settlers, two cultures that were mutually dependent. I asked our guide about this, and he told me that he and the other staff members had been encouraged by their management to develop this first section of the museum,

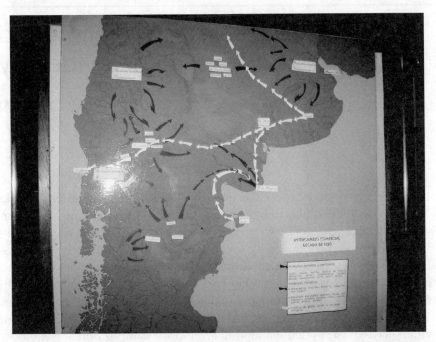

Figure 10. The Museum in Carmen de Patagones. Newly Installed Map Indicating Trade Patterns between Settlers and Indigenous Groups in the Early Nineteenth Century. © Leslie Ray

as there had been some negative comments received about it from visitors. It would seem that tourists visiting the museum are no longer content with swallowing that old chestnut about civilisation defeating barbarism. Tourism can be a force for positive change (Figure 10).

One day back in 2001 I happened to be listening to Radio Diez,[5] a talk radio station in Buenos Aires, and caught shock jock Baby Echecopar talking about Peronist politician Carlos Ruckauf. I was so taken by his words that I jotted down the following translation: 'what we need today in Argentina are modern politicians, politicians who look to Europe, and not to Formosa'. Now Formosa is one of the poorest and most neglected provinces – if not the poorest – in Argentina, with over half the population below the poverty line. In my view in Argentina the problem is that for three centuries 'modern politicians' have looked too much to Europe, and Formosa and the rest of Argentina's provinces have paid the price.

---

5 'El Ángel del Mediodía', Radio Diez, 2pm, 10 July 2001.

10

McOndo, Magical Neoliberalism and Latin American Identity

RORY O'BRYEN

I begin this chapter with an anecdote told by Alberto Fuguet and Sergio Gómez in their 1996 collection of stories, *McOndo*: A young Latin American writer obtains a scholarship to participate in an International Writer's Work-shop at a well-known university in the United States. Upon arrival he notes that in the US 'lo latino está *hot*' (anything *latino* is considered hot stuff) and that the Spanish departments and literary supplements 'están embalados con el tema' (are feverishly climbing onto this bandwagon) (Fuguet and Gómez, 1996: 9). So great is the craze that, on hearing that three young Latin American writers have been spotted wandering around the campus only a few blocks away from his office, the editor of a prestigious journal hurriedly arranges a literary lunch-party for them with the aim of putting together a special number dedicated to the *latino* phenomenon. Cool, the writers think, we're going to get published in America (and in English!), and for the simple reason that we're *latinos* who write in Spanish and were born in Latin America. Yet the editor and the three young writers are soon disappointed. Come the end of the semester, the editor rejects two of the three submissions, complaining, to the writers' dismay and disbelief, not that they lack verisimilitude, but that they lack any trace of 'magical realism', and that they could have been written anywhere in the First World (Fuguet and Gómez, 1996: 9–10).[1]

This anecdote should alert us to the currency of 'Magical Realism' both within commercial and academic circuits where the label functions simulta-neously as a positive marker of essentialised difference and as the yardstick against which the novelty of more recent Latin American writing is – by way of a curiously enduring litotes – negatively defined. As Stephen Hart and Wen-Chin Ouyang note, since 1925, when Franz Roh coined the term 'Magischer Realismus' to denote a post-Expressionist aesthetic, and since its political reinscription by the Boom in the 1960s, magical realism has become globalised to the point that it now represents, in Homi K. Bhabha's words, 'the literary language of the emergent postcolonial world' (quoted in Hart

---

1   This is my liberal rendition of the editors' anecdote. The translations are mine.

and Ouyang, 2005: 1). Yet whilst in texts like Gabriel García Márquez's *Cien años de soledad* (*One Hundred Years of Solitude*) (1967) or Alejo Carpentier's *El reino de este mundo* (*The Kingdom of this World*) (1949, 1990), magical realism's disjunctive clash of worldviews challenged the metropolis's ability to read and master the (post)colonial periphery, under the more fluid conditions of global movement and exchange described by Fuguet and Gómez, magical realism's globalisation as a postcolonial aesthetic at times clashes head-on with its value as an international commodity, and with the effect that the legibility of contemporary Latin American culture is rendered all the more complex.

Fuguet and Gómez relate this issue of legibility to Latin America's troubled contemporaneity in a globalised world in which the experience of postcolonialism is increasingly overlaid with the more uncanny experience of the post-national. After their disheartening *desencuentro*, the authors are tempted to conclude that Latin America was perhaps just an invention of North American Spanish departments ('un invento de los departamentos de español de las universidades norteamericanas'): 'Salimos a conquistar McOndo y sólo descubrimos Macondo [. . .]. Los árboles de la selva no nos dejaban ver la punta de los rascacielos' (We left to conquer McOndo but all we found was Macondo [. . .]. The trees of the jungle prevented us from seeing the tips of the skyscrapers) (1996: 12). Thus, in an ironic twist on what the postmodern anthropologist, Johannes Fabian terms 'the denial of coevalness' central to colonial knowledge-power,[2] the authors show how the popularity of a genre hailed as the hallmark of the postcolonial now prevents them from expressing the transformations of their postcolonial status under the conditions of late capitalism and globalisation. The collection produced in the light of this *desencuentro* aggressively sets out to correct this problem, and does so in its iconoclastic identification of a Latin America that they satirically term 'McOndo'. Before I offer an assessment of what is at stake in this gesture, it is necessary to pay attention to the terms in which it is made.

In an implicit resolution of the debates sparked off in the 1970s over the Boom's claims to literary autonomy,[3] Fuguet and Gómez joke that McOndo's proximity to its antecedent and homonym, 'Macondo', can be found in its status as a marketing label or 'marca registrada' (1996: 15). This contention highlights the fact that writers searching for individual and collective expression must, if they are to achieve success, learn to negotiate

---

2 *Time and the Other: How Anthropology Makes its Object.* See, in particular, Chapter 2, 'Our Time, Their Time, No Time: Coevalness Denied' (1983: 37–69).
3 See Rodríguez-Monegal (1972) for a discussion of literary and economic readings of the 'Boom', Avelar (1999: 22–38) and Martin (1984).

a global print economy that relentlessly transforms cultural capital into its libidinal and economic correlates. Yet the motivations behind *McOndo* are not only economic, but also aesthetic and ethical. Fuguet and Gómez make a claim for a new, 'virtual' realism that will give a picture of the transformations brought about by neoliberalism in the 1990s. 'McOndo', they write,

> es tan latinoamericano y mágico (exótico) como el Macondo real (que, a todo esto, no es real sino virtual). Nuestro país McOndo es más grande, sobrepoblado y lleno de contaminación, con autopistas, metro, TV-cable y barriadas. En McOndo hay MacDonald's, computadores Mac y condominios, amén de hoteles cinco estrellas construidos con dinero lavado y *malls* gigantescos. (1996: 15)

> is just as Latin American and magical (exotic) as the real Macondo (which, at the end of the day, is not real but virtual). Our McOndo is bigger, more overpopulated and polluted; it has motorways, metrosystems, cable-TV and shanties. In McOndo there are MacDonald's [*sic*], Mac computers and condominiums, as well as five-star hotels and gigantic malls built on laundered money.

Such a picture signals both the positive and negative effects of globalisation in Latin America. With flows of legitimate and illegitimate capital and commodities crossing increasingly volatile national borders, grand continental oppositions between First and Third Worlds are reproduced locally, and the view of Latin America as a kind of living museum of folklore has become obsolete. Yet McOndo is still far from constituting a homogenised 'McWorld' (*pace* Barber, 1995), as intimated by the juxtaposition of cable-TV and shanties, illicitly built five-star hotels and the realities of massive overpopulation.

Symptomatic of the aforementioned transformations of culture and society in neoliberal conditions is the fact that the stories in *McOndo* concentrate on private and individual, as opposed to collective, realities. Fuguet and Gómez present this fact – the fact that 'el gran tema de la identidad latinoamericana (¿quiénes somos?) pareció dejar paso al tema de la identidad personal (¿quién soy?)' [the grand theme of Latin American identity (who are we?) seemed to give way to the theme of personal identity (who am I?)] – as a symptom of what they call 'la fiebre privatizadora mundial' (the world-wide privatisation fever) (1996: 13). Gone are the days, they add, when 'la disyuntiva del escritor joven estaba entre tomar el lápiz o la carabina, ahora parece que lo más angustiante para escribir es elegir entre Windows 95 o Macintosh' (the writer's dilemma lay in having to choose between the pen and the rifle; now it seems the writer's greatest worry is the choice between Windows 95 and Macintosh). Neoliberal privatisation, one might glean from these remarks, seems to have emerged triumphant at the 'end' of Latin American history. These comments are in part offered tongue-in-cheek, and Fuguet and Gómez remind us that 'el nombre [. . .] McOndo es, claro, un chiste, una sátira, una talla' (the name [. . .] McOndo is, of course, a joke, a satire, a leg-pull) (1996: 15). In a later article, 'Magical Neoliberalism', Fuguet even offers something of a *mea culpa*, re-appraising these early remarks as 'a defensive and somewhat adolescent response to the user-friendly magical-realism software that politically correct writers were using to spin tales that would give world audiences exactly what they expected' (2001: 69).

Nonetheless, beneath this provocative identification of Latin America with 'MacDonald's, Macs and Condos', a more sincere expression of frustration can be heard. This brings me to the collection's ethical premise, which consists of a renewed defence of Latin American cultural *hybridity* over and against the exoticist abstractions produced by the market and the foundationalist narratives produced by traditional literary nationalisms. To deny such hybridity, they argue, is tantamount to a denial of Latin American *identity*:

> Temerle a la cultura bastarda es negar nuestro propio mestizaje. Lati-noamerica es el teatro Colón de Buenos Aires y Machu Picchu, 'Siempre en Domingo' y Magneto, Soda, Stereo y Verónica Castro, Lucho Gatica, Gardel y Cantinflas, el Festival de Viña y el Festival de Cine de La Habana, es Puig y Cortázar, Onetti y Corín Tellado, la revista *Vuelta* y los tabloides sensacionalistas. [. . .] Vender un continente rural cuando, la verdad de las cosas, es urbano [. . .] nos parece aberrante, cómodo e inmoral. (1996: 15–16)

> To fear a bastardised culture is to deny our particular *mestizaje*. Latin America is Buenos Aires's *Teatro Colón* and Machu Picchu, 'Siempre en Domingo' and *Magneto*, *Soda Stereo* and Verónica Castro, Lucho Gatica, Gardel, Cantinflas, the Viña Festival and the Havana Film Festival, it is Puig and Cortázar, Onetti and Corín Tellado, *Vuelta* and the sensationalist tabloids [. . .] To sell a rural continent which in actual fact is urban [. . .] to us seems wrong, facile and immoral.

This claim to hybridity can be located within a discursive tradition that dates back at least as far as Roberto Fernández Retamar's *Calibán* (1971), if not to Jorge Luis Borges' 'El escritor argentino y la tradición' ('The Argentine Writer and Tradition') ([1951] 1999a), or even to foundational essays like José Martí's 'Nuestra América' ('Our America') ([1891] 1979) and Simón Bolívar's 'Carta de Jamaica' ('Letter from Jamaica') ([1815] 1969). Like these, it stresses the plurality of origins, ascribes positive value to what is 'bastardised', and unravels immanent universality in the crude admixture of particulars. However, what is not clear is how such hybridity differs from its earlier formulations – how it sheds light on the inception of neoliberalism in contemporary Latin America or how neoliberalism recasts such foundational hybridity. Neither does it tell us what is at stake, under neoliberal conditions, in the equation of hybridity with Latin American *identity*.

A response to these questions is best formulated through a reading of this collection's overarching engagement with popular culture and mass consumption. In *The Art of Transition: Latin American Culture and Neoliberal Crisis* (2001), Francine Masiello notes the pivotal role played by the construction of popular subjects in intellectual debates about how local conditions are experienced under the weight of global cartographies. Latin American intellectuals have, since the 1970s, frequently turned the popular subject into a source of redemptive potential that could restore dignity to Latin America's status as a 'peripheral' culture. From Fernández Retamar's inversion of intellectual 'Arielismo' in the championing of 'Calibán' (1971), through Ángel Rama's celebration of the challenge posed to 'la ciudad letrada' (lettered city) by 'la ciudad real' (real city) (1984), to Cornejo Polar's insistence on the heterogeneity of Andean culture 'as crucial to the construction of a vision of Latin America' (Masiello, 2001: 29), popular subjects 'offered symbolic capital to intellectuals [that] allowed them to speak of their own dilemmas vis-à-vis the state' (2001: 29). Under neoliberal conditions, however, 'the popular subject often comes to be named as an embarrassing anachronism [and] the tie between intellectuals and the masses [. . .] appears irremediably severed' (2001: 23).

Now, notes Masiello, celebrations of subaltern struggle have been replaced by discourses that define equality in terms of access to a consumer-based civil sphere, whilst a return to aesthetics as part of efforts to counterbalance intellectual marginalisation, displaces endeavours to forge forms of union between popular and intellectual spheres. Beatriz Sarlo's interest in the 'poor-man's know-how' (see Sarlo, 1992), for example, was displaced by her renewed faith in political parties and a critique of the impoverishing effects of industrial mechanisation on national intellectual life (Masiello, 2001: 31).[4] One finds a similar scepticism towards subaltern struggle in Néstor García Canclini's *Culturas híbridas* (*Hybrid Cultures*) (1989) and *Consumidores y ciudadanos* (*Consumers and Citizens*) (1995), which determine citizenship according to varying degrees of consumption. 'In our current *fin de siglo*', Masiello writes, as if 'announcing a supposed end of history, critics tend to situate one another as fallen heroes expelled from paradise, exiled from the universe of modernist values that once confirmed their voice and place'

---

4   Here Masiello is referring to Sarlo's works *Escenas de la vida posmoderna* (1994) and *La máquina cultural* (1998).

(2001: 33). Against these prognoses – and despite their apparent seduction by the view of NAFTA as a stepping-stone to the 'end of history' – the authors in *McOndo* show, much as Masiello has done in her own work, how when approached from popular perspectives, neoliberalism may entail neither an impoverishment of popular creativity nor a homogenisation of cultural identity, but something quite different.

The first, and most striking, thing about *McOndo* is the ordering of its seventeen stories by nation. In the introduction, Fuguet and Gómez state their desire to 'borrar las fronteras que hicieron de esta antología no sólo una recopilación sino un viaje de descubrimiento y conquista' (blur the frontiers that made this anthology not only a compilation but also a voyage of discovery and conquest) (1996: 11). Such a desire is given expression through the formulation of what Fuguet calls 'a certain new Free Trade Area of the Americas (FTAA) sensibility' (2001: 68). He envisions this sensibility as the sensibility of a future in which 'borders will be even less explicit and influences will become so global that a new type of artist will evolve who will not be the nowhere man but, on the contrary, the here-and-now man'. He adds that such a 'sensibility-to-be' is

> less about nationality and more about empathy. Instead of trying to capture the essence of a village to show us the world, these new global souls are trying to understand the essence of our world and, thus, helping us deconstruct and, more important, care about, ourselves. (2001: 68)

The centrality accorded to the nation in *McOndo*'s structuring nonetheless suggests that, in spite of these predictions, the nation will not give in under the pressure exerted by the global without first generating resistance. Yet in line with Fuguet's view that McOndo's 'walkman morality' is 'post-everything: post-modernism, post-yuppie, post-communism, post-babyboom, post-ozone layer' (Fuguet and Gómez, 1996: 10), it seems more likely that the national will wither to the status of a mere backdrop for such 'posts', giving way to a vision of the McOndo village that is altogether more post-national in nature.

Fuguet's conjugation of a global 'empathy' with a local 'here-and-now' that lies beneath (or above) the national, resonates with Arjun Appadurai's view that the interactive nature of today's ethnoscapes,[5] and 'the loosening of

---

5   By 'ethnoscape', Appadurai means 'the landscape of persons who constitute the shifting world in which we live: tourists, immigrants, refugees, exiles, guest workers, and other moving groups and individuals constitute an essential feature

the holds between people, wealth, and territories[,] fundamentally alter[s] the basis of cultural reproduction' (Appadurai, 1996: 48–49). Rather than treating the local as a solid 'bedrock, untouched by rumours of the world at large' (1996: 63), cultural studies in a global era should instead, for Appadurai, chart the *re*-production of local identities as they register the implosion of *global* processes that leapfrog the mediations of the nation state. This implosion of the global into the local is sustained by a number of correlate processes, which include (i) the ever more fluid movement of mechanical and informational technology across previously impervious national borders; (ii) the hyper-accelerated daily transactions of 'megamonies' through currency markets, stock exchanges and speculation; and (iii) the creation of 'mediascapes' that refract these disjunctures by offering – to publics whose access to digital and electronic media increases on a daily basis – repertoires of images and narratives that allow scripts to be formed 'of imagined lives, their own as well as those of others living in other places' (1996: 35). Crucially, while these processes are all interlinked, the relationship between them is 'disjunctive and profoundly unstable because each [. . .] is subject to its own constraints and incentives' (1996: 35).

A point of departure for examining *McOndo*'s introjection of said processes, and the effects they have on its configuration of identitarian narratives, is Fuguet's story, 'La verdad o las consecuencias' ('Truth or Consequences') (Fuguet and Gómez, 1996: 109–132). This story tells of a cartographer's search for selfhood in New Mexico after a marital breakdown in his native Chile. Here the breakdown of such affective bonds provides a cipher for the destabilisation of the determinism that frames identity as a passive product of place. Pablo's inability to consolidate lasting ties with others – his inability to assume the truth or its consequences – is related to his inability to live in any other time frame than the instant, the present without future: 'Quizás ahí estuvo su error: Pablo nunca planeó nada y ahora está pagando el costo de haber vivido siempre en el presente' (Perhaps that was where he'd gone wrong: Pablo never planned anything and now he is paying the price of having always lived in the present) (1996: 113). Living in the present is a symptom of his subjection to the ephemerality of the commodity (he eats at service stations, and prefers listening to the radio to buying his own cassettes), and may also explain his abandonment of literary studies for studies in cartography, a choice that reinforces his disdain for (con)sequential thought and his subjection to the depthless, two-dimensional abstractions of the image.

---

of the world and appear to affect the politics of (and between) nations to hitherto unprecedented degree' (1996: 33).

Pablo's view that 'los Estados Unidos le [habían] colonizado su incon-sciente' (the United States [had] colonised his unconscious) (1996: 110), may tempt us further to read the dissolution of his affective ties in Chile (and indeed, his decision to travel north) as symptoms of a transformation of primal affiliations by the realm of the simulacrum that moves on an axis running from North to South. Pablo at first supports this reading. When his brand-new car begins to smell of sweat he is haunted by Chile and the thought of *empanadas* (pies). He also prefers American hotels to their Chilean counterparts: *motels* connoted with infidelity and quick, illicit sex. Yet if in the American desert all that is solid melts into the simulacrum (Truth or Consequences, the village in New Mexico where Pablo ends up, was so named after an American game-show of the same name),[6] Chile has already succumbed to a similar fate, having been turned into a virtual scenography for the enactment of New Age fantasies peddled by the BBC and the Discov-ery channel. The image of Pablo consuming these images in the communal sitting-room of a backpacker's lodge in Tucson is important as it confirms Appadurai's observation that

> As Turkish guest workers in Germany watch Turkish films in their German flats [...] and as Pakistani cabdrivers in Chicago listen to cassettes of sermons recorded in mosques in Pakistan or Iran, we see moving images meet deterritorialized viewers. These create diasporic public spheres, phenomena that confound theories that depend on the continued salience of the nation-state as the key arbiter of important social changes. (1996: 4)

As Appadurai notes, when today's migrations are accompanied by flows of mass-mediated images, these 'diasporic spheres' create 'a new order of instability in the production of modern subjectivities' (1996: 4). Yet as we shall see, the global fabric of this destabilisation of subjectivities is far from being isotropic.

The story, as I have discussed it so far, seems to suggest that the collapse of the real into the simulacrum (catalysed by flows of mass-media images from North to South) is a universal process. However, a trip to the US–Mexican border fundamentally alters such a view. When entering El Paso on the train, Pablo is tempted, by the sight of a crowd of cronies gawping in horror at 'el espectáculo del Tercer Mundo acechando a tan pocos metros' (the spectacle of the Third World lying in wait only a few metres away) (Fuguet and Gómez, 1996: 120), to imagine this scene transposed onto his native Santiago, 'como

---

6   Pablo's vision of the desert is very close to Jean Baudrillard's in *America* (1988).

si Santiago fuera dos países [...]. A un lado del Mapocho, Estados Unidos. Al otro, México. La Vega es Ciudad Juárez y Providencia es USA' (as if Santiago were two countries [...]. On one side of the Mapocho, the United States. On the other, Mexico. La Vega is Ciudad Juárez and Providencia is USA) (1996: 120). The analogy, of course, fails. When Adrián, a *latino* companion, suggests they cross the bridge to the other side (only two minutes away), Pablo is shocked by the reality of 'another world' upon which he, as a self-defined *latino*, has no purchase at all. Adrián points out that they had to get off 'el circuito para gringos' (the gringo trail) (1996: 121), but the trip to a grimy bar only confirms Pablo's inability to transcend his gringo perspective. Having been confronted with the sight of a stripper putting broken bottles up her vagina, and having emptied two bottles of *tequila* (which, like a gringo, he confuses with *mezcal*), Pablo urges Adrián that they should return to 'civilisation' (1996: 123). It is at points such as these where Fuguet's notion regarding the 'deconstructive' effects of globalisation on Latin American identity starts to become clearer.

The deconstruction of national identity is more apparent when the afore-mentioned clash of First and Third worlds is experienced locally. A Chilean may have to travel to the US to experience a shock encounter with the Third World,[7] but in Santiago Gamboa's 'La vida está llena de cosas así' ('Life is full of these things') (Fuguet and Gómez, 1996: 181–189), it seems that in cities like Bogota, people risk (even if they disavow) encounters like these on a more daily basis. In this story, Clarita, from the upper middle-class district of northern Bogota, tries to piece together a traumatic encounter with her psychoanalyst. Having knocked a homeless man off his motorcycle, she rushes him to a clinic, where she is denied access for not having a credit card. When she drives the man to the city centre she finds herself in the infernal 'Calle del Cartucho' ('Bullet Street' in popular mythology), whereupon her car is hijacked by a group of men with a pregnant beggar. Before they reach the state-run hospital, the man has an epileptic attack, the beggar starts to give birth and Clarita loses consciousness. As well as signalling the city's internal reproduction of First World–Third World divisions, this trajectory takes us into the realm of 'negative' globalisation noted by Castells when he writes that

---

7   Fuguet, of course, does not suggest that such encounters differ so greatly according to nation. In *Mala onda* (1991) his character, Matías Vicuña, ends up in a similarly 'other-worldly' part of Santiago when, having run away from home, he travels by bus around the city. Yet, the encounter is perhaps less shocking and accidental as it is experienced through the eyes of the would-be anti-hero, who models his life on that of Holden Caulfield in J. D. Salinger's *The Catcher in the Rye* ([1951] 1958).

there is more than inequality and poverty in this process of social restructuring. There is also exclusion of people and territories which, from the perspective of dominant interests in global, informational capitalism, shift to a position of structural irrelevance. This widespread, multiform process of social exclusion leads to the constitution of what I call [. . .] the *black holes of informational capitalism* [. . .], regions of society from which, statistically speaking, there is no escape from the pain and destruction inflicted on the human condition for those who, in one way or another, enter these social landscapes. (1998: 162; emphasis in the original)

Thus it is notable that Clarita's journey – significantly from North to South – is figured as a journey from a hyper-mediated middle-class world, where access to the shopping mall or country club serves as an index of citizenship, to something more akin to a 'dark continent', where people's citizenship is all the more fragile. Again, the otherness of this 'black hole' is gendered feminine when it is condensed in the abject image of the beggar-woman's gaping, bloody, vagina.

The telling of this story as a psychoanalytic session signals that Clarita's trauma derives not only from her experience of a world whose insertion in circuits of exchange and consumption is starkly asymmetrical to that of her own, but also from the shattering of the phantasmatic support that sustains her desire. When not at home or out window-shopping in Unicentro 'a ver si ya trajeron ese famoso juego de sapo electrónico que tanto anuncian' (to see if that famous electronic frog game, so heavily publicised, had arrived) (1996: 81),[8] Clarita spends time with Carlos, her boyfriend of lower social standing. '[S]us amigas tenían razón: Carlos era un poco vulgar. Pero la excitaba, todavía tenía adentro su olor' ('Her friends were right', she thinks, 'Carlos was a little vulgar. But he turned her on; she was still carrying his smell inside her') (1996: 81). When the Other's otherness is mediated televisually, as it is in her cushioned middle-class world – she admits knowing most other parts of the city only 'de haberlos visto en televisión' (from having seen them on television) (1996: 86) – the desire for otherness is safe as it is coextensive with the desire for other libidinally-mediated commodities.

Yet when the proximity of the Other's desire appears without the prosthetic support of the image (when the hijackers make her sit on the homeless man's lap, she faints when she thinks he is becoming erect), reality takes on the appearance of a bad trip: 'Yo vi la escena como si no fueran mis ojos' (I saw this

---

8   The electronic 'juego de sapo' typifies, in this instance, the *digitisation* of foundational motifs (the Incan game of 'Sapu'), and their transformation into commodities.

scene as if through someone else's eyes) (1996: 87). Moreover, when Clarita realises that the hard object is in fact a gun, the Other's desire – his attempt to escape from this 'black hole' – is translated back into the murderous desire for capital – the man, we learn, was a *sicario* (paid assassin) who had been hired to kill her friend's father. Finally, if in this story the replacement of the policeman by the psychoanalyst as mediator of Clarita's grievances stands as a synecdoche for the nation-state's waning performativity as arbiter of the social tensions produced by the uneven inception of global processes, in other stories, such tensions appear to lack even such basic mediation.

As Appadurai notes under the heading 'The Work of Reproduction in an Age of Mechanical Art', in global circumstances one can no longer assume the sort of 'transgenerational stability of knowledge' once presupposed by theories that sought to account for the reproduction of small identitarian groups (1996: 43). The absence, in *McOndo*, of any engagement with the theme of cultural reproduction amongst indigenous or other ethnic groups, may be an occasion for concern amongst foreign-language students, but many of its stories signal the pressure exerted by neoliberalism on other related transgenerational knowledge-systems, particularly those aimed at reproducing more elementary social units (such as lovers or families). Edmundo Paz-Soldán's 'Amor a distancia' ('Long-distance love') (Fuguet and Gómez, 1996: 73–78), for example, shows how, in Appadurai's words, 'global labour diasporas involve immense strains on marriages in general and on women in particular' (Appadurai, 1996: 44). If love, according to a cliché, is 'esas minucias que nos pasan mientras estamos ocupados haciendo o diciendo cosas importantes' (all the little things that we share when doing, or talking, about more important things) (Fuguet and Gómez, 1996: 73), then 'long-distance love' takes on the quality of an oxymoron. This is the tragedy of Paz-Soldán's story, where a young Bolivian studying in Berkeley – most likely to get an underpaid academic job back home – writes a letter to his lover Viviana (which he will never post), recounting details of all his infidelities. The narrator tells her (us) that when, at a party, he joyfully manages to 'olvidar el allá y el futuro, los diversos territorios y tiempos en que uno habita en una relación a distancia' (forget all about back there and the future, the different territories and time-frames that one inhabits in a long-distance relationship, and concentrate on the here and the now) (1996: 74), he is immediately plagued by guilt. Such a sentiment occurs precisely because it challenges the knowledge he has inherited from his family about relationships:

> Para alguien que nunca dudó de ninguno de los mitos que generaciones pasadas nos legaron acerca del amor esa verdad [el hecho de que yo lo pueda pasar bien sin ti] produce angustia y amargura: porque uno

cree literalmente en los mitos y cuando descubre el amor, piensa que es cierto, uno no puede vivir sin el ser amado, sin ese ser al lado hay insomnios continuos y una desgarrada [...] desesperación. (1996: 74)

For someone who never doubted any of the myths about love bequeathed to us by previous generations, this truth [the fact that I can enjoy myself without you] creates disquiet and bitterness: because you take those myths literally and when you discover love you think, it's true, you cannot live without your loved one, without your loved one at your side you experience continual insomnia and searing [...] desperation.

Such guilt leads the narrator to question whether true love is in fact possible, and to build a relationship in parallel with another student on the campus. The transformation of a long-distance love relationship into a threesome here (in Colombia, the popular adage is 'long-distance love, happy the four of us') offers yet another cipher for the ways in which, even the most apparently sacred bonds underpinning affective ties to place, dissolve to reveal a plurality of globally disseminated forces in play.

In Sergio Gómez's 'Extrañas costumbres orales' ('Strange oral Customs') (Fuguet and Gómez, 1996: 133–151), we see a similar deconstruction of the mechanisms aimed at reproducing the *habitus*, but this time within the realm of the jet-setting upper class Chilean youth. Gómez mocks a quasi-tribalist discourse of moral and cultural 'purity' by showing how the characters who utter such a thing are in fact caught up in a circuit characterised by the circulation of commodities across borders that renders such claims impure. Hence, while the title instils expectations of oral storytelling in us, what we get is instead a narrative where premodern orality (the traditional mode of reproduction for group identity) is replaced by its postmodern counterparts in casual sex and conspicuous consumption. After Charito and Seba's wedding, Florita and Silvio – who have not been invited to the reception – go to Silvio's apartment to gossip over a drink. Their conversation concerns Charito's reasons for getting married, but is also punctuated by small talk about the threats posed to personal health by certain products – Flora refuses coffee, linking it to Alzheimer's 'de lo que murió *rita heyguor*' (which is what *rita heyguor* died of) (1996: 134); Silvio likes cocktails, which he has learnt to make like '*ton cruis* en [*Cocktail*]' (*ton cruis* in [*Cocktail*]) (138). Here, reflexive consumption – significantly mediated by the cinema – constitutes the basis of a class sodality that distinguishes Florita and Silvio from an urban mass perceived as immoral and insalubrious. Yet in their unwitting creolisation of foreign terms – '*microgüey*' (135), '*yeremy airon*' (136), '*milcheic*' (140), '*greis keli*' (141), '*topgan*', '*omar charif*' (146) –, and misapplication of cultural references (Flora thinks Lisbon is in Africa, Silvio confuses Sigmund

Freud with Hermann Hesse [147]), we see the corruption of any claim to purity.

Moreover, in the playful slippage that the story enacts between different notions of orality, a more disturbing connection emerges between consumption and corruption. Silvio recounts how Charito had received a blood transfusion from her father, who later died of AIDS, but adds that she had married Seba out of love. Flora disagrees, conjecturing that Charito had married Seba to avenge a lesbian lover: her Bulgarian dance instructor, Irina Borisov, who looks like '*isidora dancan*' (144). Silvio defends Charito's 'normality' by recalling how he had had anal sex with her at a party, an interpretation of her sexuality that Flora again rejects, this time recounting how she had had cunnilingus with Charito. These details add depth to the adage, quoted by Silvio, 'Dime con quién andas y te diré quién eres' (a man is known by the company he keeps) (137), and suggest that in a neoliberal era identity is not only defined by the others with whom we keep company, but also by the more unknowable Other that leaves its spectral trace on the products and bodies we consume.

One might object that by aligning the deregulated flow of commodities with the propagation of diseases like AIDS, these stories partake of the language of political paranoia that expresses distrust of a multicultural, pluralist world;[9] especially so when both are figured in terms of the uncanny eruption of things 'foreign' into the putatively 'untainted' sanctuaries of home and nation. Yet it would be unfair to make this argument in relation to *McOndo*, where the treatment of AIDS does not advocate a militarist defence of the national from the threat posed by imagined 'primitive' foreign bodies, but points instead to its symptomaticity of postmodern processes. In fact, *McOndo*'s message seems to be that it is no longer either possible or desirable simply to opt out of the globalisation of consumer tastes and relations that characterise our everyday experience.

In David Toscana's 'La noche de una vida difícil' ('The night of a difficult life') (Fuguet and Gómez, 1996: 201–213) – the story of erstwhile rock-star, Roberto, of Los Bribones, and his attempts to make ends meet – Roberto is chided by his fellow band-members for 'prostituting' the band into doing cover-versions of hits by The Beatles, The Rolling Stones, Led Zeppelin and Dire Straits. Roberto too had once confidently refused to pander to market tastes, defiantly resolving never to lower himself to playing *Tex-Mex*,

> invento que sirve para cantar en español y cobrar en dólares a la chicaniza; basurero artístico donde caben los gordos, los feos, los cacarizos,

---

9 See Sontag (1988), who addresses the metaphors surrounding AIDS in media and political discourse.

todos los que nunca fueron aceptados dentro del rock; música para baile
[...] para quinceañera que no fue a la escuela; pasatiempo predilecto de
la gente que se cree sofisticada porque compra su ropa en Wal-Mart.
(1996: 212)

an invention designed to be sung in Spanish, and paid for in dollars
by *Chicano* plebs; an artistic rubbish-heap where all the fat, ugly, spotty
ones never accepted by the rock world end up; dancing music for [...]
fifteen-year old girls who never went to school; favourite pastime for
people who think they're sophisticated because they buy their clothes
at *Wal-Mart*.

Yet such artistic freedom was only possible thanks to state funding aimed
at building a national rock-music industry. With the denationalisation of
the music industry, Roberto now has to accept that the only way to survive
as a musician is to form mergers with other small enterprises. If in Latin
America, as Carlos Monsiváis writes, 'sin mayor oposición, la televisión
privada decide por cuenta de naciones y sociedades el significado de lo
aburrido y lo entretenido' (private television stands almost unopposed in
deciding on behalf of whole nations and societies the meaning of what is
boring and what is entertaining) (2000: 214; my translation), survival entails
negotiating the tastes and trends increasingly shaped by globalised media.
Thus, when the band object to the owner of a restaurant asking them not to
play rock music, they are replaced by a pianist who will run a quiz in which
members of the clientèle can win a free salad or pudding if they can correctly
identify the theme tunes of television programmes like *Ironside* and *Bugs
Bunny*. This last example perhaps paints a dreary picture for young Latin
American artists searching for individual and collective expression in today's
neoliberal circumstances. Yet by way of a conclusion, I would argue that
one way of tempering such pessimism, and of giving a new interpretation of
Fuguet's and Gómez's defence of cultural *hybridity* in *McOndo*, can be found
in the irreverent attitude that many of the collection's stories adopt towards
the nexuses between consumption, imitation and identity. To explore these
links further will also allow us to make more sense of what is at stake in the
passage from 'magical realism' to 'magical neoliberalism'.

The complexity of these links becomes most clear in Martín Rejtman's striking story, 'Mi estado físico' ('My state of body') (Fuguet and Gómez, 1996:
61–69), which documents a dizzying set of exchanges between young characters who spend their time hanging around in shopping malls in Buenos Aires.
Here the narrator takes his car to a garage to be repaired, telling us: 'Ya no me
queda nada [...]. El perro lo regalé cuando me mudé al departamento, que es
alquilado, y mi novia me dejó hace tres semanas por mi mejor amigo' (I've got

nothing else left in my possession [. . .]. I gave my dog away when I moved into the flat, which is rented, and my girlfriend left me three weeks ago for my best friend) (1996: 61). On returning from the garage, he places the mechanic's receipt in a frame once occupied by the photo of his ex-girlfriend, Laura. He then rings his 'ex-best friend', Leandro, to ask if he can borrow a video recording of a gym programme the latter has recorded from cable-TV. They meet at a video-bar before going to McDonald's. Here the narrator encounters Lisa, who looks similar to Laura and who is searching for an ex-boyfriend last seen in the restaurant's toilets. Later, having watched Laura practise her scales at home, the narrator visits Lisa, who is working out to Leandro's fitness programme. Lisa invites him to join her and lends him a pair of shorts belonging to Aníbal, her ex. Having collected his car from the mechanic (who tells him the receipt was unnecessary), he goes on a date with Lisa. Before they kiss, he warns her, 'lo único que tengo es un coche. Mi novia me dejó por mi mejor amigo y el apartamento en que vivo es alquilado' (All I have is a car. My girlfriend left me for my best friend, and the flat I live in is rented) (1996: 69).

This story ostensibly asks us to read these exchanges in terms of the homogenisation of identity brought about by unbridled consumerism, and as symptoms of the alienation brought about when people and bodies circulate as freely as other commodities. In this picture, lovers are swapped like any other commodities, and subjects literally have to 'sell' themselves on the basis of their exchange value in order to secure relationships with others. However, although Rejtman does not portray his characters as free agents, he does show how consumption is subject to a range of different modalities, which include selectivity, irony and even outright indifference. It is significant, for example, that the narrator prefers a vegetarian diet over the menus offered by McDonald's, and that when he sits with Leandro in the video-bar, the music videos of Genesis and Dire Straits make him feel like vomiting. It is also significant that when they go to a disco, the doorman lets them in without paying, that when he wanders around shops he rarely buys anything, and that when he shuts himself up to enjoy some 'zapping', he gets bored, musing that, 'a pesar de que [sus padres] tienen cable no hay nada' (although [his parents] have cable-TV, there is nothing worth watching) (1996: 68). When Lisa goes to the cinema, the auditorium is half empty and the experience of watching the film does not constitute consumption at all, rather its opposite, and she too feels like vomiting. Finally, and most significantly, most products and commodities consumed in this story are either borrowed, or are scavenged, and are not paid for. Such scenarios therefore suggest that the bright lights of the consumer metropolis in fact provide a thin veil that masks forms of exchange that are, in fact, more primitive.

In so many foundational Latin American works, cultural identity has been framed as the result of alternately passive or irreverent forms of imitation and consumption of foreign models and ideas. For aesthetes such as José Enrique Rodó ([1900] 1991), the imitation of North American materialism ran the risk of producing a total 'de-Latinisation' of Latin America's unique 'spirit' – an argument contradicted by the author's exhortation to 'the youth of America' to imitate Hellenic cultural paradigms. For others, Borges in particular, such imitation is always irreverent, and allows a chiasmic resignification of local by universal themes, and vice-versa ('The Argentine Writer and Tradition', 1999a: 420–427). For Fernández Retamar (1971), the mimetic inscription of colonial power is positively flawed in so far as peripheral utterances in the master's language are often 'cannibalistic' and fork-tongued, if not acts of overt warfare in which, to borrow from Homi K. Bhabha's words on the ambivalence of colonial mimesis, mimicry becomes *mockery* as it is 'threatened by the displacing gaze of its disciplinary double' (1994: 86). The appropriation of the coloniser's language in such a scenario functions like Caliban's transformation of Prospero's language into a means of cursing the master. Such paradigms remind us that there is no acculturation without a difference. Yet they start to look conspicuously anachronistic when, in relation to the complex, globalised circuits explored by works like *McOndo*, they continue to construe the big Other, against which the little Latin American other defines itself, as an identifiable metropolitan master.

As shown by the stories in *McOndo*, with the increasing implosion of the global into the local, characters encounter situations that, as well as being undoubtedly 'postcolonial', also characterise an epoch in which, to cite García Canclini's unique allegory of globalisation, 'David no sabe donde está Goliat' (David does not know where to locate Goliath). As García Canclini explains,

> durante la época del imperialismo se podía experimentar el síndrome de David frente a Goliat, pero se sabía que el Goliat político estaba en parte en la capital del propio país, en parte en Washington o en Londres, el Goliat comunicacional en Hollywood [. . .]. Hoy cada uno se disemina en treinta escenarios, con ágil ductilidad para deslizarse de un país a otro, de una cultura a muchas, entre las redes de un mercado polimorfo. (1999: 27)

> in the age of imperialism one may have felt like David facing Goliath, but one knew that the political Goliath was partly in one's own capital city and partly in Washington or London, or in the communicational Goliath of Hollywood [. . .]. Today each of these is disseminated in thirty different scenarios, and can slide with agile ductility from one country to another, from one culture to many others, among the networks of a polymorphous market. (My translation)

As García Canclini insists, this slippery dissemination of power makes it impossible to posit a clear-cut opposition between globalisation and the defence of identity. It also strengthens Appadurai's view that today's global cultural economy is a 'complex, overlapping, disjunctive order that cannot any longer be understood in terms of existing centre–periphery models (even those that might account for multiple centres and peripheries)' (1996: 32). Yet Appadurai's addendum, 'Nor is it susceptible to simple models of [...] consumers and producers' (1996: 32), should lead us to question the fetishisation of production and consumption within this picture. As so many of the stories in *McOndo* show, as well as reproducing symbolic forms of violence such as racism and class exclusion, the inception of neoliberalism in Latin America may also transform traditional patterns of production and consumption. However, in the final analysis, it may also provide something of a hollow armature, or mask, for other forms of exchange and interaction that are altogether more *sui generis*.

11

Contributors

MICHELA COLETTA holds a BA in Hispanic Studies with English from King's College London. In 2006, she was Fellow of the Department of History at the Universidad Pablo de Olavide in Seville. She is currently completing a PhD in Latin American History at University College London, with a thesis entitled *Cultural Transactions between Europe and Spanish America: Fin-de-Siècle Debates on the Concept of Degeneration*. She has taught Latin American literature and history courses at KCL and UCL, and worked as a freelance interpreter and translator.

ROBERTO IGNACIO DÍAZ is Associate Professor of Spanish and Comparative Literature at the University of Southern California. He writes on Latin American literary and cultural history with a focus on transatlantic relations in the nineteenth and twentieth centuries. He is the author of *Unhomely Rooms: Foreign Tongues and Spanish American Literature* (Lewisburg, PA: Bucknell University Press, 2002), and is presently at work on a book provisionally entitled *Abductions of Opera: Passion and Absence in Latin America, 1701–2005*.

MÓNICA DOMÍNGUEZ TORRES is Associate Professor of Art History at the University of Delaware. She received a BA in Art History from the Universidad Central de Venezuela, an MA in Museum Studies and a PhD in the History of Art from the University of Toronto. Her area of specialisation is Renaissance and Baroque art in the Hispanic World, with particular interest in the inter-action of Mesoamerican and European visual cultures during the sixteenth century. She is currently finishing the book *Military Ethos and Visual Culture in Post-Conquest Mexico* (under contract with Ashgate Publishing Group), which examines the currency of war-related imagery in the central valley of Mexico, ca. 1525–1600. She has also published articles in the *Archivo Español de Arte*, *Anales del Instituto de Investigaciones Estéticas* and *Delaware Review of Latin American Studies*.

ANNA FOCHI holds an MA from the University of Pisa and a PhD in translation studies from the University of Glasgow. She teaches Italian at the Cardiff School of European Studies (Cardiff University). She undertakes research in translation studies, autobiographical literature (letters, diaries and autobiographies), hypertextual and hypermedial writing and Italo-Australian literature. She is the editor and translator of John Keats's letters for Oscar Mondadori, and has published in several academic journals (*Studi di filologia e letteratura, Italianistica, Critica letteraria, Contesti, Lingua e letteratura, Educazione permanente, Westerly* and *Translation Studies*).

EMILSE HIDALGO holds a PhD in Critical Theory and Cultural Studies from the University of Nottingham. She is full-time researcher at IRICE-CONICET, the National Research Council of Argentina, and Lecturer of Critical Discourse Analysis at UCEL University in Rosario. Her areas of research and expertise include Argentine postdictatorial cultural expressions, human rights and museum studies, history, memory and trauma. Her current research focuses on a critical pedagogy of memory and conflict.

CHRISTINA KARAGEORGOU-BASTEA is Associate Professor of Spanish at Vanderbilt University. She is the author of *Arquitectónica de voces: Federico García Lorca y el* Poema del cante jondo (Mexico: El Colegio de México, 2008). Her main area of interest is modern Spanish and Spanish American poetry. She has published several articles on the poetry of Luis Cernuda, Pedro Salinas, Cristina Peri Rossi and Abigael Bohórquez. She is also interested in Spanish drama and has written a number of essays on Cervantes's and Valle-Inclán's theatre. At present she is working on how oblivion works in the conception and representations of authority in Hispanic Literatures.

ELENI KEFALA is a lecturer in Latin American Literature and Culture at the University of St Andrews. She received her PhD from the University of Cambridge and subsequently held a Mellon Postdoctoral Fellowship in the Humanities at the University of Pennsylvania. She is the author of *Peripheral (Post) Modernity: The Syncretist Aesthetics of Borges, Piglia, Kalokyris and Kyriakidis* (New York: Peter Lang, 2007), and of numerous articles on Latin American and comparative literature and culture. Her main area of research is twentieth-century Argentine literature and culture. She is particularly interested in issues of cultural modernity and postmodernity, postcolonial and decolonial studies, cultural identity and Borges studies. Her current project is interdisciplinary in nature and explores representations of the city in twentieth-century Argentina.

RORY O'BRYEN is University Lecturer in Latin American Literature at the University of Cambridge. He is the author of *Literature, Testimony and Cinema in Contemporary Colombian Culture: Spectres of* La Violencia (London: Tamesis, 2008). His current research focuses on the idea of the literary in the narrative works of acclaimed Chilean-Mexican writer, Roberto Bolaño.

JOHN ØDEMARK is a lecturer in Cultural History at the University of Oslo. He received his PhD from the same university, with a thesis entitled *Translating Tlaloc, Accommodating Vico: Lorenzo Boturini Benaduci and the Semiotic Character of Cultural Otherness – A Study in the History and Theory of Cultural Translation*. He has published several articles on the topic of cultural translation within the field of cultural history. He is the editor of the Norwegian edition of *Popol Vuh* (2003).

LESLIE RAY is a freelance writer and translator, and a member of the Society of Authors and the Chartered Institute of Linguists. He has translated a number of books from Italian and Spanish in the fields of architecture and art history. A regular visitor to Argentina since the late eighties, he has worked actively with Mapuche organisations in the last decade. He has published a number of articles on Argentine social, indigenous and language-related issues. His is the author of *Language of the Land: The Mapuche in Argentina and Chile* (Copenhagen: IWGIA, 2007). The Italian version of the book, *La lingua della terra. I mapuche in Argentina e Cile*, has recently been published by BFS Edizioni of Pisa. He lives in Cambridge.

VICTORIA RÍOS CASTAÑO lectures in Hispanic Studies and Translation at the University of Ulster. She received an MPhil in literary studies from the University of Salamanca and a PhD in colonial Latin America from the University of Nottingham. Her research interests lie in cultural translation during the colonisation of Mexico and literary representations of colonial Latin America. She is currently preparing a monograph on Fray Bernardino de Sahagún in which she recontextualises his work within the ideological structures of sixteenth-century Spain and America.

12

References

de Acosta, J. (1590) *Historia natural y moral de las Indias*. Impresso en casa de Juan de León: Sevilla.

Adorno, T. W. (1994) 'Bourgeois Opera' in D. J. Levin (ed.) *Opera Through Other Eyes*. Stanford University Press: Stanford, 25–44.

Agassiz, L. (1859) *An Essay on Classification*. Longman: London.

Allison, J. (2006) 'Opera Moneybags Faces the Music', *The Telegraph*, 19 February. [WWW document]. URL http://www.telegraph.co.uk/culture/3650295/Opera-moneybags-faces-the-music.htm [accessed 16 June 2010].

Álvarez, A. [1904] (1915) *¿Adónde vamos?* Vaccaro: Buenos Aires.

Ameghino, F. [1880] (1918) *La antigüedad del hombre en el Plata*. La Cultura Argentina: Buenos Aires.

Ancán Jara, J. (1997) 'Urban Mapuches: Reflections on a Modern Reality in Chile'. *Abya Yala News* **10**(3): 1–3. [WWW document]. URL http://www.mapuche.info/mapuint/ancan00.htm [accessed 17 June 2010].

de Andrade, O. (1991) 'Cannibalist Manifesto' (trans. L. Bary). *Latin American Literary Review* **19**(38): 35–47.

Anglicus, B. [1494] (1992) *De las propriedades de las cosas* (trans. M. C. Seymour et al.). Micronet: Madrid.

Anglicus, B. (1975–1988) *On the Properties of Things: John Trevisa's Translation of Bartholomaeus Anglicus De Proprietatibus Rerum* (trans. S. Maurice Charles *et al.*). Clarendon Press: Oxford.

Anzaldúa G. (1987) *Borderlands/La Frontera*. Aunt Lute Books: San Francisco.

Apel, F. (2008) 'Tradurre come strategia di mutamento'. *Testo a fronte* **XIX**(39): 5–29.

Appadurai, A. (1996) *Modernity at Large: Cultural Dimensions of Globalization*. University of Minnesota Press: London.

Apter, E. (2006) *The Translation Zone*. Princeton University Press: Princeton.

Aquinas, T. (1963–1981) *Summa Theologiae: Latin Text and English Translation, Introductions, Notes, Appendices, and Glossaries*. Vol. 42. (ed. and trans. T. Gilby), Blackfriars: London.

Ardao, A. (1980) *Génesis de la idea y el nombre de América Latina*. Centro de Estudios Latinoamericanos Rómulo Gallegos: Caracas.

Ardao, A. (1992) *España en el origen del nombre América Latina*. Biblioteca de Marcha: Montevideo.

Arguedas, A. (1909) *Pueblo enfermo. Contribución a la psicología de los pueblos hispanoamericanos*. Vda. de Luis Tasso: Barcelona.

Arguedas, J. M. (1985). 'The Novel and the Problem of Literary Expression in Peru' in *Yawar Fiesta* (trans. F. Horning Barraclough). University of Texas Press: Austin, xiii–xxi.

Argyrou, V. (2002) *Anthropology and the Will to Meaning. A Postcolonial Critique*. Pluto Press: London.

Aronna, M. (1999) *Pueblos Enfermos: The Discourse of Illness in the Turn-of-the-Century Spanish and Latin American Essay*. U.N.C. Department of Romance Languages: Chapel Hill.

Arreguine, V. (1900) *En qué consiste la superioridad de los latinos sobre los anglosajones*. La Enseñanza Argentina: Buenos Aires.

Asad, T. (1986) 'The Concept of Cultural Translation in British Social Anthropology' in J. Clifford and G. E. Marcus (eds.) *Writing Culture: The Politics and Poetics of Ethnography*. University of California Press: Berkeley, 141–164.

Asad, T. (1993) *Genealogies of Religion: Discipline and Reasons of Power in Christianity and Islam*. Johns Hopkins University Press: Baltimore.

Avelar, I. (1999) *The Untimely Present: Postdictatorial Latin American Fiction and the Task of Mourning*. Duke University Press: London.

Baker, M. (1995) 'Corpora in Translation Studies: An Overview and Some Suggestions for Future Research'. *Target* **7**(2): 223–243.

Balderston, D. (1993) *Out of Context: Historical Reference and the Representation of Reality in Borges*. Duke University Press: Durham.

Balderston, D. (1994) 'Introduction' in R. Piglia *Artificial Respiration* (trans. D. Balderston). Duke University: Durham, 1–3.

Balderston, D. and Schwartz, M. E. (eds.) (2002) *Voice-Overs: Translation and Latin American Literature*. SUNY Press: Albany.

Barber, B. (1995) *Jihad vs. McWorld*. Ballantine Books: New York.

Baudrillard, J. (1988) *America*. Verso: London.

BBC News (2005) 'Opera House Drops Benefactor Name'. *BBC News*, 20 September. [WWW document]. URL http://news.bbc.co.uk/1/hi/entertainment/arts/4262918.stm [accessed 16 June 2010].

Benjamin, W. (1999) *Illuminations* (ed. and intro. H. Arendt, trans. H. Zorn). Pimlico: London.

Benjamin, W. (2000) 'The Task of the Translator' in L. Venuti (ed.) *The Translation Studies Reader*. Routledge: London and New York, 15–25.

Berlin, I. (1990) *The Crooked Timber of Humanity: Chapters in the History of Ideas*. Murray: London.

Berlin, I. (2002) *Three Critics of the Enlightenment: Vico, Hamann, Herder*. Princeton University Press: Princeton.

Berman, A. (2000) 'Translation and the Trials of the Foreign' in L. Venuti (ed.) *The Translation Studies Reader*. Routledge: London and New York, 285–297.

Betto, F. (2001) 'Globalização ou globocolonização?' *ALAI, América Latina en Movimiento*, 16 July. [WWW document]. URL http://alainet.org/active/1354&lang=es [accessed 11 June 2010].

Betto, F. (2004) 'Fracassa a globalização'. *ALAI, América Latina en Movimiento*, 12 March. [WWW document]. URL http://alainet.org/active/5779&lang=es [accessed 11 June 2010].

Bhabha, H. K. (1994) *The Location of Culture*. Routledge: London and New York.

Blanco Fombona, R. (1902) *La americanización del mundo*. Amsterdam.

Bolívar, S. [1815] (1969) 'Carta de Jamaica' in *Escritos politicos, Selección e introducción de Graciela Soriano*. Alianza: Madrid, 61–90.

Borges, J. L. (1998) 'The South' in *Collected Fictions* (trans. A. Hurley). Penguin: New York, 174–179.

Borges, J. L. (1999a) 'The Argentine Writer and Tradition' in *Selected Non-Fictions* (ed. E. Weinberger, trans. E. Allen, S. J. Levine and E. Weinberger). The Penguin Press: Middlesex, 420–427.

Borges, J. L. (1999b) 'The Homeric Versions' in *Selected Non-Fictions* (ed. E. Weinberger, trans. E. Allen, S. J. Levine and E. Weinberger). The Penguin Press: Middlesex, 69–74.

Borges, J. L. (1999c) 'The Translators of *The Thousand and One Nights*' in *Selected Non-Fictions* (ed. E. Weinberger, trans. E. Allen, S. J. Levine and E. Weinberger). The Penguin Press: Middlesex, 92–109.

Boturini Benaduci, L. (1746) *Idea de una nueva historia general de America septentrional fundada sobre material copioso de Figuras, Symbolos, Caractères y Geroglificos, Cantares y Manuscritos de Autores Indios ultimamente descubiertos.* La imprenta de Juan de Zúñiga: Madrid.

Brecht, B. (1964) *Brecht on Theatre: The Development of an Aesthetic* (ed. and trans. J. Willett). Methuen: London.

Brennan, T. (2004) 'From Development to Globalization: Postcolonial Studies and Globalization Theory' in N. Lazarus (ed.) *The Cambridge Companion to Postcolonial Literary Studies.* Cambridge University Press: Cambridge, 120–138.

Browne, W. (2000) *Sahagún and the Transition to Modernity.* University of Oklahoma Press: Norman.

Budick, S. (1996) 'Crises of Alterity: Cultural Untranslatability and the Experience of Secondary Otherness' in S. Budick and W. Iser (eds.) *The Translatability of Cultures: Figurations of the Space Between.* Stanford University Press: Stanford, 1–22.

Budick, S. and Iser, W. (eds.) (1996) *The Translatability of Cultures: Figurations of the Space Between.* Stanford University Press: Stanford.

Buffon, G.-L. Leclerc, Comte de (1749–1788) *Histoire naturelle, générale et particulière.* Imprimerie Royale: Paris.

Bunge, C. O. (1903) *Nuestra América.* Impr. de Henrich y Cia: Barcelona.

Burke, P. (1997) *Varieties of Cultural History.* Polity Press: Cambridge.

Busquets, L. (1996) 'Don Álvaro, o la fuerza de la Historia'. *Cuadernos Hispanoamericanos* **547**: 61–78.

Bustamante García, J. (1989) *La obra etnográfica y lingüística de fray Bernardino de Sahagún.* Universidad Complutense: Madrid.

Caldera, E. (1995) 'La polémica sobre el *Don Álvaro*'. *Crítica Hispánica* **XVII**: 22–35.

de Campos, H. (1982) 'Mephistofaustian Transluciferation (Contribution to the Semiotics of Poetic Translation)' (trans. G. S. Wilder and H. de Campos). *Dispositio* 7(19–20): 181–187.

de Campos, H. (1986) 'The Rule of Anthropophagy: Europe under the Sign of Devoration' (trans. M. T. Wolff). *Latin American Literary Review* **14**(27): 42–60.

Cañizares-Esguerra, J. (2001) *How to Write the History of the New World: Histories, Epistemologies and Identities in the Eighteenth-Century Atlantic World.* Stanford University Press: Stanford.

Caparrós, M. (2008) *A quien corresponda.* Anagrama: Barcelona.

Carpentier, A. (1949) *El reino de este mundo.* Seix Barral: Barcelona.

Carpentier, A. (1990) *The Kingdom of this World* (trans. H. de Onís and H. Martin). Andre Deutsch: London.

Carrasco, D. (1990) *Religions of Mesoamerica: Cosmovision and Ceremonial Centers.* Harper and Row: San Francisco.

Carrasco, D. (2000) *Quetzalcoatl and the Irony of Empire: Myths and Prophecies in the Aztec Tradition.* University Press of Colorado: Boulder.

Castañeda de la Paz, M. (2009) 'Central Mexican Indigenous Coats of Arms and the Conquest of Mesoamerica'. *Ethnohistory* **56**(1): 125–161.

Castells, M. (1998) *The Information Age, Volume III – End of Millennium.* Blackwell: Oxford.

Castro-Gómez, S. (2007) 'Decolonizar la universidad. La hybris del punto cero y el diálogo de saberes' in S. Castro-Gómez and R. Grosfoguel (eds.) *El giro decolonial: reflexiones para una diversidad epistémica más allá del capitalimo global.* Iesco-Pensar-Siglo del Hombre Editores: Bogota, 79–91.

Catford, J. C. (1967) *A Linguistic Theory of Translation: An Essay in Applied Linguistics.* Oxford University Press: London.

Cedeño, A. (1997) 'Don Álvaro o la carnavalización del héroe'. *Romance Languages Annual* **9**: 438–443.

Césaire, A. (1998) 'Discourse on Colonialism' in E. Chukwudi Eze (ed.) *African Philosophy: An Anthology.* Blackwell: Oxford, 222–227.

Chavero, A. and Baranda, J. (eds.) (1892) *Antigüedades Mexicanas publicadas por la Junta Colombina de México en el cuarto centenario del descubrimiento de América.* Oficina Tipográfica de la Secretaría de Fomento: Mexico City.

Chong, A., Linger, R. and Zahn, C. (eds.) (2003) *Masterpieces from the Isabella Stewart Gardner Museum.* Isabella Stewart Gardner Museum and Beacon Press: Boston.

Chueh, H.-C. (2004) *Anxious Identity: Education, Difference and Politics.* Praeger Publishers: Westport.

Clarín (2005) *Viva* (colour supplement of newspaper, editor-in-chief Ernestina Herrera de Noble), 20 March.

Clifford, J. (1997) *Routes: Travel and Translation in the Late Twentieth Century.* Harvard University Press: Cambridge.

Columbus, C. (1969) *The Four Voyages* (ed. and trans. J. M. Cohen). Penguin: London.

Cornejo Polar, A. (2004) '*Mestizaje*, Transculturation, Heterogeneity' in A. del Sarto, A. Ríos and A. Trigo (eds.) *The Latin American Cultural Studies Reader.* Duke University Press: Durham, 116–119.

Coronil, F. (2004) 'Latin American Postcolonial Studies and Global Decolonization' in N. Lazarus (ed.) *The Cambridge Companion to Postcolonial Literary Studies.* Cambridge University Press: Cambridge, 221–240.

Cortázar, J. (2002) 'Translate, Traduire, Tradurre: Traducir' in D. Balderston and M. E. Schwartz (eds.) *Voice-Overs: Translation and Latin American Literature.* SUNY Press: Albany, 21–22.

Cortés, H. (2001) *Letters from Mexico* (ed. and trans. A. Pagden). Yale University Press: New Haven.

Cuadriello, J. (1999) 'El origen del reino y la configuración de su empresa: episodios y alegorías de triunfo y fundación' in J. Soler Frost (ed.) *Los pinceles de la historia: el origen del Reino de la Nueva España, 1680–1750.* Museo Nacional de Arte; Banamex: Mexico City, 50–107.

Cuddon, J. A. (ed.) (1988) *The Penguin Dictionary of Literary Terms and Literary Theory.* Penguin Books: London.

Dejbord, P. T. (1998) *Cristina Peri Rossi: escritora del exilio.* Editorial Galerna: Buenos Aires.

Delabastita, D. (1993) *There's a Double Tongue: An Investigation into the Translation of Shakespeare's Wordplay, with Special Reference to 'Hamlet'.* Rodopi: Amsterdam.

Demolins, E. [1897] (1901) *À quoi tient la supériorité des Anglo-Saxons.* Firmin-Didot et Cie.: Paris.

Derrida, J. (1981) *Positions* (trans. A. Bass). University of Chicago Press: Chicago.

Derrida, J. (1992) *Acts of Literature* (ed. D. Attridge). Routledge: New York and London.

Diablo familia y propiedad (1999) Documentary film. Directed by Fernando Krichmar. Grupo de Cine Insurgente: Buenos Aires.

Díaz, R. I. (2004) 'Silencios de Caruso o la ópera en La Habana'. *América: Cahiers du CRICCAL (Sorbonne Nouvelle)* **31**: 153–159.

Dizikes, J. (1993) *Opera in America: A Cultural History.* Yale University Press: New Haven and London.

Dowling, J. (1989) 'Time in *don Álvaro'. Romance Notes* **3**: 355–361.

Duncan, C. (1995) *Civilizing Rituals: Inside Public Art Museums.* Routledge: New York.

Durán, D. (1971) *Book of the Gods and Rites and the Ancient Calendar* (ed. and trans. F. Horcasitas and D. Heyden). University of Oklahoma Press: Norman.

Dussel, E. (1995) *The Invention of the Americas: Eclipse of the Other and the Myth of Modernity* (trans. M. D. Barber). Continuum: New York.

Dussel, E. (1996) *The Underside of Modernity: Apel, Ricœur, Rorty, Taylor, and the Philosophy of Liberation* (trans. E. Mendieta). Humanity Books: New York.

Dussel, E. (2000) 'Europe, Modernity, and Eurocentrism' (trans. J. Krauel and V. C. Tuma). *Nepantla: Views from the South* **1**(3): 465–478.

Dussel, E. (2002) 'World-System and "Trans"-Modernity' (trans. A. Fornazzari). *Nepantla: Views from the South* **3**(2): 221–244.

Encina, F. A. (1912) *Nuestra inferioridad económica: sus causas, sus consecuencias.* Imprenta Universitaria: Santiago.

Escobar, A. (2003) '"Mundos y conocimientos de otro modo": el programa de investigación de modernidad/colonialidad latinoamericano'. *Tabula Rasa* **1**: 51–86.

Fabian, J. (1983) *Time and the Other: How Anthropology Makes its Object.* Columbia: New York.

Fanon, F. (1963) *The Wretched of the Earth* (trans. C. Farrington). Grove Press: New York.

Fanon, F. (1967) *Black Skins, White Masks* (trans. C. Farrington). Grove Press: New York.

Fernández de Recas, G. (1961) *Cacicazgos y nobiliario indígena de la Nueva España.* Instituto Bibliográfico Mexicano: Mexico City.

Fernández Retamar, R. (1971) *Calibán.* Diógenes: Mexico.

Ferrero, G. (1897) *L'Europa giovane. Studi e viaggi nei paesi del Nord.* Treves: Milano.

Ferrero, G. (1902–1906) *Grandezza e decadenza di Roma.* Treves: Milano.

Fiedler, J. (2003) *Molto Agitato: The Mayhem Behind the Music at the Metropolitan Opera.* Anchor Books: New York.

Fisher, W. F. and Ponniah, T. (eds.) (2003) *Another World is Possible: Popular Alternatives to Globalization at the World Social Forum.* Zed Books: London and New York.

Fochi, A. (1982) 'Traduttori del Verga in lingua inglese'. *Italianistica* **11**(1): 35–47.

Foster, D. W. (1990) *The Argentine Generation of 1880: Ideology and Cultural Texts.* University of Missouri Press: Columbia.

Francis, W. N. (1942) *The Book of Vices and Virtues: A Fourteenth-Century English Translation of the* Somme le Roi *of Lorens d'Orléans.* Early English Text Society, Oxford University Press: London.

Fuguet, A. (1991) *Mala onda.* Suma de Letras: Santiago.

Fuguet, A. (2001) 'Magical Neoliberalism'. *Foreign Policy* **125**: 66–73.

Fuguet, A. and Gómez, S. (1996) *McOndo.* Mondadori: Barcelona.

Gaines, S. (2002) 'Britain's Super-Rich Are Miserly, Says Philanthropist'. *The Guardian*, 6 February. [WWW document]. URL http://www.guardian.co.uk/society/2003/feb/06/fundraising.uknews [accessed 16 June 2010].

García Canclini, N. (1989) *Culturas híbridas: estrategias para entrar y salir de la modernidad*. Grijalbo: Mexico City.

García Canclini, N. (1995) *Consumidores y ciudadanos: conflictos multiculturales de la globalización*. Grijalbo: Mexico City.

García Canclini, N. (1997) *Hybrid Cultures: Strategies for Entering and Leaving Modernity* (trans. C. L. Chiappari and S. L. López). University of Minnesota Press: Minneapolis.

García Canclini, N. (1999) *La globalización imaginada*. Paidós: Mexico City.

García Canclini, N. (2004) 'Aesthetic Moments of Latin Americanism'. *Radical History Review* **89**: 13–24.

García Márquez, G. (1967) *Cien años de soledad*. Sudamericana: Buenos Aires.

García Márquez, G. (1981) *Crónica de una muerte anunciada*. Plaza and Janes: Barcelona.

García Márquez, G. (1996) *Chronicle of a Death Foretold* (trans. G. Rabassa). Penguin Books: London.

García Márquez, G. (2002) 'The Desire to Translate' in D. Balderston and M. E. Schwartz (eds.) *Voice-Overs: Translation and Latin American Literature*. SUNY Press: Albany, 23–25.

Gazmuri, C. (ed.) (2001) *El Chile del Centenario, los ensayistas de la crisis*. Instituto de Historia, Pontificia Universidad de Chile: Santiago.

Gemelli Careri, G. F. (1728) *Giro del mondo del Dottore D. Gio. Francesco Gemelli Careri. Nuova edizione accresciuta, ricorretta, e divisa in nove volumi. Con un Indice de ' Viaggiatori, e loro opera. Tomo sesto. Contenute le cose più ragguardevoli vedute nella Nuova Spagna*. Presso Sebastiano Coleti: Venice.

Gemelli Careri, G. F. (1976) *Viaje a la Nueva España*. UNAM: Mexico.

Gerbi, A. (1983) *La disputa del nuovo mondo*. R. Ricciardi: Milano.

Ghiraldo, A. (1904) 'Los salvajes'. *Caras y Caretas*, 30 January.

Gibbons, F. (2003) 'Tate Chief Attacks "Save for the Nation" Art Policy'. *The Guardian*, 12 November. [WWW document]. URL http://www.guardian.co.uk/uk/2003/nov/12/arts.artsnews3 [accessed 16 June 2010].

Gibson, C. (1964) *The Aztecs Under Spanish Rule: A History of the Indians of the Valley of Mexico, 1519–1810*. Stanford University Press: Stanford.

Gillespie, J. (1999) *Saints and Warriors: Tlaxcalan Perspectives on the Conquest of Mexico*. University Press of the South: New Orleans.

Glass, J. (1975) 'The Boturini Collection'. *Handbook of Middle American Indians*, Vol. 15. University of Texas Press: Austin, 473–486.

Glissant, É. (1992) *Caribbean Discourse: Selected Essays* (trans. J. M. Dash). University of Virginia Press: Charlottesville and London.

Glissant, É. (1993) *Tout-monde*. Gallimard: Paris.

de Gobineau, A. [1853–1855] (1967) *Essai sur l'inégalité des races humaines*. Éditions Pierre Belfond: Paris.

von Goethe, J. W. (2007) 'Translations' in L. Venuti (ed.) *The Translation Studies Reader* (trans. S. Sloan). Routledge: New York, 64–66.

González, J. A. and Pitt, C. (1992) 'Cuba' in S. Sadie (ed.) *The New Grove Dictionary of Opera*, Vol. 1. Macmillan Press: New York, 1022–1023.

Gordon, A. (1985) 'The Seaport beyond Macondo'. *Latin American Literary Review* (special issue on Gabriel García Márquez) **13**(25): 79–89.

Grafton, A. (1999) 'Introduction' in G. Vico *New Science* (trans. D. Marsh). Penguin: London, xi–xxxiii.

Grafton, A. (2001) *Bring Out Your Dead. The Past as Revelation.* Harvard University Press: Cambridge.

Grandmontagne, F. (1899) 'El bachiller'. *Caras y Caretas*, 15 April.

Grandmontagne, F. (1902) 'La máscara en el desierto'. *Caras y Caretas*, 15 February.

Guebel, D. (2004) *La vida por Perón.* Booket: Buenos Aires.

Hanke, L. (1974) *All Mankind is One: A Study of the Disputation between Bartolomé de Las Casas and Juan Ginés de Sepúlveda in 1550 on the Intellectual and Religious Capacity of the American Indians.* Northern Illinois University Press: DeKalb.

Hart, S. M. (2007) *A Companion to Latin American Literature.* Tamesis: London.

Hart, S. M. and Ouyang, W.-C. (2005) *A Companion to Magical Realism.* Tamesis: London.

Haskett, R. (1996) 'Paper Shields: The Ideology of Coats of Arms in Colonial Mexican Primordial Titles'. *Ethnohistory* **43**(1): 99–126.

Hauser, I. (2005) 'El Congreso no anula, sólo deroga'. *Página/12*, 19 June.

Hegel, G. W. F. (1969) *Science of Logic* (trans. A. V. Miller). Humanity Books: New York.

Heinz, W. and Frühling, H. (1999) *Determinants of Gross Human Rights Violations by State and State-sponsored Actors in Brazil, Uruguay, Chile and Argentina (1960–1990).* Martinus Nijhoff Publishers: The Hague.

Hernández, J. [1872–1879] (2004) *El gaucho Martín Fierro y la vuelta de Martín Fierro.* Stockcero: Buenos Aires.

Hilferty, R. (2002) 'A Knight at the Opera'. *New York*, 21 January. [WWW document]. URL http://nymag.com/nymetro/arts/music/features/5616/ [accessed 16 June 2010].

Hinnels, J. R. (1984) *Penguin Dictionary of Religion.* Penguin: Hammondsworth.

Huidobro Valdés, A. (1898) 'A qué se debe la superioridad de los anglosajones'. *Revista de Chile* **1**(5): 296–301.

Iarocci, M. (2006) *Properties of Modernity: Romantic Spain, Modern Europe, and the Legacies of Empire.* Vanderbilt University Press: Nashville.

Iser, W. (2000) 'Il concetto di traducibilità: le variabili dell'interpretazione'. *Testo a Fronte* **22**(1): 13–29.

James, H. (1978) 'Preface to the New York Edition (1907)' in *The American* (ed. J. W. Tuttleton). W. W. Norton and Company: New York, 1–15.

James, H. (1981) *The American.* Penguin Books: New York.

James, H. (2002) *The Outcry.* New York Review Books: New York.

Jameson, F. (1989) 'Regarding Postmodernism' in D. Kellner (ed.) *Postmodernism/ Jameson/Critique.* Maisonneuve: Washington, 43–76.

Jameson, F. (1994) *The Political Unconscious: Narrative as a Socially Symbolic Act.* Cornell University Press: Ithaca.

Joffe, J. G. (2003) 'Letter'. *The Times*, 8 February. [WWW document]. URL http://www.timesonline.co.uk/tol/comment/letters/article871824.ece [accessed 16 June 2010].

Jos, E. (1927) *La expedición de Ursúa al Dorado y la rebelión de Lope de Aguirre según documentos y manuscritos inéditos* (intro. A. Millares Carlo). Talleres Gráficos Editorial V. Campo: Huesca.

Katra, W. H. (1996) *The Argentine Generation of 1837: Echeverría, Alberdi, Sarmiento, Mitre.* Associated University Press: London.

Kefala, E. (2007) *Peripheral (Post) Modernity: The Syncretist Aesthetics of Borges, Piglia, Kalokyris and Kyriakidis*. Peter Lang: New York.

Kefala, E. (2008) 'Diez preguntas a Noé Jitrik'. *Revista Iberoamericana* **74**(222): 263–272.

Kefala, E. (2009) 'Συνομιλία με τον τελευταίο αναγνώστη' (Conversation with the last reader – interview with Ricardo Piglia). *Planodion* **11**(47): 616–619.

Kennedy, M. (2004) 'Jubilation in the National Gallery Over Deal to Retain Raphael Masterpiece'. *The Guardian*, 14 February. [WWW document]. URL http://www.guardian.co.uk/uk/2004/feb/14/arts.artsnews [accessed 16 June 2010].

Khatibi, A. (1983) *Maghreb pluriel*. Denoël: Paris.

Kingwell, M. (2006) 'Crossing the Threshold: Towards a Philosophy of the Interior, I'. *Queen's Quarterly* **113**(1): 91–104.

Klor de Alva, J. J. (2006) 'Forward' in M. León Portilla (ed.) *The Broken Spears: The Aztec Account of the Conquest of Mexico* (trans. L. Kemp). Beacon Press: Boston, xi–xxii.

Knight, L. (1994) *Collins English Dictionary and Thesaurus*. Harper Collins: Glasgow.

Kohan, M. (2002) *Dos veces junio*. Anagrama: Barcelona.

Kohan, M. (2006) *Museo de la revolución*. Mondadori: Buenos Aires.

Kohan, M. (2007) *Ciencias morales*. Barcelona: Anagrama.

Kontopoulos, K. (1993) *The Logic of Social Structures*. Cambridge University Press: Cambridge.

Kowii, A. (2005) 'Barbarie, civilizaciones e interculturalidad' in C. Walsh (ed.) *Pensamiento crítico y matriz (de)colonial*. Universidad Andina/Abya Yala: Quito, 277–296.

Kozinn, A. (2000) 'So You Can Buy Love After All'. *The New York Times*, 8 October. [WWW document]. URL http://www.nytimes.com/2000/10/08/arts/music-so-you-can-buy-love-after-all.html [accessed 16 June 2010].

Kusch, R. (1970) *El pensamiento indígena y popular en América*. Hachette: Buenos Aires.

Labanyi, J. (2004) 'Love, Politics and the Making of the Modern European Subject: Spanish Romanticism and the Arab World'. *Hispanic Research Journal* **3**: 229–243.

Lacan, J. (1999) 'The Mirror Stage as Formative of the Function of the I as Revealed in Psychoanalytic Experience' in A. Elliott (ed.) *The Blackwell Reader in Contemporary Social Theory*. Blackwell: Oxford, 61–66.

de Landa, D. (1941) *Relación de las cosas de Yucatan* (ed. and trans. A. M. Tozzer). Harvard University Press: Cambridge.

Lander, E. (2000) '¿Conocimiento para qué? ¿Conocimiento para quién? Reflexiones sobre la universidad y la geopolítica de los saberes hegemónicos' in S. Castro-Gómez (ed.) *La reestructuración de las ciencias sociales en América Latina*. Instituto Pensar: Bogota, 49–70.

Le Bon, G. [1895] (1905) *Psychologie des foules*. Félix Alcan: Paris.

Lebrecht, N. (2000) *Covent Garden, The Untold Story: Dispatches from the English Culture War, 1945–2001*. Pocket Books: London.

Lebrecht, N. (2001) 'Alberto Vilar: On Money and Opera'. *Culturekiosque*, 23 May. [WWW document]. URL http://www.culturekiosque.com/opera/intervie/albertovilar.htm [accessed 16 June 2010].

Leguizamón, M. (1900) 'La raza vencida'. *Caras y Caretas*, 14 July.

Leguizamón, M. (1908) *De cepa criolla*. Establecimiento Gráfico de Joaquín Sesé: La Plata.

León Portilla, M. (1999a) *Bernardino de Sahagún: pionero de la antropología*. Universidad Nacional Autónoma: Mexico.

León Portilla, M. (1999b) 'De la oralidad y los códices a la *Historia general*. Transvase y estructuración de los textos allegados por fray Bernardino de Sahagún'. *Estudios de Cultura Náhuatl* **29**: 65–141.

León Portilla, M. (ed.) (2006) *The Broken Spears: The Aztec Account of the Conquest of Mexico* (trans. L. Kemp). Beacon Press: Boston.

Lilla, M. (1993) *G. B. Vico: The Making of an Anti-Modern*. Harvard University Press: Cambridge.

Lipp, S. (1975) *Three Chilean Thinkers*. Wilfrid Laurier University Press: Waterloo.

López Austin, A. (1974) 'The Research Method of Fray Bernardino de Sahagún: The Questionnaires' in M. S. Edmonson (ed.) *Sixteenth-Century Mexico: The Work of Sahagún*. University of New Mexico Press: Albuquerque, 111–149.

Lovett, G. (1977) *The Duke of Rivas*. Twayne Publishers: Boston.

Lugones, L. (1915) *Elogio de Ameghino*. Otero: Buenos Aires.

Lugones, L. (1916) *El payador*. Otero: Buenos Aires.

Luque Talaván, M. and Castañeda de la Paz, M. (2006) 'Escudos de armas tlaxcaltecas: iconografía prehispánica y europea'. *Arqueología mexicana* **14**(82): 68–73.

Madureira, L. (2005) *Cannibal Modernities: Postcoloniality and the Avant-Garde in Caribbean and Brazilian Literature*. University of Virginia Press: Charlottesville.

Magaloni-Kerpel, D. (2004) *Images of the Beginning: The Painted Story of the Conquest of Mexico in Book XII of the Florentine Codex*. Yale University: Diss.

Maldonado-Torres, N. (2007) 'Sobre la colonialidad del ser: contribuciones al desarrollo de un concepto' in S. Castro-Gómez and R. Grosfoguel (eds.) *El giro decolonial: reflexiones para una diversidad epistémica más allá del capitalismo global*. Iesco-Pensar-Siglo del Hombre Editores: Bogota, 127–167.

Mansur, G. P. (1989) 'Concerning Rivas's Unexplained Localization of *Don Álvaro* in the Eighteenth Century'. *Romance Notes* **3**: 349–354.

Mariscal, G. (2001) 'The Figure of the *Indiano* in Early Modern Spanish Culture'. *Journal of Spanish Cultural Studies* **1**: 55–68.

Martí, J. [1891] (1979) 'Nuestra América'. *Tres discursos de nuestra América*, Havana: Casa de las Américas (original in *La Revista Ilustrada de Nueva York* 10 January 1891).

Martin, G. (1984) 'Boom, Yes; "New" Novel, No: Further Reflections on the Optical Illusions of the 1960s in Latin America'. *Bulletin of Latin American Research* **3**(2): 53–63.

Martin, G. (2002) 'Translating García Márquez, or, The Impossible Dream' in D. Balderston and M. E. Schwartz (eds.) *Voice-Overs: Translation and Latin American Literature*. SUNY Press: Albany, 156–163.

Martínez Sarasola, C. (1992) *Nuestros paisanos los indios: vida, historia y destino de las comunidades indígenas en la Argentina*. Emecé: Buenos Aires.

Masiello, F. (1992) *Between Civilization and Barbarism: Women, Nation and Literary Culture in Modern Argentina*. University of Nebraska Press: Lincoln.

Masiello, F. (2001) *The Art of Transition: Latin American Culture and Neoliberal Crisis*. Duke University Press: London.

Mateo, F. (1997) *El otro Borges: entrevistas (1960–1986)*. Equis Ediciones: Buenos Aires.

Materna, L. (1994) 'Ideología y la representación de lo femenino en Don Álvaro o la fuerza del sino'. *Modern Language Studies* **3**: 14–27.

Materna, L. (1998) 'Prodigal Sons and Patriarchal Authority in Three Plays by the Duque de Rivas: *Lanuza, Don Álvaro o la fuerza del sino,* and *El desengaño en un sueño'. Letras Peninsulares* **2**: 603–623.

Mathes, M. (1982) *Santa Cruz de Tlatelolco: la primera biblioteca académica de las Américas.* Secretaría de Relaciones Exteriores: Mexico.

Mayans y Siscar, G. (2002) *Obras Completas, Epistolario, Bibliografía* [CD-ROM, no pagination]. Digibis: Madrid.

Merlos, S. R. (1914) *América Latina ante el peligro.* Imprenta Nueva de Gerardo Matamoros: San José.

Meschonnic, H. (2000) 'Poetica del tradurre – Cominciando dai principi' and 'Il traduttore e l'odio della poetica'. *Testo a fronte* **XI**(23): 5–36.

Mignolo, W. (1995) *The Darker Side of the Renaissance: Literacy, Territoriality and Colonization.* The University of Michigan Press: Ann Arbor.

Mignolo, W. (1996) 'Beyond Occidentalism: Toward Nonimperial Geohistorical Categories'. *Cultural Anthropology* **11**(1): 51–87.

Mignolo, W. (ed.) (2001) *Capitalismo y geopolítica del conocimiento: el eurocentrismo y la filosofía de la liberación en el debate intelectual contemporáneo.* Ediciones del Signo: Buenos Aires.

Mignolo, W. (2003) *Historias locales/diseños globales: colonialidad, conocimientos subalternos y pensamiento fronterizo.* Akal: Madrid.

Mignolo, W. (2005) *The Idea of Latin America.* Blackwell: Oxford.

Minguet, C. (1989) 'América hispánica en el siglo de las luces'. *Cuadernos Americanos* **466**: 30–41.

Minorities at Risk Project (2003) 'Assessment for Indigenous Peoples in Argentina'. [WWW document]. URL http://www.cidcm.umd.edu/mar/assessment.asp?group Id=16002 [accessed 11 June 2010].

de Molina, A. [1555] (1571) *Vocabulario en lengua mexicana y castellana.* Antonio de Spinosa: Mexico.

de Molina, A. [1569] (1984) *Confessionario mayor en lengua mexicana y castellana* (ed. R. Moreno). Universidad Nacional Autónoma de Mexico: Mexico City.

Monsiváis, C. (2000) *Aires de familia: cultura y sociedad en América Latina.* Anagrama: Barcelona.

Montoto de Sedas, S. (1927?) *Nobiliario hispano-americano del siglo XVI.* Compañía Ibero-Americana de Publicaciones: Madrid.

Morel, B. A. (1857) *Traité des dégénérescences physiques, intellectuelles et morales de l'espèce humain et des causes qui produisent ces variétés maladives.* Baillière: Paris.

Moreno, F. P. (1994) *Reminiscencias de Francisco P. Moreno* (ed. E. V. Moreno). Secretaría de Cultura de la Nación and Ediciones Devenir: Buenos Aires.

Moreno, M. (ed.) (1810) *Gazeta de Buenos Ayres*, n.d. Buenos Aires.

Moynihan, C. (2010) 'Arts Patron Is Sentenced to 9 Years for Fraud'. *The New York Times*, 5 February. [WWW document]. URL http://www.nytimes.com/2010/02/06/nyregion/06vilar.html?scp=1&sq=Alberto%20Vilar&st=cse [accessed 16 June 2010].

Muñoz Camargo, D. (1981) *Descripción de la ciudad y provincia de Tlaxcala de las Indias y del Mar Océano para el buen gobierno ennoblecimiento dellas* (ed. R. Acuña). Universidad Nacional Autónoma de México: Mexico City.

Muñoz Camargo, D. (1998) *Historia de Tlaxcala: Ms. 210 de la Biblioteca Nacional de París* (eds. L. Reyes García and J. Lira Toledo). Gobierno del Estado de Tlaxcala; Centro de Investigaciones y Estudios Superiores en Antropología Social; Universidad Autónoma de Tlaxcala: Tlaxcala.

Nicholson, H. B. (2001) *Topiltzin Quetzalcoatl: The Once and Future King of the Toltecs.* University Press of Colorado: Boulder.

Ødemark, J. (2004) 'Making the Paintings of the Ancestors Speak. The Father of Anthropology and the Translation of Mesoamerican Cultural Heritage in Miguel León Portilla and Francisco Javier Clavijero'. *ARV, Nordic Yearbook of Folklore* **60**: 61–106.

Orr, M. (2003) *Intertextuality: Debates and Contexts.* Polity Press: Cambridge.

Ortega, J. (2006) *Transatlantic Translations: Dialogues in Latin American Literature* (trans. P. Derbyshire). Reaktion Books: London.

Ortiz, F. (1987) *Contrapunteo cubano del tabaco y azúcar.* Biblioteca Ayacucho: Caracas.

Paine, T. (1776) *Common Sense.* W. and T. Bradford: Philadelphia.

Palacios, N. (1904) *Raza chilena: libro escrito por un chileno i para los chilenos.* Imprenta i litografía alemana de Gustavo Schäfer: Valparaíso.

Palacios, N. (1908) *Decadencia del espíritu de nacionalidad.* Salón Central de la Universidad de Chile, Extensión Universitaria: Santiago.

Pastor, B. (1983) *Discursos narrativos de la conquista: mitificación y emergencia.* Ediciones del Norte: Hanover.

Paz y Meliá, A. (1892) *Nobiliario de conquistadores de Indias.* Imprenta y Fundición de M. Tello: Madrid.

Pérez Firmat, G. (1994) *Life on the Hyphen: The Cuban-American Way.* University of Texas Press: Austin.

Pérez-Rocha, E. and Tena, R. (2000) *La nobleza indígena del centro de México después de la conquista.* Instituto Nacional de Antropología e Historia: Mexico City.

Peri Rossi, C. (2002) 'A Translator in Search of an Author' in D. Balderston and M. E. Schwartz (eds.) *Voice-Overs: Translation and Latin American Literature.* SUNY Press: Albany, 58–60.

Piglia, R. (1981) 'Ideología y ficción en Borges' in A.-M. Barrenechea, J. Rest and J. Updike (eds.) *Borges y la crítica.* Centro Editor de América Latina: Buenos Aires, 87–95.

Piglia, R. (1994) *Artificial Respiration* (trans. D. Balderston). Duke University Press: Durham.

Piglia, R. (1995) 'Memoria y tradición' in A. Pizarro (ed.) *Modernidad, posmodernidad y vanguardias: situando a Huidobro.* Fundación Vicente Huidobro: Santiago, 55–60.

Piglia, R. (2000) *Crítica y ficción.* Seix Barral: Buenos Aires.

Piglia, R. (2001) *Respiración artificial.* Planeta: Buenos Aires.

Plimpton, G. (ed.) (2003) *Latin American Writers at Work.* The Modern Library: New York.

Powell, K. (2001) *New London Architecture.* Merrell: London.

Preston, K. K. (1993) *Opera on the Road: Traveling Troupes in the United States, 1825–1860.* University of Illinois Press: Champaign.

Prieto, A. (1988) *El discurso criollista en la formación de la Argentina moderna.* Editorial Sudamericana: Buenos Aires.

Quesada, E. (1902) *El criollismo en la literatura argentina.* Imprenta y Casa Editora de Coni Hermanos: Buenos Aires.

Quijano, A. (1993) 'Raza, etnia y nación en Mariátegui' in R. Forgues (ed.) *José Carlos Mariátegui y Europa: el otro aspecto del descubrimiento.* Empresa Editora Amauta S.A: Lima, 167–187.

Quijano, A. (2000a) 'Colonialidad del poder, eurocentrismo y América Latina' in E. Lander (ed.) *La colonialidad del saber. Eurocentrismo y ciencias sociales: perspectivas latinoamericanas.* CLACSO: Caracas, 201–245.

Quijano, A. (2000b) 'Colonialidad del poder y clasificación social'. *Journal of World-System Research* 6(2): 342–386.

Quinn, D. (1975) 'Rivas's Unexplained Localization of *Don Álvaro* in the Eighteenth Century'. *Romance Notes* 2: 483–485.

Rabassa, G. (2002) 'Words Cannot Express ... The Translation of Cultures' in D. Balderston and M. E. Schwartz (eds.) *Voice-Overs: Translation and Latin American Literature.* SUNY Press: Albany, 84–91.

Rama, Á. (1982) *Transculturación narrativa en América Latina.* Siglo XXI: Mexico.

Rama, Á. (1984) *La ciudad letrada.* Ediciones del Norte: Hanover.

Rampini, F. (2001) 'Argentina, l'agonia di una nazione'. *La Repubblica*, 21 December. [WWW document]. URL http://www.repubblica.it/online/mondo/argentinauno/rampini/rampini.html [accessed 17 June 2010].

Random House Webster's Unabridged Dictionary (2001). Random House Reference: New York.

Ray, L. (2007) *Language of the Land: The Mapuche in Argentina and Chile.* IWGIA: Copenhagen.

Remnick, D. (1999) 'The Imperial Stagehand'. *The New Yorker*, 22 February, 104–118. [WWW document]. URL http://www.newyorker.com/archive/1999/02/22/1999_02_22_104_TNY_LIBRY_000017598 [accessed 16 June 2010].

Renan, E. (1882) *Qu'est-ce qu'une Nation?* Calmann Lévy: Paris.

Ricœur, P. (2003) *The Rule of Metaphor.* Routledge: London and New York.

Río Prado, E. (2001) *Pasión cubana por Giuseppe Verdi: la obra y los intérpretes verdianos en La Habana colonial.* Ediciones Unión: Havana.

de Rivas, D. (Ángel de Saavedra) [1835] (1990) *Don Álvaro, o la fuerza del sino* (ed. A. Suárez). REI: Mexico.

de Rivas, D. (Ángel de Saavedra) (2005) *Don Álvaro or the Force of Fate* (trans. R. M. Fedorchek and intro. J. Tolliver). The Catholic University of America Press: Washington.

Rivera, A. (1984) *En esta dulce tierra.* Alfaguara: Buenos Aires.

Robertson, D. (1966) 'The Sixteenth-Century Mexican Encyclopedia of Fray Bernardino de Sahagún'. *Cahiers d'Histoire Mondiale* 9: 617–627.

Rodó, J. E. [1900] (1991) *Ariel.* Austral: Madrid.

Rodríguez, J. (2006) *Civilizing Argentina: Science, Medicine and the Modern State.* University of North Carolina Press: Chapel Hill.

Rodríguez-Monegal, E. (1972) *El boom de la novela latinoamericana.* Tiempo Nuevo: Caracas.

Roskamp, H. (2001) 'Warriors of the Sun: The Eagle Lords of Curicaueri and a Sixteenth-Century Coat of Arms from Tzintzuntzan, Michoacan'. *Mexicon* 23(1): 14–17.

Rowe, J. C. (2003) 'Henry James and Globalization'. *The Henry James Review* 24(3): 205–214.

Ruggiero, K. (2004) *Modernity in the Flesh: Medicine, Law, and Society in Turn-of-the-Century Argentina.* Stanford University Press: Stanford.

Ruiz de Alarcón, H. [1629] (1984) *Treatise on the Heathen Superstitions that Today Live Among the Indians Native to this New Spain* (eds. and trans. J. R. Andrews and R. Hassig). University of Oklahoma Press: Norman.

Saccomanno, G. (2008) *77*. Planeta: Buenos Aires.

de Sahagún, B. (1950–1982) *Florentine Codex: General History of the Things of New Spain*, Vol. 1–13 (eds. and trans. A. J. O. Anderson and C. E. Dibble). University of Utah: Santa Fe.

de Sahagún, B. [1579] (1993) *Adiciones, apéndice a la postilla y exercicio quotidiano* (ed. and trans. A. J. O. Anderson). Universidad Nacional Autónoma: Mexico.

de Sahagún, B. [ca. 1577] (2000) *Historia general de las cosas de Nueva España*, Vol. 1–3 (eds. J. García Quintana and A. López Austin). Consejo Nacional para la Cultura y las Artes: Mexico City.

Said, E. (1975) 'Conclusion: Vico in His Work and in This' in *Beginnings: Intentions and Methods*. Johns Hopkins University Press: Baltimore, 345–381.

Salinger, J. D. [1951] (1958) *The Catcher in the Rye*. Penguin: London.

Santiago, S. (1978) 'O entre-lugar do discurso latino-americano' in *Uma literatura nos tropicos: essaios sobre dependencia cultural*. Editora Perspectiva: São Paulo, 11–28.

Sarlo, B. (1987) 'Política, ideología y figuración literaria' in D. Balderston, D. W. Foster and T. Halperin Donghi (eds.) *Ficción y política: la narrativa argentina durante el proceso militar*. Alianza: Buenos Aires, 30–35.

Sarlo, B. (1992) *La imaginación técnica: sueños modernos de la cultura argentina*. Nueva Visión: Buenos Aires.

Sarlo, B. (1994) *Escenas de la vida posmoderna: intelectuales, arte y videocultura en la Argentina*. Ariel: Buenos Aires.

Sarlo, B. (1998) *La máquina cultural: maestras, traductores y vanguardistas*. Ariel: Buenos Aires.

Sarmiento, D. F. (1883) *Conflicto y armonías de las razas en América*. S. Ostwald Editor: Buenos Aires.

Sarmiento, D. F. (1948) *Obras Completas*, Vol. II. Luz del Día: Buenos Aires.

Sarmiento, D. F. [1845] (2001) *Facundo: civilización y barbarie*. Altamira: Buenos Aires.

Schleiermacher, F. (2007) 'On the Different Methods of Translating' in L. Venuti (ed.) *The Translation Studies Reader* (trans. S. Bernofsky). Routledge: New York, 43–63.

Schurlknight, D. E. (1995) 'Toward a Rereading of *Don Álvaro*' in C. J. Paolini (ed.) *La Chispa '95: Selected Proceedings*. Louisiana Conference on Hispanic Languages and Literatures, Tulane University Press: New Orleans, 337–346.

Schwarz, R. (1992) *Misplaced Ideas: Essays on Brazilian Culture* (ed. J. Gledson). Verso: London and New York.

Sergi, G. (1900) *La decadenza delle nazioni latine*. Bocca: Torino.

Shumway, N. (1991) *The Invention of Argentina*. University of California Press: Oxford.

Simerka, B. (2003) *Discourse of Empire: Counter-Epic Literature in Early Modern Spain*. Pennsylvania State University Press: University Park.

Solberg, C. E. (1970) *Immigration and Nationalism: Argentina and Chile, 1890–1914*. The University of Texas Press: Austin.

Sontag, S. (1988) *Illness as Metaphor and AIDS and its Metaphors*. Penguin: London.

Spengemann, W. (1981) 'Introduction' in H. James *The American* (ed. W. Spengemann). Penguin Books: New York, 7–25.

Stepan, N. Leys (1991) *'The Hour of Eugenics': Race, Gender and Nation in Latin America*. Cornell University Press: Ithaca.

Stevenson, R. (1992) 'Havana' in S. Sadie (ed.) *The New Grove Dictionary of Opera*, Vol. 2. Macmillan Press: New York, 669–670.

Stewart, J. B. (2006) 'The Opera Lover'. *The New Yorker*, 13 February, 108–123.

Sublette, N. (2004) *Cuba and its Music: From the First Drums to the Mambo*. Chicago Review Press: Chicago.

Suriano, J. (2000) *La cuestión social en Argentina, 1870–1943*. La Colmena: Buenos Aires.

Taine, H. (1864) *Histoire de la littérature anglaise*. Hachette: Paris.

Taine, H. (1876–1893) *Les origines de la France contemporaine*. Paris.

Terán, O. (ed.) (1996) *Escritos de Juan Bautista Alberdi: El redactor de la ley*. Universidad Nacional de Quilmes: Buenos Aires.

Thierry, A. (1825) *Histoire de la conquête de l'Angleterre par les Normands*. Firmin Didot: Paris.

Todorov, T. (1993) *On Human Diversity: Nationalism, Racism, and Exoticism in French Thought*. Harvard University Press: Cambridge.

Torop, P. (2000) *La traduzione totale* (trans. B. Osimo). Guaraldi: Rimini.

Torres Revello, J. (1936) 'Documentos relativos a D. Lorenzo Boturini'. *Boletín del Archivo General de la Nación (Mexico)* **VII**(1): 5–45.

Trenner, R. (ed.) (1983) *E. L. Doctorow: Essays and Conversations*. Ontario Review Press: Princeton.

Turner, V. (1984) 'Liminality and the Performative Genres' in J. J. MacAloon (ed.) *Drama, Festival, Spectacle: Rehearsals Toward a Theory of Cultural Performance*. Institute for the Study of Human Issues: Philadelphia, 19–41.

Venegas, A. (1910) *Sinceridad: Chile íntimo en 1910*. Imprenta Universitaria: Santiago.

Venuti, L. (1998) *The Scandals of Translation: Towards an Ethics of Difference*. Routledge: London and New York.

Venuti, L. (ed.) (2000) *The Translation Studies Reader*. Routledge: London and New York.

Venuti, L. (2008) *The Translator's Invisibility: A History of Translation*. Routledge: London and New York.

Venuti, L. (2009) 'Translation: Between the Universal and the Local'. *Testo a fronte* **XX**(40): 7–18.

Verene, D. P. (2002) 'Giambattista Vico' in S. Nadler (ed.) *A Companion to Early Modern Philosophy*. Blackwell: Malden, 562–570.

Vico, G. [1719–1721] (1936) *Il diritto universale* (ed. F. Nicolini). Laterza and Figli: Bari.

Vico, G. [1744] (1968) *The New Science of Giambattista Vico* (trans. T. G. Bergin and M. H. Fisch). Cornell University Press: Ithaca.

Vico, G. [1710] (1988) *On the Most Ancient Wisdom of the Italians: Unearthed from the Origins of the Latin Language: Including the Disputation with the Giornale de' letterati d'Italia*. Cornell University Press: Ithaca.

Vico, G. [1744] (1990) *Principi di Scienza Nuova d'intorno alla commune natura delle nazioni, Opere Volume 1* (ed. A. Battistini). Arnoldo Mondadori Editore: Milano.

Vico, G. [1719–1721] (2000) *Universal Right* (trans. G. Pinton and M. Diehl). Rodopi: Amsterdam.

Vico, G. [1725] (2002) *The First New Science* (trans. L. Pompa). Cambridge University Press: Cambridge.

Videla, J. R. (1979) 'Conferencia de prensa'. *Clarín*, 14 December.

de Villar Villamil, I. (1933) *Cedulario heráldico de conquistadores de Nueva España*. Talleres Gráficos del Museo Nacional de Arqueología, Historia y Etnografía: Mexico City.

Viñas, D. (1979) *Cuerpo a cuerpo*. Siglo XXI: Madrid.

Vogel, C. (2002) 'Ardent Rivals for a Raphael'. *The New York Times*, 8 February. [WWW document]. URL http://www.nytimes.com/2002/11/08/arts/inside-art.html [accessed 16 June 2010].

Wagner, R. (1981) *The Invention of Culture*. The University of Chicago Press: Chicago and London.

von der Walde Moheno, L. (1993) 'Indiano, simple embustero' in L. von der Walde Moheno and S. González García (eds.) *Dramaturgia española y novohispana (siglos XVI-XVII)*. UAM Iztapala: Mexico, 149–158.

Walsh, C. (2005) '(Re)pensamiento crítico y (de)colonialidad' in C. Walsh (ed.) *Pensamiento crítico y matriz (de)colonial: reflexiones latinoamericanas*. Universidad Andina Simón Bolívar/Abya-Yala: Quito, 13–35.

Walsh, C. (2006) 'Interculturalidad y (de)colonialidad: diferencia y nación de otro modo' in C. Walsh (ed.) *Desarrollo e interculturalidad, imaginario y diferencia: la nación en el mundo andino*. Academia de la Latinidad: Quito, 27–43.

Walsh, C. (2007) '¿Son posibles unas ciencias sociales/culturales otras? Reflexiones en torno a las epistemologías decoloniales'. *Nómadas* **26**: 102–113.

Weber, M. (1969) *The Methodology of the Social Sciences* (eds. and trans. E. Shils and H. Finch). The Free Press: New York.

Weckmann, L. (1992) *The Medieval Heritage of Mexico*. Fordham University Press: New York.

White, H. (1976) 'Vico: A Study of the "New Science"'. *History and Theory* **15**(2): 186–202.

Williams, R. (1977) *Marxism and Literature*. Oxford University Press: Oxford and New York.

Wortham, S., Murillo, E. G. and Hamann, E. T. (2001) *Education and the New Latino Diaspora: Policy and the Politics of Identity*. Greenwood: Westport.

Yao, S. G. (2002) *Translation and the Languages of Modernism. Gender, Politics, Language*. Palgrave Macmillian: New York.

Young, R. C. (1995) *Colonial Desire: Hybridity in Theory, Culture and Race*. Routledge: London and New York.

Zamora, L. Parkinson (1985) 'Ends and Endings in García Márquez's *Crónica de una muerte anunciada*'. *Latin American Literary Review* (special issue on Gabriel García Márquez) **13**(25): 104–116.

Zaragoza, G., Darras, G., Marcandier-Colard, C. and Samper, E. (2002) *Héroïsme et marginalité: Friedrich Schiller*, Les Brigands, *Victor Hugo*, Hernani, *Duc de Rivas*, Don Álvaro ou la force du destin. Atlande: Paris.

Zimmermann, E. A. (1992) 'Racial Ideas and Social Reform: Argentina, 1890–1916'. *Hispanic American Historical Review* **72**(1): 23–46.

Zumeta, C. (1899) *El continente enfermo*. New York.

Index